ACROSS THE ATLANTIC
NORWEGIAN PENTECOSTAL MISSIONARY WORK IN THE AMERICAS

ACROSS THE ATLANTIC

NORWEGIAN PENTECOSTAL MISSIONARY WORK IN THE AMERICAS

GEIR LIE

CPT PRESS
Cleveland, Tennessee

Across the Atlantic
Norwegian Pentecostal Missionary Work in the Americas

Published by CPT Press
680 Walker Street NE
Cleveland, TN 37311, USA

email: cptpress@pentecostaltheology.org
ISBN xxxxxx

TABLE OF CONTENTS

FOREWORD BY MIGUEL ÁLVAREZ

A few years ago, my friend Dr. Harold Hunter, introduced me to Geir Lie. He told me very specifically: 'I want you to meet this brother. He is a Norwegian theologian dedicated to cross-cultural missions. His friendship will do you much good'. And, needless to say, as time went by, I got to know Geir better and, indeed, his friendship and fellowship have been a blessing to me, not only professionally, but in some projects that we later undertook together. Some colleagues did well to call him the Latino Noruego.

In January 2019, we both agreed to begin publishing the *Hechos* journal, which was unique in its academic genre and, due to its biblical, theological, and ministerial content, of great help to contemporary readers. For six years, Geir and I were able to publish twelve volumes that narrated the Pentecostal experience of Latin American writers to the rest of the world. Without a doubt, this project caused interest, especially among young theologians, to publish their ideas through *Hechos*. In addition to that publication, I also had the honor of serving as editor of his *Un compendio contemporáneo del Nuevo Testamento* as well as his *Un compendio contemporáneo del Antiguo Testamento* (CPT Press), volumes that are now available to the public interested in these topics.

Now that Geir is publishing this work, to tell the story of Norwegian Pentecostal missions in the Americas, the public in this region will have the opportunity to learn about some of the primary sources that established Pentecostal missions in this continent. I personally met some Norwegian missionaries in my country, Honduras, who were instrumental in strengthening Pentecostal missions in that country. This was happening back in the 1970s and has continued until today. The work grew and the new generations have expanded the mission throughout the country and beyond.

Furthermore, I have read about Norwegian missionary work in Brazil, Argentina, Bolivia, Peru, Cuba, and other countries in the area. It is impressive to see how the Holy Spirit motivated and paved the way for several Norwegian missionaries to plant churches and pastoral training centers in Latin America.

As I write these lines, I am convinced that through this volume the reader will be able to see a model of cross-cultural mission that involves Norwegian and North American Pentecostals in the planting of churches in the different countries of Central and South America. I hope that Geir's hope, by publishing this work, will serve to inspire others to do more research on the historical background of Pentecostal churches in Latin America, preferably with a historical and sociological approach at the same time.

Together with the author, I hope that the volume will be read with positive interest, not only by Norwegians, but also by Latin American Pentecostals. This could contribute to the documentation of the history of Pentecostalism in the region. The emerging Pentecostal generations need to know their history. With all that said, I would like to say thank you Geir Lie for this contribution to Norwegian and Latin American Pentecostalism.

INTRODUCTION

For many years, Norway was known as 'the leading country in sending missionaries in proportion to its population'.[1] This has made it an even greater joy to work on this book, beginning with reading through year after year of *Korsets Seier* and *Det Gode Budskap*. The learning curve has been steep, as I initially had limited knowledge of the contributions of Norwegian Pentecostal missionaries to the church history of the Americas.

Descriptions of missions in earlier times, often with a particular focus on the exotic differences between life at home and what awaited on the mission field, could easily blur the lines between a missionary calling and a desire for travel or adventure. These portrayals also contributed to unrealistic expectations about what constituted the daily life of a traditional missionary.[2] Laila and Oddvar Bauge, sent to Bolivia in 1979, illustrate some of these challenges:

> The best way to prepare is to talk to older and experienced missionaries — and that's what we did. We also read travel accounts and other literature. Some of the books were helpful, while others were too adventurous and unrealistic. [...] One often has very high ideals for missionaries, but it didn't take long for us to realize that they, too, are just people. There were disappointments as well, mostly in not being able to live up to our

---

[1] 'Norge er ikke lenger verdensmester i misjon', *Korsets seier* 25 July 1997, p. 24.

[2] 'In the stories, geographical information was mixed together with ethnology and history and composed to bring out strong emotions. This was the best way to collect monetary gifts. Later, when I got to know the conditions, I found it distasteful. You can forgive me when I can say today that there was little from the mission stories that corresponded to reality'. Tarald Rike, *Blyfoten. Historien om misjonær Leif Andersen* (Hovet: Hermon Forlag, 1993), p. 14.

own ideals. But meeting the missionaries was interesting in many ways. The environment included many strong and colorful personalities, and the conditions were good. The work, however, involved more practical tasks than we had anticipated before departure. At times, one could easily spend more time repairing engines than preaching.[3]

This book is, of course, not complete, partly because every author must be selective in terms of material and emphasis. The book focuses on Norwegian Pentecostal missionaries on the American continent.[4] This focus is both a strength and a weakness. The weakness, which I hope others will address in future publications, is that the significant contributions of local collaborators are scarcely mentioned — whether it be Bruno Müller (1939–77),[5] born and raised in Paraguay, or his compatriot Milton Laranjera, who at one point worked with Anna Strømsrud,[6] or the Argentine couple Martha and Juan José ('Tito') Rosotto.[7] Many more could — and should — be acknowledged and credited.

To provide a more accurate picture of Norwegian Pentecostal missions in the Americas, this book needs an alternative perspective, drawing on available sources or through interviews with current Pentecostal leaders in the countries discussed here.[8] Several

---

[3] Einar Vestvik, 'Møtet med folk og kultur i Bolivia sjokkartet', *Korsets seier* 17 February 1982, p. 9.

[4] When Norwegian Pentecostal missionaries are not explicitly referred to as representatives of either the Free Evangelical Assemblies, Maran Ata or New Life Mission, they will be representatives of *Pinsebevegelsen*.

[5] For further biographical information, cf. Inge Bjørnevoll, 'Bruno Müller til minne', *Korsets seier* 18 January 1978, p. 14.

[6] Ingebjørg Tveito, 'Misjonærene i Paraguay trenger hjelp', *Korsets seier* 31 January 1968, p. 8.

[7] The couple came up to northern Argentina from the Buenos Aires area and were of great help in the mission in the north. When missionaries returned home, they often took charge of places such as Tartagal, Salta, San Pedro de Jujuy and Ingeniero Juárez. They were given the status of missionaries and had support from Brevik/Stathelle for many years.

[8] 'Completely correct', as G. Leonard Pettersen writes, 'such an overview cannot be, and for many reasons. Our mission field today flows in most fields right into the national congregations that have gradually arisen and are led by the national brothers. It will be difficult to keep statistics on the "Norwegian mission", which we are not at all sorry for'. And still, in 1970 there were 65 missionaries in Latin America, more than 20 mission stations and more than 80 outposts. They also had four infirmaries, and the year before there were around 18,000 treatments.

significant leaders from Latin America have visited Norway, and some biographical information about them can be found in *Korsets Seier* and *Det Gode Budskap*. However, I suspect that to give these local collaborators and leaders the attention and recognition they deserve, primary sources must be sought in their home countries. National authors are likely best qualified to supplement my contribution to Pentecostal history in their respective countries

Another weakness of this book is that it does not cover the contributions of Norwegian emigrant Pentecostal missionaries, particularly Norwegian Americans. The Assemblies of God's Flower Pentecostal Heritage Center in Springfield, Missouri — the world's largest Pentecostal archive, housing sources in over 170 languages — holds a wealth of material on Norwegian-American Pentecostals, including missionaries. A book dedicated to the Norwegian-American contributions to Pentecostal missions should take its foundation precisely from the source material available primarily in Springfield.

It has not been possible to devote much attention to Norwegians who made short visits to Norwegian mission stations, whether as friends, family, or representatives of the Norwegian Pentecostal Movement. In addition to these, there were short-term missionaries who may have traveled on their own initiative[9] or through Team Action, started by Helge Adolfsen, as well as individual believers who spent shorter or longer periods in Latin America and may have been involved in church activities without holding formal missionary status.[10] These aspects will be addressed only minimally, if at all, in this book.

In addition, there were four orphanages, four schools and two boarding schools, as well as river missions in Bolivia and Peru. Furthermore, evangelical radio programs were broadcast on more than 20 stations. As an extension of the radio work, correspondence courses in Bible teaching were also run. Pettersen claims that in 1969 alone, over 2,000 people were baptized as believers under the auspices of the Norwegian Pentecostal mission, and many national workers were connected to this activity. 'Norsk pinsemisjon representert i 7 land: Sterk utvikling i Latin-Amerika', *Korsets seier* 25 July 1970, p. 8.

[9] An elderly Norwegian woman with connections to *Sarons Dal* has even written a book about her short-term stays in Puerto Rico during the period 1988–91. Ruth Gylthe, *Frie fanger: Blant fanger og uteliggere på Puerto Rico* (Kvinesdal: Logos forlag, 1992).

[10] Former boarding school parents at the Norwegian school in Paraguay and

This book primarily examines Norwegian Pentecostal missions up until the point when the work largely became self-sufficient, and missionaries increasingly took on roles more equal to their national counterparts. In many mission countries, this trend emerged in the 1970s, coinciding with an ongoing emphasis on the need for a new type of missionary:[11] companions who support local efforts, assist with teaching, take central roles in NORAD-supported projects, or pioneer work in areas where the gospel had rarely, if ever, been preached. It can also be said that the book's lack of a systematic account of the many projects channeled through the Norwegian Pentecostal Mission (PYM)[12] represents an additional weakness. For example, in 1995, NORAD funding for Latin American projects amounted to 7.2 million Norwegian kroner, distributed across thirteen different projects. Six of these were in Paraguay, five in Bolivia, one in Peru, and one in Nicaragua. Some were health projects, while others focused on education or agriculture.[13]

Latin America has fascinated me since the early 1980s, and for a period, I was part of the Hispanic group at the Salem Church in Oslo. This group was established in 1980 and has, for extended periods, been led by Pentecostal missionaries on home leave in Norway.[14] In 1980, the number of missionaries in Latin America representing the Norwegian *Pinsebevegelsen* was approximately 90, accounting for 30% of the total number of Norwegian Pentecostal missionaries that

---

later teachers at Hedmarktoppen folk high school, Eldbjørg and Vidar Børjesson, have also been initiators of Global Mission Camps, bases 'where volunteers can live and help in local projects for shorter or longer periods'. Rakel E. Berntzen and Kristin B. Karlsen, 'En verden av muligheter', *M2 Misjons-magasinet* no. 2 2013, pp. 16-17. Supplement to *Korsets seier* 17 May 2013.

[11] It can be difficult to distinguish between what should be properly defined as missionaries and surrendered Christians living abroad for a shorter or longer time. This book does not have a focus on short-term missionaries, either if one is formally sent from (1) the *Pinsebevegelsen*, the Free Evangelical Assemblies or possibly other Pentecostal denominations or (2) interdenominational missionary organizations such as Youth With A Mission, Operation Mobilization, or others.

[12] In 1996, *Stiftelsen Pinsevennenes Ytre Misjon* was disbanded and instead became an association called *Norske Pinsemenigheters Ytre Misjon*, with its own board of five representatives in addition to the former chairmen of the working committees.

[13] 'Store beløp til Latin-Amerika', *Korsets seier* 27 September 1996, p. 16.

[14] Geir Lie, 'Spansk– og portugisisktalende menigheter i Norge: En rapport', in Lemma Desta and Stian Sørlie Eriksen (eds.), *Migrasjon og misjon: Refleksjon og praksis* (Oslo: Norges Kristne Råds Skriftserie – No. 24), pp. 59-69.

year. [15] Naturally, questions arise concerning this, such as what
screening processes were conducted and what should have been
implemented. Without trivializing illegitimate actions—some
rightfully criminal—it is not surprising, considering the high number
of missionaries sent out by both the *Pinsebevegelsen* and the Free
Evangelical Assemblies, that missionaries were occasionally sent who,
in hindsight, should not have been cleared for such assignments.

Many children and young people have had positive,[16] while others
have had mixed, sometimes heartbreaking, experiences as students at
our schools and/or boarding schools.[17] This also applies in Latin
America. However, these matters will not be a focus area in this book,
which primarily seeks to provide a descriptive introductory account
of Norwegian long-term missionaries' contribution to American
church history in the countries where we have been represented.

It is my hope that this book can inspire others to go deeper into
the work with a focus either on individual *nations* or *individuals* and
preferably with both a historical and sociological approach. I
therefore hope that the book will be read with positive interest by
Norwegian Pentecostals and that a Portuguese and Spanish-language
version will be able to attract similar interest among Latin American

---

[15] 'Sør-Amerika – feltet med 30% av våre misjonærer', *Korsets seier* 12 April 1980,
p. 1. The high number of missionaries who have worked in Latin America also
means that it is beyond the scope of this book to give a detailed description of all
of them. A separate appendix lists the missionaries, but the book as such only
follows a selective number of missionaries' specific work.

[16] Hilde Stuksrud, 'Misjonærbarn i Atyra: Vi trives bedre i Sør-Amerika enn i
Norge', *Korsets seier* 12 April 1980, p. 9.

[17] In 1983, the Norwegian school in Paraguay had 18 students divided into nine
grades, and of these, seven of the children had their parents in Argentina and one
of the children had parents as far away as in the northern part of Bolivia: 'Here
[the missionary children] form bonds of friendship with other Nor-wegian children
who later in life prove to be very strong. But many have probab-ly also cried
themselves to sleep every now and then, missing their mother and father'. Of
course, it was 'difficult for the missionaries to send e.g. first-graders miles away
from home,' but how harmful such separation has been for the children was
probably little understood at the time. Aina Førland, 'Jeg er verdens heldigste, for
jeg treffer mamma og pappa hver helg!' *Korsets seier* 12 October 1983, p. 7. Cf. also
Ole Mats Gjervoldstad, 'Misjonærbarn og internatbarn', *Korsets seier* 3 August 2007,
p. 17. Perhaps in response to Gjervoldstad's article, the then general secretary Svein
Jacobsen of PYM admitted that 15-20 years ago the respect for one's calling was
'so overwhelming that it could often put human needs in the shade. Often the
children just accompanied their parents, without anyone asking the critical
questions'. Lars Christian Gjerlaug, 'PYM vil høre fra misjonærbarna', *Korsets seier*
22 June 2007, pp. 2-3.

readers, including people with an interest in writing their own country's Pentecostal history and where relevant sources about Norwegian Pentecostal missionaries have not been available in their own language.

I would like to express my deep gratitude to the *Pinsebevegelsen* in Norway for the invaluable support they have given me, not least through their positive interest throughout the process and their valuable feedback during the writing phase. Of course, I alone remain responsible for the final result, including any errors or misunderstandings.

1

NORWEGIAN PENTECOSTAL MISSIONARIES ARE SENT OUT

Neither during the Reformation nor the period of the consolidation of doctrinal teachings that has become known as *Orthodoxy* was anyone much concerned with the concept of missions. To the extent that this was dealt with, it was common to claim that the missionary assignment itself had already been completed in the apostolic age – and with alleged support in Paul's epistle to the Romans, chapter 10 and verse 18: 'But I say, Have they not heard? Yes verily, their sound went into all the earth, and their words unto the ends of the world'. It was not until the 17th century that the concept of missions was 'articulated', although it still took time before this concept was 'translated into practical action'.[1]

It is interesting to note that it was King Frederick IV (1671-1730) of Denmark-Norway who took the initiative for change, as his Pietist court preacher Franz Julius Lütkens asked for 'suitable missionary candidates' for the then Danish colony of Trankebar in India. The first two German Pietist missionaries Bartholomäus Ziegenbald and Heinrich Plütschau arrived there in July 1706. This in turn led to a massive missionary awakening among German-Lutheran Pietists, both among Moravians and Halle Pietists.[2] Ziegenbald and Plütschau were truly pioneers in that almost 90 years passed before the British Baptist minister William Carey, often referred to as the founder of

---

[1] Geir Lie, *Tro og tanke før og nå. En selektiv gjennomgang av den kristne menighets historie* (Wyoming, MI: Akademia forlag, 2024), p. 60.

[2] Lie, *Tro og tanke*, pp. 60-62.

the modern missionary movement, with his wife and children left his homeland and, like the above-mentioned German Pietists, set a course for India.

Also in Norway, the missionary revival was Pietist-inspired, largely influenced by Haugeans and Moravians. In 1827, Danish Niels Johan Holm (1778-1845) started the publication of *Norsk Misjons-Blad*, which also appealed to many within the clergy. Local missionary associations arose ahead of the establishment of *Det norske Misjonsselskap* (The Norwegian Missionary Society) in 1842, followed by *Forening af Israels venner* (Society for Friends of Israel), later with a name change to *Den norske Israelsmisjon* (the Norwegian Missions to Israel), founded in 1844, and *Santalmisjonen* (the Mission to the Santal), founded in 1867. In connection with the founder of the China Inland Mission, the medical missionary James Hudson Taylor (1832-1905), visiting Kristiania in 1889, as well as thanks to considerable preparatory work by schoolmaster Otto Treider, rider Hans Guldberg and clockmaker Johannes Jørgensen, the Norwegian China Mission saw the light of day the same year. As early as 1884 the first two Norwegian missionaries had been sent to China, and they immediately agreed to join the new organization, which later changed its name to *Norsk Orient Misjon* (the Norwegian Orient Mission).

One of the Norwegian China Mission's missionaries, Ludvig Eriksen, also founded the Chihli mission in 1901, later with a name change to *Norsk Misjonsallianse* (the Norwegian Mission Alliance).[3] Following the Swedish-American Fredrik Franson's visit to Norway in 1883, which caused a country-wide revival which in turn became a catalyst for the creation of the *Misjonsforbundet* (now the *Misjonskirken* in Norway), he took the initiative in 1891 to establish the missionary organization Scandinavian Alliance Mission, which also recruited *Norwegian* missionaries.[4]

With this as a brief historical background, we now turn our attention to the beginning of the Pentecostal movement in the U.S. Several scholars have identified the early American Pentecostal movement as a missionary-eschatological movement. Charles Fox

---

[3] Lie, *Tro og tanke*, pp. 118-23.
[4] 'Our history', *https://www.team.org/ourstory#:~:text=TEAM%20began%20under %20the%20name,East%20Africa%2C%20Swaziland%20and%20Mongolia.* [Accessed 15 March 2024].

Parham (1873-1929) is considered the movement's founder as one of his Bible school students in Topeka, Kansas, Agnes Ozman, was prayed for by the laying on of hands to receive the baptism in the Holy Spirit accompanied by the gift of tongues on January 1, 1901.[5] Five years later, the movement was brought to Los Angeles, California through the African-American Holiness minister William Joseph Seymour (1870-1922), who, through the meetings at 312 Azusa Street, became a catalyst for the movement's global impact.[6] From a Norwegian perspective, it is also interesting to note that the American Pentecostal movement has a precursor in an independent Scandinavian revival in Minnesota, North and South Dakota from the 1890s and with elements of both faith healing and speaking in tongues. Several of the ministers within the Scandinavian revival agreed to join the American Pentecostal movement, as it began later.[7] This Scandinavian phenomenon was first documented in book form by Darrin J. Rodgers, Director of the Assemblies of God's Flower Pentecostal Heritage Center in Springfield, Missouri, in 2003.[8]

The first American scholar to identify the original Pentecostal movement as an end-times movement was Robert M. Anderson, through his book *Vision of the Disinherited* (1979). He correctly pointed out that, although speaking in tongues is the most visibly distinguishing feature of the movement, it is the eschatology and ecclesiology that shaped the focus on tongues during the movement's early years. Speaking in tongues was initially regarded as an earthly language that the first Pentecostals would use on the mission field to communicate their message of conversion and thus hasten the return of Jesus. Parham was influenced in this regard by the holiness preacher Frank Weston Sandford (1862–1948), with whom he spent

---

[5] James R. Goff, Jr., *Fields White Unto Harvest. Charles F. Parham and The Missionary Origins of Pentecostalism* (Fayetteville, AR: The University of Arkansas Press, 1988), p. 71.

[6] Cecil M. Robeck, *The Azusa Street Mission & Revival. The Birth of the Global Pentecostal Movement* (Nashville, TN: Nelson Reference & Electronic, 2006).

[7] Geir Lie, *Fra hellighetsbevegelse til norsk karismatikk*. Vol. 1 (Wyoming, MI: Akademia forlag, 2024), p. 58.

[8] Darrin J. Rodgers, *Northern Harvest: Pentecostalism in North Dakota* (Bismarck, ND: North Dakota District Council of the Assemblies of God, 2003). Rodger's pioneer research contributed to and gave direction to Gary B. McGee's book *Miracles, Missions, & American Pentecostalism* (Maryknoll, NY: Orbis Books, 2010).

six weeks in 1900.[9] The previous year, Parham had read about one of Sandford's followers, Jenny Glassey, in Sandford's publication *The Everlasting Gospel*. Glassey had received the gift of tongues in 1895 and felt a missionary calling to Sierra Leone in Africa. Parham referred to this story in his own publication, *The Apostolic Faith*, that same year.[10] However, it seems that a woman named Mary Johnson, 'of the Swedish Free Mission in Moorhead, Minnesota', who appears to have had no contact with either Parham or Seymour, became the first 'Euro-American "Pentecostal" missionary of the twentieth century'. Having spoken in tongues, she arrived in Durban, South Africa, as early as January 1905.[11]

The beginning of Pentecostalism in Norway

The early history of the Norwegian Pentecostal movement is inseparably tied to the British-born Methodist preacher Thomas Ball Barratt (1862-1940), who, through the Methodist Church, was ideologically prepared by reading works by representatives of the 19th-century Holiness movement in both the United States and Britain.[12] Also, the founder of Norwegian Methodism, Ole Peter Petersen (1822–1901), experienced his Christian conversion in the United States in 1846 and, two years later, had a specific sanctification experience in line with the teachings of the Holiness movement.[13]

As pastor of the 3rd Methodist Church in Kristiania (Oslo) from 1889 to 1891, Barratt began considering organizing an outreach effort to reach the unconverted through both gospel preaching and social work.[14] This idea took clearer form when, in 1892, he became

---

[9] David William Faupel, *The Everlasting Gospel. The Significance of Eschatology in the Development of Pentecostal Thought* (Sheffield: Sheffield Academic Press, 1996), p. 164.

[10] Faupel, *Everlasting Gospel*, p. 174.

[11] Rodgers, *Northern Harvest*, pp. 13-14.

[12] The most comprehensive study of Barratt can be found in Rakel Ystebø Alegre's *The Pentecostal Apologetics of T. B. Barratt: Defining and Defending the Faith 1906-1909* (PhD thesis, Regent University, 2019).

[13] Lie, *Tro og tanke*, p. 124; Tore Meistad, *Methodism as a carrier of the Holiness tradition in Norway* (Alta: ALH-forskning, 1994:2), p. 108.

[14] Barratt was likely inspired by the work carried out from the Methodist 'Central Hall' in London, which he had the opportunity to observe during his stay in England from 1890–1891. The work in London, in turn, seems to have drawn inspiration from Australia. David Dale Bundy, *Visions of Apostolic Mission. Scandinavian Pentecostal Mission to 1935* (PhD thesis, Uppsala Universitet, 2009), pp. 147, 159.

'presiding elder,' or district superintendent, for the entire Kristiania district, and from 1898, pastor of the 1st Methodist Church. In 1902, the Kristiania City Mission was officially established with an inaugural meeting at the Tivoli Theatre. Subsequent meetings were 'held in concert halls, the student society, the Grand Hotel, theaters, open air venues, *and wherever we could reach the masses with the gospel*.'[15] Gradually, Barratt succeeded in recruiting co-workers. The work was anticipated to be divided into seven 'departments':

> 1) Evangelical work. 2) Social work. 3) A literary department to spread good literature and educate the public through lectures, etc. 4) Comprehensive music, singing, entertainment, etc. 5) Work among youth and children, including the Epworth League, Sunday school, and Boys' Brigade. 6) Correspondence. 7) Finances.

In 1904, Barratt launched the magazine *Byposten* to promote the work of the Kristiania City Mission. Many were converted to the Christian faith without necessarily leaving the Church of Norway for the Methodist Church. Barratt now began considering constructing a building in the capital 'to serve as the base for his activities'.[16] Well known is his one year stay in America to raise funds for *Håkonsborgen*, the proposed name for the City Mission's headquarters in Kristiania, which had already received advance approval from King Haakon VII.[17]

Despite written recommendations from several American Methodist bishops and nearly a year-long stay in America, the fundraising campaign ultimately failed. Barratt later claimed that his encounter with the emerging American Pentecostal movement during this time was of far greater significance.[18] Barratt had left Norway for the United States in September 1905.[19] While staying at A.B. Simpson's Alliance House at 250 W. Forty-fourth Street in New York City, he came across the first issue of William J. Seymour's *Apostolic Faith* newsletter from Azusa Street in Los Angeles, published in September 1906. That same month, Barratt initiated

---

[15] Thomas Ball Barratt, *Erindringer* (Oslo: Filadelfiaforlaget, 1941), p. 83.
[16] Barratt, *Erindringer*, p. 91.
[17] Barratt, *Erindringer*, p. 94.
[18] '*Håkonsborgen* was gone forever, but in its place, the Holy Spirit had come!' Barratt, *Erindringer*, p. 129.
[19] Martin Ski, *Fram til urkristendommen. Pinsebevegelsen gjennom 50 år*. Vol. 1 in a 3 vols. series (Oslo: Filadelfiaforlaget, 1956), p. 8.

correspondence with several staff members at Azusa Street. He received six letters in total from Ida May Throop, Glen Cook, Clara Lum, and Benjamin Hardin Irwin, in addition to one from Seymour himself. Then, when Barratt on November 15, at a meeting at Maude Williams' mission at 250 W. Fourteenth Street in New York City, was prayed for personally by her and later, during the evening service, by Lucy Leatherman and an unknown Norwegian man, Barratt spoke in tongues for the first time.

In his diary entry on Sunday, November 25, Barratt noted that he had met the former Angola missionaries Samuel and Ardella Mead the previous Wednesday.[20] They had arrived in New York City with eight other Pentecostal missionaries (and three small children) in route to Angola and Liberia. Barratt spent time with them in New York City until December 8 and accompanied them as a fellow passenger on the British ocean liner RMS *Campania* from December 8 to 15, when the ship docked in Liverpool.[21] It is reasonable to assume that Barratt was instructed in and initially recognized the original Pentecostal teaching of missionary tongues. It was not, however, the American researcher Robert Mapes Anderson, but rather the Norwegian clergyman Thorstein Gunnarson, who first identified the doctrine of missionary tongues as the primary constitutive element of the early Pentecostal movement's self-understanding. He did this in 1928 in a lengthy but relatively obscure footnote in a book seldom consulted within Pentecostal circles, titled *Dommedagsventing* (Expectation of Doomsday), with the subtitle *Millennismen og dens innslag i norsk kristendom* (Millennialism and its Influence on Norwegian Christianity).[22]

Even prior to Barratt's spiritual experience in New York City, he had written an article in *Byposten* about the Azusa Street revival.[23] By

---

[20] Thomas Ball Barratt, *When the fire fell and an outline of my life* (Oslo: Privately published, 1927), pp. 135-6; *Erindringer, p.* 127; Lie, *Fra hellighetsbevegelse til norsk karismatikk*, p. 64.

[21] According to the passenger list, a copy of which is deposited in the Norwegian Pentecostal Historical Archive, *NPA-PA/Barratt T.B./F/L0001*, the Azusa Street missionaries, in addition to the Mead couple, included Julia Hutchins and Lucy Farrow.

[22] Geir Lie, 'Apostler og aposteltjeneste i internasjonal pinsekristendom', *Refleks – med karismatisk kristendom i fokus* 1-1 2002, p. 6 (note 6); Lie, *Fra hellighetsbevegelse til norsk karismatikk, pp.* 58-67.

[23] It is interesting to note that while Barratt's first article about the revival at

the time he returned to Norway on December 18 and attended his first Christian meeting the very next day, many were already ideologically prepared for the new movement. Laura, Barratt's wife, had already started attending meetings with Erik Andersen Nordquelle in Torvgaten 7, as well as on the second floor of Citypassasjen, where Kristiania Bymission rented space.[24] It is perhaps unsurprising, then, that Nordquelle was present at Barratt's first meeting in the Kristiania Bymission *Hjælpe-forening's* 'clothing festival for poor children'.[25]

In the very beginning, the meetings were primarily held in Turnhallen, Citypassasjen, and Møllergata 20. However, due to complaints from neighboring offices about the noise levels during the midday prayer meetings in Citypassasjen, preacher Bot Nyborg—who was then speaking in Nordquelle's venue in Torvgaten 7—suggested that Barratt also start holding meetings there. The first meeting at Nordquelle's rented location took place on Saturday, December 29, and lasted from 10:30 a.m. until midnight.[26]

Nordquelle himself had moved to the capital in 1899, and his congregation was the result of a merger between two house fellowships dating back to around 1887. Both appear to have been called 'Den frie venneflokken' (The Free Fellowship of Friends), and they merged in 1894. Nordquelle also maintained contact with approximately 100 similar fellowships across the country, with an estimated combined following of just under 4,000 people. Therefore, when Nordquelle and his congregation in Torvgaten 7 opened themselves to Barratt's preaching and the practice of speaking in tongues, it is difficult to conclude otherwise than that Nordquelle's network of congregations became the first Pentecostal denomination like community in Norway. Both Nordquelle himself and the publication *Det gode Budskap*, first issued in 1904, played a unifying role for the movement. Through Nordquelle, Barratt gained access to this network, although it would later become apparent that the two had differing understandings of the baptism in the Spirit. For

---

Azusa Street was published in *Byposten* on October 6, 1906, the first Swedish article (by A. Linn) was published in *Närkesbladet* as early as September 18.

[24] Laura Barratt, *Minner* (Oslo: Filadelfiaforlaget, 1946), pp. 74-75.

[25] Nils Bloch-Hoell, *Pinsebevegelsen. En undersøkelse av pinsebevegelsens tilblivelse, utvikling og særpreg med særlig henblikk på bevegelsens utforming i Norge* (Oslo: Universitetsforlaget, 1956), p. 140; Barratt, *Erindringer*, p. 134.

[26] Bloch-Hoell, *Pinsebevegelsen*, p. 143.

Nordquelle, the experience seemed to be identifiable with a particular manifestation of God's love, while Barratt made speaking in tongues the normative criterion for knowing that one had experienced the baptism in the Spirit.[27]

Another distinction between Nordquelle's Free Evangelical Assemblies and the *Pinsebevegelsen* movement that Barratt would later found was that Nordquelle and his movement did not require formal membership, as they did not have a church register.

In early 1907, people began traveling to the capital to attend the meetings, and soon services were being held in surrounding towns such as Drammen and Fredrikshald (Halden): 'There are constantly new reports from rural areas and towns saying that the revival has struck there'.[28] Severin Larsen, with ministerial back-ground both in the Methodist Church and the *Misjonsforbundet*, had become the pastor of the Baptist congregation in Fredrikshald in 1907 and experienced his personal baptism in the Holy Spirit that same year, although he 'remained a member of the Norwegian Baptist Union for the rest of his life'.[29]

The first independent *Pinsebevegelsen* congregation was established in Skien in 1908, following Baptist pastor Carl Magnus Seehuus' resignation from his position as Baptist pastor in January. He started an independent ministry on March 22, forming an 'organized congregation' with 26 members. This is today's Tabernaklet in Skien.[30] It wasn't until 1910 that an organizational split occurred between Nordquelle and Barratt, as the latter began independent meetings that same year at Møllergt. 38, where about 200 people from Nordquelle's congregation followed him.[31] That same year, the magazine *Byposten* changed its name to *Korsets Seir*, later to *Korsets Seier*.[32]

---

[27] Asbjørn Froholt, *Erik Andersen Nordquelle. Mannen som med god grunn kunne vært kalt pinsebevegelsens 'mor' og den frie evangeliske bevegelsens 'far' i Norge. En biografi* (Moss: Eget forlag, 1981), p. 118.

[28] Barratt, *Erindringer*, p. 149.

[29] Oddvar Nilsen, 'Larsen, Severin', in Geir Lie (ed.), *Norsk pinsekristendom og karismatisk fornyelse. Ettbinds oppslagsverk* (Oslo: Refleks-Publishing, 2nd. edn., 2008), pp. 97-98.

[30] Bloch-Hoell, *Pinsebevegelsen*, p. 192.

[31] Lie, *Tro og tanke før og nå*, p. 136.

[32] For a short period in 1911, the magazine was also published in Finnish as *Ristin Voitto*. A few issues were also released in Swedish as *Korsets Seger* and in

Many of the Pentecostal believers had been baptized by Nord-quelle early on, but Barratt, as a Methodist, held to infant baptism until 1913. That year, he and Laura were baptized by Lewi Pethrus in the Filadelfia congregation in Stockholm. This, alongside Barratt's independent meeting activities starting in 1910, likely helped consolidate the movement. Barratt performed his first believer's baptism on November 17, 1913, 'at the friends' place on St. Olavs Gate 6, as there was no baptismal pool at Møllergaten 38'.[33] The friends were an independent Pentecostal group led by figures such as Knud Martin Hansen Sæther, known as M.H. Sæther, and Ludvig Bratlie. They had previously rented a venue at Møllergt. 9 and merged with Barratt's group in 1914.[34]

It wasn't until 1916 that Barratt considered the work he was leading as an organized church. On June 26, the first church service was announced, and 200 members were registered. In parallel with this, Barratt and his family formally withdrew from the Methodist Church.[35]

Already during the meetings at Nordquelle's congregation in Torvgaten 7, there were foreign visitors. To some extent, this was due to coverage, often negative, in both Norwegian and foreign publications. In January 1907, the first Swedish and Finnish ministers arrived. From Denmark, Thorvald Plum came from the Kirkeklokken publishing house, and from England, vicar A.A. Boddy, who also invited Barratt to his Anglican church in Sunderland a few months later.[36] Barratt also visited Copenhagen during the period of June–July 1907, with subsequent visits in August and December, as well as in March 1908. It was during the latter visit that he prayed for the Danish actress Anna Larssen Bjørner,[37] who, alongside her husband Sigurd, became influential figures both in the *Pinsebevægelsen* and in the Apostolic Church in their home country.

Russian as *Pabeda Krista*. Barratt, *Erindringer*, pp. 200-201. A Spanish-language version, *Victoria de la Cruz*, was also published from Barcelona, Spain, according to a note in *Korsets Seir* dated November 15, 1915.

[33] Barratt, *Erindringer*, p. 206.

[34] Lie, *Tro og tanke før og nå*, p. 136. The letter 'S' in Sæther likely refers to the crofter's farm Laakesæter in Ullensaker, where Sæther was born. This con-clusion is based on Arnold Ruud's not published research.

[35] Barratt, *Erindringer*, pp. 208-209.

[36] Bundy, *Visions of Apostolic Mission*, p. 178.

[37] Bundy, *Visions of Apostolic Mission*, pp. 193-97.

Leaders within the German holiness movement showed early interest in Barratt's meetings in Kristiania, and it was Emil Meyer, leader of the Hamburg Strandmission, who invited Barratt's colleagues Agnes Thelle and Dagmar Gregersen to Germany in June 1907. Through Meyer, the two women were also introduced to Heinrich Dallmeyer, who opened the doors for a month-long series of meetings in Kassel. Through this, the Pentecostal movement was introduced to Germany.[38] It was also Thelle and Gregersen, through their preaching on the baptism of the Holy Spirit, who became the first to introduce the Pentecostal movement to Switzerland.[39] The following year, they traveled to A.B. Simpson's Bible school in New York City, preparing for planned missionary work in India. Barratt had visited India already in 1908, and two years later, Thelle and Gregersen set out for the mission field. Gregersen soon married Henrik Engstrøm. During a visit to Norway in 1913-14, the Banda Mission was founded, with guidelines developed in collaboration with Barratt.

1910 was the year when several Norwegian Pentecostals went out into the service of missions. As Oddvar Nilsen writes, there was

> no established organization behind these missionaries. Some of them had the support of congregations, but regular promises of financial support were few and far between. No one had given them directives about where they should go or how they should carry out their work. Everything was left to the missionaries themselves – including, for the most part, securing their own livelihood. The funds that came in were directed to the missionaries personally, 'and they rarely or never accounted for how they spent the money'.[40]

Although this was the same year Barratt left Torvgt. 7 and established independent meetings in Møllergt. 38, it was too early to speak of a confessional divide between the *Pinsebevegelsen* as a distinct entity (which did not yet exist) and the Free Evangelical Assemblies (which also did not yet exist as a defined denomination separate from

[38] Alegre, *The Pentecostal Apologetics of T. B. Barratt*, pp. 101-107.

[39] Jean-Daniel Plüss, *Vom Geist Bewegt. Die Geschichte der Schweizerischen Pfingst-mission* (Kreuzlingen: Schweizeriche Pfingstmission, 2015); Bloch-Hoell, *Pinsebevegelsen*, p. 274.

[40] Oddvar Nilsen, *Ut i all verden. Pinsevennenes ytre misjon i 75 år* (Oslo: Filadelfia-forlaget, 1985), p 31.

the *Pinsebevegelsen*). Therefore, the first Pentecostal missionaries were also unaware that they belonged to one 'movement' rather than the other, and they would often send mission reports to both Barratt's magazine (which in 1910 changed its name from *Byposten* to *Korsets seir*), *Det gode Budskap*, and from 1914, also to *Misjonæren*.[41] *Misjons-Røsten*, published by Gustav Iversen from Sarpsborg, was first released in 1929 and was incorporated into *Det gode Budskap* in 1948.[42]

During a missionary conference in Skien in September 1914, Barratt expressed a desire for more organized conditions for missionaries, possibly following the model of the Banda mission. In late January 1915, Barratt invited people to a missionary conference in Kristiania where the organization *Norges Frie Evangeliske Missionsforbund* (Norway's Free Evangelical Missionary Society), with a change of name to *Norges Frie Evangeliske Hedningemisjon* (Norway's Free Evangelical Mission to the Gentiles) in 1920, was founded. At this time, there were only 'six "formally structured" Pentecostal congregations in the country'.[43]

In connection with an illness during a stay at a cabin in Mesnalien outside Lillehammer in 1929, Barratt concluded that he no longer believed in the missionary model he had helped define in 1915. On the contrary, he now felt that 'any plan for a joint organization for the churches was in direct conflict with the practice of the apostles and the early Christian congregations'. This marks a significant shift in Barratt's thinking. Initially, he had been a proponent of creating a more structured, organized approach to missionary work and church activities, but by 1929, he seemed to reject institutionalized structures

---

[41] *Misjonæren* published its first issue in 1889 and initially served as a voice for the *Det norske Misjonsforbund*. The first editor was Mons Andersen from Larvik, who was replaced in 1904 by A.J. Anthony (later affiliated with the *Pinsebevegelsen*. In 1914, Carl Magnus Seehuus became the editor, giving the magazine a more distinctly Pentecostal profile. The final editor, Alf Kasborg, held the position from 1935 until the publication ceased in 1957.

[42] Froholt, *Erik Andersen Nordquelle*, p. 175. Gustav Iversen's son Paul Iversen writes in the article 'Misjonsrøsten. En epoke i DFEF's misjonshistorie', *Det gode Budskap* 11-15 June 1984, p. 20: 'The publication of *Misjonsrøsten* was initiated by my father, encouraged by several suggestions and motivations from others. A significant contributing factor was the discontinuation of the mission magazine "Misjonsbreve", which had been published by missionary Dagmar Engstrøm. Without "Misjonsbreve" the independent missionaries lacked a dedicated mission journal, although both *Det gode Budskap* and *Misjonæren* occasionally included letters from missionaries'.

[43] Nilsen, *Ut i all verden*, p. 46.

in favor of a more decentralized and independent model, one that aligned more closely with his understanding of early Christian practice.[44] *Norges Frie Evangeliske Hedningemisjon* was formally dissolved in 1931, and during a transitional period, 'all the remaining missionaries with their stations and fields ... were transferred to the congregation in Filadelfia, Oslo'.[45] The Norwegian *Pinsebevegelsen's* strictly congregational model of church organization, combined with Barratt's leadership influence, were the main reasons why missionaries thereafter were quickly sent out and financially supported by local congregations. Even though these congregations were often numerically small, several churches would collaborate to financially support a missionary or missionary family.

In 1946, however, a missionary secretary was appointed, Gunnerius Tollefsen, who was succeeded by Hans Svartdahl in 1965. At the same time, PYM – The Foreign Mission of the Norwegian *Pinsebevegelsen* churches was established.[46] In 2008, there were regional secretaries for Asia, Europe, Africa, and America who '[coordinated] the work in the new contact churches and country committees established for each country where Norwegian *Pinsebevegelsen* churches operate'.[47] The same year, a collaboration agreement was signed with *Gå Ut-Senteret* in Hurdal, which is operated by *Normisjon*. Several *Pinsebevegelsen* missionaries had previously taken mission preparation courses there, but from now on, their representatives also contributed with teaching staff.[48] A name change from *PYM* to *Pinsemisjonen* occurred in 2017.[49] In 2020, *Pinsemisjonen* became an

---

[44] Solveig Barratt Lange, *T.B. Barratt. Et Herrens sendebud* (Oslo: Filadelfia-forlaget, 1962), p. 275.

[45] Nilsen, *Ut i all verden*, p. 64.

[46] *Pinsemisjon i 100 år* (Oslo: De norske pinsemenigheters ytremisjon, 2010), p. 53. In 1996. the *Stiftelsen Pinsevennenes Ytre Misjon* was dissolved and replaced by an association called the *Norske Pinsemenigheters Ytre Misjon*, with its own executive board consisting of five representatives, in addition to the former chairpersons of the working committees. 'Store forandringer i Pinsevennenes Ytre Misjon', *Korsets seier* 4 October 1996, p. 4; Oddvar Johansen, 'Ja til ny struktur i PYM', *Korsets seier* Christmastime 1996, p. 3.

[47] 'Nye regionssekretærer i PYM', *Korsets seier* 11 July 2008, p. 24.

[48] Anne Gustavsen, 'PYM-avtale med Gå Ut-senteret', *Korsets seier* 4 April 2008, p. 23.

[49] Anne Gustavsen, 'Pinsemisjonen', *Korsets seier* 29 September 2017, p. 4; Deborah Selbekk Lunde, 'PYM endrer navn', *Korsets seier* 29 September 2007, pp. 10-11.

implemented department under the *Pinsebevegelsen* in Norway and was renamed *Pinse Misjon* the following year.

As already pointed out, the Free Evangelical Assemblies and the *Pinsebevegelsen* had a 'shared missionary history' in the early years.[50] Without any missionary organization behind them, each missionary 'had to provide for their own finances and find their own treasurer'.[51] Many sought partial support by writing reports to *Det gode Budskab*, *Korsets Seir*, and *Missionæren*. Malla Moe, who had been working in Swaziland since 1892, was one of many who received support from both the circle around Nordquelle and Barratt.

Similar to the *Pinsebevegelsen*, there were several within the Free Evangelical Assemblies who eventually desired more structure for the missionary work. A 'Brethren Council' was formed in 1929 to oversee the financial matters. This council only lasted for one year, but in 1935 a Mission Committee was established. Two years after World War II ended in 1945, at the Free Evangelical Assemblies' mission conference in Drammen, a new mission committee, the Mission and Home Committee (MHU), was created.[52] The missionaries were, however, as in the *Pinsebevegelsen*, sent out and supported by local congregations.

In 2023, most of the congregations within the Free Evangelical Assemblies (DFEF) chose to join the *Pinsebevegelsen* in Norway. Perhaps it can be said that the local DFEF congregations that have *not* chosen to join the *Pinsebevegelsen* represent the oldest Pentecostal denomination in Norway.[53] In addition to these two denominations, there are several smaller Pentecostal groups. Apostolic Faith (Portland, OR), with its headquarters in Stavanger, began its work in Norway in 1912, while the Apostolic Church started operations in the late 1940s through Denmark. Brunstad Christian Church, still commonly known as Smith's Friends, is a Norwegian-born

---

[50] Asbjørn Froholt, *De Frie Evangeliske Forsamlingers Misjon. 75 år. Et jubileumsskrift* (Moss: Elias forlag, 1985), p. 5.

[51] Froholt, *De Frie Evangeliske Forsamlingers Misjon*, p. 7.

[52] Froholt, *De Frie Evangeliske Forsamlingers Misjon*, pp. 123-30.

[53] Two of the oldest *local* congregations in the *Pinsebevegelsen*, the congregation in Berger outside Drammen and in Nærsnes, date back to 1887 and 1888 respectively, as they originally started as *Kristi Menigheter* (Churches of Christ) and were later affiliated with the *Pinsebevegelsen*.

Pentecostal denomination founded in the early 20th century,[54] while Maran Ata established its first congregation in 1959. The Foursquare Church formally established itself in Norway in 1983, and a Church of God congregation was founded outside Ålesund in 2004. In addition to these, there are also several small Oneness Pentecostal churches and denominations. Furthermore, various Pentecostal traditions are reflected in and through the many migrant churches.

The charismatic renewal first made its mark in Norway starting in 1970, and various organizations such as Agape, Youth With a Mission, and Oase are a fruit of this renewal. One characteristic of the original charismatic renewal was the desire not to form independent congregations, but to remain within their original churches and denominations in order, if possible, to bring about charismatic renewal there. The missionary work of charismatic groups falls outside the scope of this book.

In the 1980s, what is commonly referred to as the Word of Faith movement emerged in Norway. Several of its churches have since been incorporated into the *Pinsebevegelsen* in Norway, while others remain independent local congregations, and some have been dissolved.

As is evident in the following chapters, there was extensive cooperation between missionaries from, not least, the Scandinavian countries, often due to a shared congregationalist-ecclesiological understanding of the importance of planting independent churches in collaboration with national workers. At the same time, it should not be overlooked that the missionaries were largely products of their time, and many of the earliest descriptions reflect a paternalistic attitude toward the local population[55] and at times an insensitive and often elitist attitude toward both Catholic theology, spirituality, and

---

[54] Their work on the American continent has been described in the book *Menighetens utvikling i Nord– og Sør-Amerika* (Tananger: Stiftelsen Skjulte Skatters Forlag, 2022).

[55] 'But don't you have native workers there?' some may ask. "Yes, of course, but a native pastor or evangelist cannot, and does not have, the qualifications to work in the same way a missionary can.'" Gerda Lillian Aardalen, 'Fra arbeidet i Nord-Parana, Brasil', *Korsets seier* 29 August 1959, pp. 555-56. It is a relief to read from the Latin America Conference in 1997, where Finn Røine addressed 'the missionaries' attitudes toward the nationals'. Oddvar Johansen, 'Latin-Amerikakonferansen i Heddal med oppsiktsvekkende klar tale', *Korsets seier* 25 April 1997, p. 6.

folk religion.[56] I believe I see a shift from the 1970s onwards as the work entered a phase of consolidation, where perhaps more than before, there was a greater emphasis on involving national ministers who could more easily reach the country's population with the gospel message.[57] At the same time, we must also be nuanced in our reflections on the first pioneer missionaries. Anne Lise Søvde, the then executive director of NORME, wrote in 2013 – and rightly so:

> My claim is that in most places, missionaries and their work have made a positive difference and uplifted the dignity of individuals. Western missionaries in Argentina, in the early 20th century, helped the indigenous people acquire identification numbers so they were not left without rights and vulnerable to being exploited by landowners in the country. Even today, a clear geographical boundary can be seen in Argentina: where the missionaries came from the north, there are still indigenous people, but south of this boundary, all the indigenous people were either killed or forcibly relocated. [...] If missionaries do not influence the cultures they are sent to, market forces and the cultural imperialism of mass media will shape the mission fields. But if we believe we have a better way to offer, we owe it to the world to present it.[58]

The 1970s were, in many ways, the golden age of Norwegian Pentecostal missions in terms of the number of long-term missionaries sent abroad. Within the *Pinsebevegelsen* as much as 1 percent of the movement's members were foreign mission- aries. Since then, the number has drastically decreased. Nonetheless,

---

[56] An illustrative quote can be found from the Argentine missionary Helga Mjåvatn, 'Hilsen fra Argentina', *Korsets seier* 12 May 1956, p. 298 – 'The year 1947, one morning when I woke up, a voice said to me: "You shall flee, but your small children shall be left behind and handed over to the Pope in Rome, under his power to be tormented and denied the right to serve God." Ask for revival!' It is not until 1996 that we get a clear distinction between official Catholic doctrine and popular Catholic folk religiosity: 'In Latin America, Catholicism is often mixed with primitive paganism, which often results from being so-called nominal Christians, and not having received the necessary teaching,' Roger Samuelsen states. 'Katolikkene i Latin-Amerika er ikke som de europeiske', *Korsets seier* 27 September 1996, p. 15.

[57] '[Emiliano Vera] takes part in everything that happens and is involved as an elder in the Council working to nationalize the work, i.e., to hand over the work to the nationals'. Josef Iversen, 'Gud gjør under i Paraguay', *Korsets seier* 23 March 1977, p. 16.

[58] Anne Lise Søvde, 'Toleranse og misjon', *Korsets seier* 11 January 2013, p. 7.

mission engagement has taken on various forms: retirees who have chosen to settle abroad and become involved in missions, even though they have not been formally sent by PYM, is one variant. In addition, there is tentmaking and short-term missions. However, none of these forms of mission will be the focus of attention in this book.

It is also interesting to note the South America conferences in Norway, which undoubtedly contributed to the increasing interest in South America year by year',[59] which not only contributed to growing interest in the conferences themselves, with attendance increasing year by year, but also indirectly helped more people become aware of their own missionary calling, leading to them being sent out as missionaries later on.

---

[59] 'Sør-Amerika-konferansen i Halden', *Korsets seier* 9 June 1951, pp. 275-76.

2

ARGENTINA

The first Norwegian Pentecostal missionaries left the country as early as 1910. This also applies to Latin America, as Berger N. Johnsen (1888–1945) traveled to Argentina in August of the same year.

Johnsen had experienced a Christian conversion in 1905 and received his missionary calling in America the following year. In New York City, he encountered the Pentecostal movement and also became acquainted with the Canadian-born minister Alice Wood (1870–1961).[1] She originally had a Quaker background but later became part of A.B. Simpson's Christian and Missionary Alliance. Prior to her encounter with the Pentecostal movement, she had served as a CMA missionary in both Puerto Rico and Venezuela. Along with May Kelty and her mother Harriet, Wood arrived in Argentina in 1910. She quickly settled in the city of Gualeguaychú in the province of Entre Ríos, about 160 kilometers north of Buenos Aires.[2]

Wood was not the first Pentecostal missionary to arrive in Argentina. If we disregard a spontaneous and unsuccessful mission attempt in 1907 led by an unknown Thomas O'Reilly,[3] Luigi Francescon (1866-1964), along with his two coworkers Giacomo

---

[1] Cf. Alice Wood's diary entries for December 19, 1909, which are deposited in the Flower Pentecostal Heritage Center's archive in Springfield, Missouri. 'Berger Johnsen & I went to Brooklyn by the subway & ... to attend Norwegian Pentecostal meeting'. Also cf. Bundy, *Visions of Apostolic Mission*, p. 239.

[2] Allan H. Anderson, 'Primeras misiones pentecostales en América Latina', *Hechos – una perspectiva pneumatológica* 4-1 (Enero) 2022, p. 15.

[3] McGee, *Miracles*, pp. 94-95.

Lombardi and Lucia Menna, had initiated a work in Buenos Aires four months before Wood's arrival, in October 1909.

Francescon played a significant role within the First Italian Presbyterian Church in Chicago when he had his Pentecostal experience in 1907 at William H. Durham's Full Gospel Mission at 943 W. North Avenue in the same city.[4] The three Italians moved on from Argentina to Brazil as early as March 1910,[5] after being released from Argentine detention.[6] Thus, Alice Wood founded the first Pentecostal church in Argentina.

Berger Johnsen arrived in 1910,[7] with 15 kroner (less than 2 USD) when he 'disembarked in Gualeguaychú',[8] where he initially worked alongside Wood.[9] However, he soon felt that God was calling him 'toward the inland to the Indians', and in an article, he asked if there might be 'someone in Norway' with a missionary calling to Argentina who could work alongside him.[10]

In 1914, Johnsen went to the town of Embarcación in the northern part of Argentina, in the province of Salta, where he purchased land to begin evangelical work among the indigenous population. Embarcación was a strategic hub, as travelers between Argentina, Brazil, and Bolivia passed through the town. Later in 1914, Johnsen went back in Norway, one of his reasons being to raise funds

---

[4] Joseph Coletti, 'Francescon, Luigi', in Stanley M. Burgess and Eduard M. van der Maas (eds.), *The New International Dictionary of Pentecostal Charismatic Movements. Revised and expanded edition* (Grand Rapids, MI: Zondervan Publishing House, 2002), p. 646.

[5] J. Norberto Saracco, 'Argentine Pentecostalism: Historical Roots, Current Developments, and Challenges for the Future', in Vinson Synan, Amos Yong and Miguel Álvarez (eds.), *Global Renewal Christianity*. Vol. 2: *Latin America* (Lake Mary, FL: Charisma House, 2016), pp. 259-60.

[6] Kathleen M. Griffin, *Luz en Sudamérica: Los primeros pentecostales en Gualeguaychú, Entre Ríos, 1910-1917* (PhD thesis. Instituto Universitario ISEDET, Buenos Aires, Argentina, 2014), p. 33. Griffin writes that the work was resumed when the two Italian Pentecostal preachers Narciso Natucci and Francesco Anfuzzo arrived via the USA in 1916. The work quickly picked up, and vibrant congregations were established.

[7] Berger Johnsen, 'Fra Argentina', *Det gode Budskab* 15 December 1910, pp. 95-96.

[8] Berger N. Johnsen, 'Argentina', *Korsets seir* 15 July 1912, p. 110.

[9] For a systematic presentation and analysis of Berger Johnsen's ministry in Argentina, cf. Rakel Ysteb's master's thesis, *La misión pentecostal en Embarcación. Conversiones y cambios socio-culturales entre los indígenas afectados por la misión de Berger Johnsen (1916-1945)* at the Universidad Nacional de San Martín in Buenos Aires, Argentina in 2010.

[10] Berger Johnsen, 'Fra Sydamerika', *Det gode Budskab* 1 June 1911, p. 42.

and, if possible, recruit missionary candidates. [11] One of the candidates would turn out to be Albin Gustavsson from Sweden, whom Johnsen had met in Halden in 1916. Gustavsson did not arrive until 1920, however. Another missionary candidate was Per G. Talaasen, who, through his encounter with Johnsen in 1915, 'received his life's calling' and came to Embarcación in the fall of 1916. Talaasen, however, contracted malaria and returned to Norway the same year.[12]

A group of Swedish missionaries worked for a short period with Johnsen in Embarcación, and one of these was Hedvig Berg. She would become Johnsen's wife in 1921. Together they had the children Miriam, Débora and Benjamín.

In their first years, the Johnsen couple hardly saw any results from the missionary activities among the natives, and the first conversions did not occur until around 1922. One of the first to accept the preaching of the gospel was Santos Aparicio, who soon identified himself as a candidate for leadership and followed Johnsen on evangelistic tours both as an independent minister and as an interpreter to various native indigenous languages.[13] Aparicio was not the only one to do this.

In 1928, Sigurd Grønvold arrived,[14] who stayed only one year in Argentina, but after getting married, returned in 1932. Unfortunately, he died in 1937.

---

[11] Berger Johnsen was, in other words, in Norway in 1915 when the *Pinsebevegelsens* 'Norges Frie Evangeliske Missionsforbund' was founded. The missions organization changed its name to 'Norges Frie Evangeliske Hedningemission' five years later. 'Fra Argentina', *Det gode Budskab* 15 September 1936, p. 2 Johnsen writes: 'I was probably the only missionary who was at Dalen and protested when "Norges frie hedningemisjon" was formed, and I had to bite my tongue in some cases, but I am glad that those who did this had the courage and strength to overturn their own work'. Johnsen is likely referring to the fact that 'Norges Frie Evangeliske Hedningemission' was dissolved in 1930, and its associated mission council in 1932.

[12] Berger Johnsen, 'Fra Argentina', *Det gode Budskab* 1 August 1917, p. 58. 'Malaria fever drove me home the following year, and then I became a missions treasurer instead of a missionary'. Per G. Talaasen, 'Mangeårig misjonskasserer trekker seg tilbake', *Korsets seier* 8. January 1972, p. 7. However, we read that Oscar Halvorsen was Johnsen's treasurer in 1915. 'Syd-Amerika', *Korsets seir* 15 March 1915, p. 47.

[13] Marcos Delgado is a grandson of Santos Aparicio. He is also the current pastor of Misión Evangélica in Embarcación, which was founded by Berger Johnsen in 1915. Oddwin Solvoll, 'Tredjegenerasjons indianerpastor', *Korsets seier* 5 March 2010, p. 22.

[14] Sigurd Grønvold, 'Argentina', *Det gode Budskab* 15 April 1928, p. 7.

After the civil war between Bolivia and Paraguay ended in 1935, Johnsen was finally able to travel to Pilcomayo, which he had previously received an invitation to visit, about 225 kilometers from Embarcación. Here he preached, together with, among others, Santos Aparicio. Nevertheless, about a year passed without seeing visible results. However, in what had been announced as their farewell meeting, some women were moved by the message and began shouting for sheer joy and clapping their hands. A man with eyes filled with tears cried out repeatedly and in a loud voice: 'Heavenly Father, have mercy on us!' This set off a chain reaction among the more than 2,000 people present, and Johnsen and his colleagues witnessed a great revival among the various Indian tribes on the Pilcomayo river. Johnsen wrote home to Norway:

> In less than two minutes this entire congregation was under a very Spirit-like weather. Such a thing cannot be described, but they heard us 18 kilometers away, so you can understand for yourselves! They came from across the Bolivian border to watch, because they could hear the song and the praise.[15]

The very next day, Johnsen returned to Embarcación, but several of his co-laborers, including Santos Aparicio, remained behind to establish the new converts in the faith. After one year, over 2,000 of the natives chose to move to Embarcación, many of these at least partially due to a desire to be close to Johnsen. As a result, Johnsen was probably for many years pastor of the country's largest Pentecostal congregation.

Johnsen had health challenges all these years, and the war years in Europe meant that contact with his homeland was largely cut off. Although Johnsen had no formal connection to the Norwegian *Pinsebevegelsen*, he was supported by several free groups, and Gustav Iversen, who was an active minister within the Free Evangelical Assemblies, served for many years as Johnsen's treasurer and maintained correspondence with him.[16] Since Iversen 'was in partial opposition' to Erik Andersen Nordquelle,[17] partly because, according

[15] Berger N. Johnsen, 'Argentina', *Korsets seier* 22 August 1936, p. 5.

[16] G. Sønstebø had been Johnsen's treasurer since 1915 but was replaced by Gustav Iversen in 1938. Berger N. Johnsen, 'Argentina', *Korsets seier* Eastertime 1938, pp. 10-11.

[17] Asbjørn Froholt, 'Iversen, Gustav', in Lie (ed.), *Norsk pinsekristendom og karismatisk fornyelse*, p. 78.

to Iversen, missionary material was not sufficiently prioritized in *Det gode Budskap*, the Free Evangelical Assemblies' main organ, Johnsen was regularly profiled in the magazine *Misjons-Røsten*.[18] Here, Iversen was the editor. Iversen also wrote a biography on Johnsen in 1946. This was translated into Spanish by Rakel Ystebø Alegre in 2009 and entitled *35 años entre los indígenas: El trabajo misionero de Berger N. Johnsen en Argentina.*

After Johnsen's death in 1945, Hedvig continued the work for a time, in cooperation with Santos Aparicio. However, Hedvig desired relief and asked Per A. Pedersen to take over the leadership of the work. Together with his wife Palma, he left Norway in 1948, but due to visa issues, they had a three-year stay in Brazil before finally moving to the city of Rosario in Argentina in 1951. While still there, Hedvig passed away. About a week before her death, however, fellow countryman Olof Jonsson had arrived in Embarcación to assist with the work. When Per Pedersen arrived in the city in 1952, a conflict arose regarding who should have decision-making authority. This was partly due to the fact that Hedvig was Swedish. Lewi Pethrus visited them the same year and stated that since all financial support from Europe had come through Norway, except for the last few years after Johnsen's death,[19] the Swedish missionaries should find a new mission field. They then moved to Tartagal, while Per and Palma remained and continued the work for several more years.

Swedish Pentecostal missionaries

We have already been introduced to Albin Gustavsson, who together with his wife Fanny and six other Swedish Pentecostal missionaries arrived in Argentina in 1920. At first, they worked alongside Berger Johnsen in Embarcación. One of them, Hedvig Berg, became Johnsen's wife in 1921, as we have already seen.

Some of the Swedish missionaries went on to Bolivia, but most remained in Argentina. Axel Severin and his wife moved in 1921 to

---

[18] As of January 1, 1948, the magazines *Misjonsrøsten* and *De unges blad* were merged with *Det gode Budskap*, which then became the official publication of the Free Evangelical Assemblies.

[19] Johnsen built the mission station 'primarily with money that one of his relatives had given him'. Kaleb Hansen, 'Berger Johnsen – misjonær i 25 år', *Korsets seier* 14 September 1935, p. 5.

Buenos Aires where a small Pentecostal congregation was founded on 26 February the following year. In 1925, they returned to Sweden but were replaced by Beda and Gunnar Svensson as the new pastors.[20] From the beginning there seems to have been good relations and regular interaction between the Scandinavian missionaries. This also applied to Danish-born Annina Kjælstrup and compatriot Niels Sørensen. They had both arrived as early as 1913, and a few years after they married, they set up their own ministry in Bolívar outside the city of Buenos Aires. The Scandinavian missionaries shared the same theological understanding, often called the Swedish congregational model, with free, independent congregations instead of the congregations being subject to some foreign missionary organization.[21]

Erling and Alvina Andresen

Erling Andresen had worked as an evangelist in Northern Norway in the period 1922-25.[22] This partly coincided in time with Berger Johnsen's stay in Norway, which seems to have been instrumental to Andresen's sensing a missionary call to Argentina.

His original plan was to leave at the same time as Johnsen.[23] However, it did not work out that way. Instead, Andresen went temporarily to the United States where, on 22 June 1926, he married Alvina, who was from Nordhordaland, but belonged to a local Pentecostal congregation in Chicago. He himself was a member of the Filadelfia congregation in Oslo but had received ordination papers as a missionary through the Scandinavian Assemblies of

---

[20] Gunnar Svensson's successor in Buenos Aires was reportedly Karl Fredriksson, who published the magazine *El Heraldo Pentecostal* which later changed its name to *El Heraldo de Paz*. Helga Mjåvatn, 'Argentina', *Korsets seier* 30 April 1949, p. 187.

[21] Bengt Samuel Forsberg, *Svensk Pingstmission i Argentina* (Huddinge: Missions-Institutet-PMU, 2000), pp. 33-43.

[22] However, already in 1919, i.e., before the period in northern Norway, Andresen had worked as an evangelist. Alvina and Erling Andresen, 'Hilsen fra misjonær Erling Andresen og hustru', *Korsets seier* 26 January 1946, pp. 63-64.

[23] Erling Andresen, 'Ut til 'Argentina', *Korsets seir* 20 April 1925, p. 3.

God.[24] The newlyweds therefore took the boat route from New York via Rio de Janeiro and on to Buenos Aires.[25]

Erling and Alvina spent some time with Berger Johnsen in Embarcación and considered moving on to Bolívar to work with the Sørensen couple. While they were visiting Beda and Gunnar Svensson in Buenos Aires, they became acquainted with the Spaniard Gerardo Pérez, who in 1913 had moved from Brazil to Argentina where he now resided in the town of Río Tercero in Córdoba. His wife had won several of the neighbors over to the Christian faith, and they were aware of the need for assistance. This was the reason why they approached Gunnar Svensson to ask for a foreign missionary to be sent, which coincided in time with Erling and Alvina's visit.[26]

Thus, Erling and Alvina's first own field of activity became Río Tercero, where the first public meeting was held on Christmas Day 1927.[27] They combined public meetings with door to door visiting, as well as handing out tracts and parts of Scripture on the streets. In 1928 they already gathered around 100 people for church services, and in February 1929 they held the first baptism meeting where four people were baptized. In October of the same year, they bought land to build their own church premises. The mission station could be built because they received an interest-free loan from the Canadian Pentecostal missionary C.M. Wortman, who had replaced Annina and Niels Sørensen in Bolívar.[28]

In the same year, they received reinforcements via Albin Gustavsson and his family, who had returned from Bolivia, and soon after they started preparations for the construction of their own mission station.[29] Bengt Forsberg writes:

> The missionaries experienced success in their work and the congregation grew. Many young people came to faith. For a long

---

[24] In 1931, however, we read that they are 'supported by contributions from the congregation in Brooklyn, NY, and friends in Norway'. 'Følgende misjonærer', *Korsets seier* 16 May 1931, p. 5. The congregation in Brooklyn refers to the Salem Scandinavian Pentecostal Assembly, where Arne Dahl was the congregation's first pastor.

[25] 'Fra fjern og nær', *Korsets seier* 30 October 1926, pp. 2-3.

[26] Forsberg, *Svensk Pingstmission i Argentina*, pp. 53-54.

[27] Erling Andresen, *Blant indianere og katolikker i Argentina* (Oslo: Filadelfia-forlaget [n.d.]), p. 36.

[28] Alvina and Erling Andresen, 'Argentina', *Korsets seier* 24 June 1939, p. 403.

[29] Erling Andresen, *Blant indianere og katolikker i Argentina*, pp. 11, 23, 31, 35-38.

time to come, the congregation became a center for church work in the province. From there the blessing was to extend far beyond the local scene. No fewer than twenty of the congregation's young people became ministers and pastors in different parts of the country. A further ten married ministers.[30]

In connection with Erling and Alvina's home leave in 1930, Albin and Fanny Gustavsson took the main responsibility at the mission station – this despite the fact that their 3-year-old daughter died only two weeks before Erling and Alvina left Río Tercero.[31] In September 1932, Erling and Alvina were back in Argentina,[32] now with the Pentecostal congregation in Sarpsborg as partly responsible for their financial support,[33] and in their absence the congregation had grown by about 30 people.[34]

Several Norwegian Pentecostals sensed a missionary calling to Argentina, and in 1930 Signora Dragland came to Río Tercero before moving to Buenos Aires the following year.[35] Sigurd Grønvold, already mentioned, also worked for a period with them.[36] So did Kaleb Hansen, from Lillehammer, who ministered briefly alongside Erling and Alvina, and then visited Albin and Fanny Gustavsson, who now worked in the city of Córdoba, before he expressed his desire to continue up to Embarcación where Berger Johnsen had his mission station.[37] However, he only stayed there for a month and a half before moving on temporarily to Las Lomitas in the province of Formosa.[38]

In 1938, Albin and Fanny Gustavsson broke away from Córdoba in favor of neighboring Chile, which led Alvina and Erling to take over their work. Córdoba at this time had around 300,000 inhabitants,

[30] Forsberg, *Svensk Pingstmission i Argentina*, p. 54.

[31] Alvina and Erling Andresen, 'Argentina', *Korsets seier* 18 April 1931, p. 5.

[32] Alvina and Erling Andresen, 'Fra Argentina', *Korsets seier* 14 January 1933, p. 6.

[33] Gustav Søderberg, 'Underhold av misjonær Erling Andresen, Argentina', *Korsets seier* 22 October 1932, p. 5.

[34] Gustav Søderberg, 'Vedrørende misjonær Erling Andresens underhold', *Korsets seier* 28 January 1933, p. 6.

[35] 'Fra Argentina', *Korsets seier* 30 August 1930, pp. 6-7; Signora Dragland, 'Argentina', *Korsets seier* Christmastime 1931, p. 12.

[36] Sigurd Grønvold, 'Misjon Evangelia', *Det gode Budskab* 15 February 1932, p. 3.

[37] Kaleb Hansen, 'Fra Argentina', *Korsets seier* 17 August 1935, p. 5.

[38] Kaleb Hansen, 'Argentina', *Korsets seier* 2 November 1935, p. 6.

and despite a distance of 100 kilometers between this city and Río Tercero, Erling and Alvina chose to travel on a monthly basis to Río Tercero both to 'give [the church members] the communion', but also in order to continue supervising the congregation.[39] Helga Mjåvatn, with the Espa Pentecostal congregation outside Hamar as a sending church, had also recently come out and was with them in Córdoba, but with an intended function in Río Tercero.[40]

Already in 1939, Alvina and Erling had baptized 30 people, and the congregation had over 100 members.[41] In the same year, they were replaced by Swedish missionary Karl Fredriksson while *they* replaced Canadian missionary C.M. Wortman in Bolívar. Wortman had taken over from Annine and Niels Sørensen earlier. Through this we see how Norwegian, Swedish, Danish and Canadian Pentecostal missionaries collaborated in a common goal of planting and building autonomous and self-supporting local congregations. [42] As an extension of this collaboration, a separate magazine, *Heraldo Pentecostal,* was published, then with a name change to *Heraldo de Paz,* in addition to the children's magazine *Heraldo de los Niños.*[43]

In 1952, Alvina and Erling were in Teodoro García, Buenos Aires. At some point, Erling had become part of the Pentecostal Assemblies of Canada (PAOC), which in Argentina merged with the Assemblies of God in 1947 and took the name *la Unión de las Asambleas de Dios.* [44] Here, Niels Sørensen and Erling Andresen became the first superintendents. They reported positively on American healing minister Tommy Hicks' meetings in the Argentine capital. Already back in 1952 a committee had been formed with the

---

[39] Alvina and Erling Andresen, 'Argentina', *Korsets seier* 24 September 1938, p. 6.

[40] After some time in Río Tercero, Mjåvatn seems to have moved to the city of Villa María and she thought about moving to the city of San Francisco. In both of these two cities, as well as six other places, the Córdoba congregation had outpost activities. Mjåvatn also writes that she received part of her maintenance from Norway and part from North America. Helga Mjåvatn, 'Argentina', *Kor-sets seier* 13 July 1946, p. 446.

[41] Alvina and Erling Andresen, 'Argentina', *Korsets seier* 25 February 1939, pp. 122-23.

[42] Alvina and Erling Andresen, 'Argentina', *Korsets seier* 24 June 1939, pp. 403-404.

[43] Alvina and Erling Andresen, 'Hilsen fra misjonær Erling Andresen og hustru', *Korsets seier* 26 January 1946, pp. 63-64.

[44] Louie W. Stokes, *Historia del Movimiento Pentecostal en la Argentina* (Buenos Aires, Argentina: the author, [n.d.], p. 31.

intention of getting T.L. Osborn to come, but when this had not succeeded, Hicks arrived instead.[45] He stayed over two months in Buenos Aires, and after about 4 weeks the meetings were transferred from the soccer stadium Atlanta to Huracán, where at times hundreds of thousands of participants were present.[46] Alvina and Erling Andresen wrote shortly afterwards:

> The whole of Buenos Aires with its more than 4 million inhabitants was affected by the revival. Thousands confessed Jesus as their Savior for the first time in their lives. Thousands reportedly also got to know God's healing power. 80,000 handed in their cards where they listed their name and address as a sign that they had received Jesus as their Savior and wanted to know more about the Christian faith.[47]

In 1959, Alvina and Erling wrote to Norwegian Pentecostals that the Scandinavian congregations in Argentina were also part of *Unión de las Asambleas de Dios en Argentina*. However, this did not apply to the congregations in the North – *la misión noruega* – which did not want to join the UAD.[48] One of the reasons why Erling and Alvina, as well as the congregations in the south, chose to join the organization was that without national recognition, they were no longer allowed to hold meetings, and UAD had been granted this recognition. Alvina and Erling continued to write about revivals around them, not least through evangelist Juan Carlos Ortiz, who had attended their Bible school.[49] Around 1963, Alvina and Erling moved

---

[45] Alvina and Erling Andresen, 'Vekkelse i Buenos Aires', *Korsets seier* 24 - 31 July 1954, p. 475.

[46] Arnt Twetan, 'Vekkelsen i Argentina', *Det gode Budskap* 20 April 1955, p. 90; Arnt Twetan, 'Vekkelsen i Argentina', *Det gode Budskap* 1 May 1955, pp. 101, 104.

[47] Alvina and Erling Andresen, 'Mer om vekkelsen i Buenos Aires', *Korsets seier* 12 March 1955, pp. 162-63.

[48] It was not until 2023 that the Norwegian mission in the north entered into a collaboration with UAD.

[49] Alvina and Erling Andresen, 'Misjonsarbeidet bærer frukt i Argentina', *Korsets seier* 11 July 1959, p. 444. Both Alvina and Erling had been teachers at the Assemblies of God Bible school where Erling 'was also the first school Director' in addition to the fact that he was for several years superintendent of the denomination. Finn Jensen, 'Festdager i Embarcacion', *Korsets seier* 10 September 1969, p. 5. In 1976 Ortiz was warned against, as he was not part of the *Asambleas de Dios*, that his 'presence in Argentina, Paraguay, Chile and other countries in South America has led to the division of several congregations' and that 'his books and

to the city of Rosario[50] and then to Córdoba in 1968[51] before the following year they 'were ready to go to North America, where they [had] their children and family'.[52]

Steady influx of new missionaries

In 1946, perhaps as an extension of the South American conference at Ski in January, Bergljot Nordmoen from Trysil announced her missionary call to Argentina.[53] A new South American conference, this time under the auspices of the congregation Sion in Lillestrøm, was held in October of the same year.[54]

Little by little there was a steady influx of new missionaries. Palma and Per A. Pedersen had traveled to Brazil in 1949 and three years later to Argentina, where they worked for at least two periods in Embarcación, the old mission field of Berger and Hedvig Johnsen.[55] It was Per Talaasen who for many years was their treasurer and who made sure that they eventually received both permanent support and a sending congregation. When he and his wife Gerda spent a year in Latin America in the period 1959-60 and in the city of Embarcación personally observed Palma and Per '[standing] with the medical treatment of the Indians in a corner of the veranda that is used as a

---

writings are strongly destructive and directly non-Scriptural in several areas'. 'Sør-Amerikakonferansen i Sarpsborg viser framgang', *Korsets seier* 2 June 1976, pp. 20, 19. Cf. also Nils Kastberg, 'Juan Carlos Ortiz forandrer menighetslivet', *Korsets seier* 25 May 1977, p. 2, as well as Lazaro Herrera and Ivar Vingren, 'Argentinske predikanter sier sin mening om Ortiz', *Korsets seier* 25 June 1977, p. 12. Ortiz would later become superintendent of the Spanish speaking members of Robert Schuller's Crystal Cathedral in Garden Grove, California. 'Juan Carlos Ortiz fra pinsebevegelsen til presbyterianerne', *Korsets seier* 6 August 1993, p. 6.

[50] Gunnvald Opheim, '40 år i misjonens tjeneste', *Korsets seier* 7 December 1966, p. 4; Henry W. Spjøtvold, 'Vekkelsens vinder blåser i Argentina', *Korsets seier* 13 May 1967, p. 12.

[51] Hanne-Berit and Finn Jensen, 'Frelsesmøter og dåp i Argentina', *Korsets seier* 27 July 1968, p. 12.

[52] Finn Jensen, 'Festdager i Embarcacion', *Korsets seier* 10 September 1969, p. 5.

[53] 'Til Argentina', *Korsets seier* 19 October 1946, pp. 674, 678.

[54] 'Sør-Amerika konferansen i Lillestrøm', *Korsets seier* 16 November 1946, pp. 739-40.

[55] Jarle Reite, 'Guds kraft forandrar indianarane', *Korsets seier* 22 September 1971, pp. 4-5; Gustav Iversen, 'Fra Argentina', *Det gode Budskap* 20 May 1953, p. 115; Palma and Per A. Pedersen, 'Hilsen fra Sør-Amerika', *Korsets seier* 15 March 1952, pp. 130-31. Per A. Pedersen's book *Blant indianere i Chaco* (Oslo: Filadelfia-forlaget, 1972) contains descriptions of his travel activities in northern Argen-tina.

living room,' he began immediately after returning to Norway 'to collect [money] for the infirmary and sent out funds as he received them'. [56] The infirmary was completed in 1964 and was then expanded.

Two years earlier, Finn Jensen had announced his missionary call to Argentina after having worked as an evangelist in Finnmark. [57] In 1964, his fiancée, Hanne-Berit Johansen, announced *her* call. [58] They married upon her arrival in Argentina on 31 October. [59] By then he had already been out for almost two years while she completed her education as a nurse in Drammen. [60] Similarly, Frantz Mangersnes worked in 1963 in Juárez, in the province of Formosa about 350 kilometers from Embarcación after having had his first missionary assignment in Brazil starting in 1948. [61] 1963 was also the year that Cyril Pedersen, son of Palma and Per, as a 19-year-old was sent out on an independent basis by the congregation Tabernaklet in Skien. [62] He eventually started up in Rivadavia, a short distance from Embarcación. [63] More or less at the same time, Finn and Hanne-Berit Jensen began ministry in the town of Jujuy, [64] where they had Gunnvald and Julie-Marie Opheim as colleagues. They had been recognized as missionary candidates by the Pentecostal congregation

---

[56] Ranveig Annie Edvardsen, 'Takk til Per Talaasen', *Korsets seier* 26 April 1972, p. 4.

[57] Finn Jensen, 'Til Argentina', *Korsets seier* 9 June 1962, p. 359.

[58] 'Til Argentina', *Korsets seier* 19 January 1964, p. 37; 'Avskjedsfest for Hanne-Berit Johansen', *Korsets seier* 24 October 1964, p. 678.

[59] 'Våre misjonærer', *Korsets seier* 13 March 1965, p. 6.

[60] Hanne-Berit Jensen, *Minner fra et helt liv* (Private publication, 2016), p. 6.

[61] Frantz Mangersnes, 'Hilsen fra Formosa, Nord-Argentina', *Korsets seier* 23 March 1963, p. 187.

[62] 'Ny misjonær', *Korsets seier* 23 November 1963, pp. 738-39. Cyril's parents had been advised against taking the children with them when they were going out to Brazil for the first time in 1949. As a 5-year-old, he and his four-year-younger brother were therefore left with their grandparents. It wasn't until eight months later that he was allowed to travel abroad. This happened because his grandfather followed him to Oslo, where Erling Rydse, contact person for South America, followed the 5-year-old to Copenhagen, where he was left to a flight attendant at SAS. Thus, Cyril traveled alone, with a stopover in the African country of Senegal. However, his grandmother had attached a note to his backpack with the PO box address of missionary Leonard Pettersen in Rio de Janeiro. 'Med merkelapp på ryggen til postboks i Brasil', *Korsets seier* 5 November 1999, p. 32.

[63] G. Leonard Pettersen, 'Glimt fra et nytt misjonsfelt i Sør-Amerika', *Korsets seier* 20 November 1965, p. 7.

[64] Hanne-Berit and Finn Jensen, 'Nye framstøt i Argentina', *Korsets seier* 12 March 1966, p. 12.

in Vestby already back in 1955 and came out to Argentina the following year.[65]After about two and a half years in the central part of the country, they had then moved up to Embarcación in 1958. The subtropical heat probably contributed to Julie-Marie becoming seriously ill, and they had then moved to the city of Salta[66] before a new relocation to San Salvador de Jujuy in 1965. In connection with Hanne-Berit and Finn going to Norway on furlough, Julie-Marie and Gunnvald were given the main responsibility in Jujuy.[67] With the assistance of Hardy Mossberg in Chile, weekly devotional programs were soon broadcast over the radio announcing the congregation's meetings in Jujuy. [68] Later, Opheim began producing their own programs instead of, as previously, receiving ready-made programs from Mossberg.[69]

In 1967, Ingjerd Øvrum, a member of Tabernaklet, Skien, announced a missionary call to Argentina after working for over a year in the Betania home in Alta.[70] So did Martha Kvalsvik, from Filadelfia, Hammerfest.[71] The next year, Solfrid and Roar Eriksen announced *their* call to Argentina.[72]

In 1969 there was a marriage between Palma and Per A. Pedersen's daughter Evelyn and evangelist Pedro Draganchuk, whose parents had left Eastern Europe many years before in favor of Argentina due to difficult conditions for Christians in their home country.[73] Pedro and Evelyn had their assignment in Tartagal.[74] A few years later, an

---

[65] 'Til Argentina', *Korsets seier* 28 July – 4 August 1956, pp. 474-75.

[66] Julie-Marie and Gunnvald Opheim, 'Hilsen fra Salta, Argentina', *Korsets seier* 23 May 1959, pp. 328-29.

[67] Hanne-Berit and Finn Jensen, 'Avskjedsmøter i Paraguay', *Korsets seier* 15 October 1966, p. 6.

[68] Julie and Gunnvald Opheim, 'Misjonen tar radioen i bruk i Nord-Argentina', *Korsets seier* 3 January 1968, pp. 3, 6.

[69] Thor J. Thoresen, 'Sentralisering av vårt radioarbeid i Sør-Amerika', *Korsets seier* 30 June 1973, p. 9.

[70] 'Ny misjonær til Argentina', *Korsets seier* 8 April 1967, p. 12. In 1968 we read that she works together with Ranveig Edvardsen in the infirmary at the mission station in Embarcación. Ingjerd Øvrum, 'Blant skogens indianere lyder evangeliet', *Korsets seier* 6 March 1968, p. 8.

[71] 'Nymisjonær', *Korsets seier* 18 October 1967, p. 3.

[72] 'Nye misjonskandidater for Argentina', *Korsets seier* 16 March 1968, p. 9.

[73] Finn Jensen, 'Festdager i Embarcacion', *Korsets seier* 10 September 1969, p. 5; Jarle Reite, 'Guds kraft forandrar indianarane', *Korsets seier* 22 September 1971, pp. 4-5.

[74] Håkon Haug, 'Unge misjonærer til Argentina', *Korsets seier* 5 February 1972, p. 12.

area of land was bought where indigenous people could live safely and no one could take it from them again. Almost immediately, 29 families from 4 different tribes moved into the area.[75]

Evelyn's brother Carlos, who was born in Argentina and already in his teens, began to work as a traveling evangelist[76] and would eventually, together with his wife Adela, be officially sent out by a Norwegian church.[77] In 1978, they had taken up operations in Aguaray and Pocitos.[78]

After a furlough in Norway, Finn and Hanne-Berit embarked on a new field of activity in the town of Orán in 1974.[79] A congregation was founded there two years later.[80] This was led by a national pastor. Mention should also be made of Henry William Spjøtvold and his wife Mildrid, who were missionaries in Argentina under the auspices of the Salvation Army when they experienced a charismatic renewal through contact with Alvina and Erling Andresen and later became Pentecostal missionaries.[81] They were instructors at an evangelist school in Río Cuarto, the *Centro Evangelístico*, which in turn was part of a local congregation in Rosario and had about 1,500 members in 1971.[82] We first read about them in 1965 when Henry, together with Finn Jensen, was visiting the town of Tartagal, 60 kilometers from the Bolivian border.[83] Before Henry and Mildrid were officially sent out by a Norwegian Pentecostal congregation, Per Talaasen was their treasurer.[84] Later, Zion, Stavanger became their sending church.

---

[75] 'Hjelp indianerne med lokalbygg i Tartagal!' *Korsets seier* 4 August 1973, p. 6.

[76] Kjetil Haugstøl, 'Med evangeliet til indianerne i Argentinas skoger', *Korsets seier* 24 October 1970, p. 7.

[77] 'Nye misjonærer', *Korsets seier* 19 January 1977, p. 8; 'Til Argentina', *Korsets seier* 2 July 1977, p. 2.

[78] 'Stort behov for nytt lokale i Aguaray, Argentina', *Korsets seier* 15 February 1978, p. 6.

[79] Hanne-Berit and Finn Jensen, 'Nytt virke i Argentina', *Korsets seier* 28 December 1974, p. 6.

[80] Hanne-Berit and Finn Jensen, 'Menighet dannet i Oran, Argentina', *Korsets seier* 17 November 1976, pp. 1, 15.

[81] Alvina and Erling Andresen, 'Arbeidet i Argentina går fram', *Korsets seier* 10 September 1966, p. 7.

[82] Henry William Spjøtvold, 'Karismatisk vekkelse i Argentina: Stort behov for undervisning', *Korsets seier* 13 January 1971, pp. 6-7.

[83] Henry William Spjøtvold, 'Besøk på en utpost i Argentina', *Korsets seier* 11 December 1965, p. 10.

[84] Ranveig Annie Edvardsen, 'Takk til Per Talaasen', *Korsets seier* 26 April 1972, p. 4; Gottfred Leonard Pettersen, 'Utsendermenighet for misjonærene Spjøt-vold', *Korsets seier* 14 December 1966, p. 15.

The Spjøtvold family received assistance from Solfrid and Roar Eriksen, who were sent to Argentina in 1970.[85] After two years with them in Río Cuarto, the Eriksen family moved in 1972 to Laboulaye, which then had a population of about 20,000.[86] During their first furlough in 1974, they were replaced by the Opheims.[87] On their return, they also took up work in the small town of Levalle, about 50 kilometers from Laboulaye. In Laboulaye itself, in the center of the city, they were also able to buy land for the congregation.[88] The church was formally founded as *Asamblea de Dios – Laboulaye* in 1977 with 34 members.[89]

In connection with a furlough in Norway, Roar and Solveig were replaced by Martha and Helge Magne Øya in 1978,[90] who two years later handed over the church to the Argentine Juan Cáceres,[91] who had been converted six years earlier and after three years had become an elder in the congregation.[92] In 1987, the congregation counted more than 150 baptized including the outposts.[93] Similarly, we read

---

[85] Solfrid and Roar Eriksen, 'Nye misjonærer møter Argentina', *Korsets seier* 4 November 1970, p. 4.

[86] 'På besøk i Argentina', *Korsets seier* 13 January 1973, p. 2; Solfrid and Roar Eriksen, 'Guds ord forvandler', *Korsets seier* 1973, p. 9.

[87] 'Hjem etter første periode i Argentina', *Korsets seier* 5 January 1974, p. 2.

[88] Solfrid and Roar Eriksen, 'Begivenhetsrike år i Laboulaye, Argentina', *Korsets seier* 7 February 1976, p. 5. Helge Magne Øya had already announced to have a missionary call to Argentina in 1972, and together with his wife Martha he had for a time beginning in 1974 been ministering in San Pedro de Jujuy. 'Ny misjonær til Argentina', *Korsets seier* 23 September 1972, p. 4; Martha and Helge Magne Øya, 'Framsteg i Argentina', *Korsets seier* 1 September 1976, p. 7. Astrid and Roald Jensen also came to Jujuy the same year, and in 1975 a congregation was founded. In 1993, the Argentinian couple Efraín and Olga Gonzáles became the pastors of the church. Else Johannesen, 'Nasjonal ledelse av menigheten i San Pedro', *Korsets seier* 7 May 1993, p. 15.

[89] 'Ny menighet dannet i Argentina', *Korsets seier* 21 May 1977, p. 2.

[90] Martha and Helge Magne Øya, 'Til ny periode i Argentina', *Korsets seier* 13 September 1978, p. 2.

[91] Birger Sandli, 'Avskjed for Martha og Helge Magne Øya i Argentina', *Korsets seier* 15 October 1980, p. 14. Cáceres spent almost three months in Norway in 1989 where he was preaching in Norwegian Pentecostal churches. 'Argentina-besøk i norske menigheter', *Korsets seier* 10 March 1989, p. 5.

[92] Solfrid and Roar Eriksen, 'Framgang for Guds Ord i Laboulaye, Argentina', *Korsets seier* 12 November 1980, p. 10.

[93] Solfrid and Roar Eriksen, '10-årsjubileum i Argentina', *Korsets seier* 3 April 1987, p. 14. In 1994 Adela and Gabriel Gorjón became pastors in the congregation, and in 2022 their son Rodrigo and his wife Yanina were sent out as missionaries to Spanish speakers in Canada. In the same year, the congregation in

from the small town by the name Ing. Juárez, where PYM had carried out work since 1956, not least through Frantz Mangersnes, and which from 1986 had national pastors, Mary and Adolf Tasuni.[94]

Strategic thought was given to the training of future national ministers, and in 1987 Finn Jensen was chosen to lead an itinerant Bible school in northern Argentina. The school would be held for one month each in various churches, thus avoiding additional costs for suitable premises. They initially envisioned one or two-year studies which included church practice, with the intended goal 'to get national pastors for all the congregations both in Argentina and the additional South American countries'.[95]

Finn and Hanne-Berit's son Benjamin also became involved in the Bible school when *he* was sent out as a missionary. Initially he spent six months at the Norwegian school in Paraguay and then a couple of months in Cochabamba, Bolivia before establishing himself in northern Argentina where his parents were.[96]After marriage to Linda in Norway in 1991, they were sent out as missionaries, this time to

---

Laboulaye had 'activity in 15 places in Argentina, in addition to having congregations in Brazil'. Roar Eriksen, '"Norsk"' kirkevekst i Argentina', *Korsets seier* 26 August 2016, p. 35. Besides Rodrigo and Yanina were sent to Spain in 2022 and are financially supported through Norwegian contacts. Rodrigo's parents have also visited Brazil on various occasions, and through that they have made acquaintances with Brazilian missionaries in Mozambique, who are now being supported by the congregation in Laboulaye. The congregation also supports a Chilean woman whom they met during a visit to Norway. The woman was actively involved in the Hispanic group within the Salem Church, Oslo and is now a missionary in India. Geir Lie, interview with Roar Eriksen, 4 April 2024.

[94] Britt and Birger Sandli, 'Vekkelsesrapporten fra Ing. Juarez', *Ekko. Korsets seiers utenriks– og misjonsmagasin* May 1987, p. 4. There was still a Norwegian Pentecostal presence within the city, however, and in 1991 Vidar Bullen and Ranveig A. Edvardsen reported from 'the inauguration of a NORAD-supported housing project of 65 simple houses', nonetheless described as 'a big transition for most of the indigenous people – from a poor dirt hut to a house with two rooms and a large terrace'. Vidar Bullen and Ranveig A. Edvardsen, 'Stor dag for indianerne i Ing. Juarez, Argentina', *Korsets seier* 18 January 1991, p. 1.

[95] Hans Svartdahl, 'Betel bibelinstitutt i Argentina', *Korsets seier* 12 June 1987, pp. 5, 21. 'Most [Norwegian missionaries] went home in the 90s and the work has been nationalized. [...] The first period after the missionaries left the country, the national leaders used the time to consolidate their position and find their own identity. Today you find a vibrant church that wants to stand on its own two feet'. Jørgen Cloumann, 'Fattige indianere vil misjonere blant unådde', *Korsets seier* 16 January 2009, p. 22.

[96] 'Benjamin O. Jensen ønsket velkommen hjem etter første periode i Argentina', *Korsets seier* 4 November 1988, p. 16.

the city of Salta in Argentina.[97] There was already a Pentecostal congregation there, the *Iglesia Betania*, but it had experienced a marked decline and only had about 20 people, including the children. The congregation experienced significant growth after Benjamin and Linda came and started public meetings in the district of Santa Ana I.[98] Together with Else Palma Øgaard, Benjamin and Linda also founded a congregation in *Penal Villa las Rosas*, Salta's prison. This congregation, *La verdadera libertad*, was pastored by one of the inmates and grew in a few years from 30 to 300 people.[99]

In 1997 Benjamin and Linda left Argentina, but after four years in Norway they moved to Spain where, in addition to church planting, they founded, in collaboration with the American Assemblies of God couple Dana and David Santiago, the disciple-training school Masters Commission. The teaching was based on the Assemblies of God Berean School of Ministry (now: Berean School of the Bible) and consisted of both theoretical teaching and evangelistic praxis. In 2007, Benjamin and Linda moved back to Argentina where the discipleship school was conducted in the city of Salta in the period 2007-2009. The evangelistic praxis in Argentina was largely 'children's ministry, street evangelism, social work, and church related activities'.[100]

During the first year they had 18 students, but when that figure dropped to 4 the next year, the school was restructured for year 3. They used the same material but now made 5 course modules and initiated 8 different congregational Bible schools with 180 students in total. After each completed module, Benjamin traveled around to the various congregations to hold the exam. About 160 students completed the five modules. In addition to Masters Commission, they also offered a church leaders program, using a Spanish-language

[97] 'Pionerarbeid i Argentina', *Korsets seier* 31 May 1959, p. 9.

[98] In 1997 there were about 200 members in Iglesia, Betania. Magne Losnegård, 'Fest og glede i Salta', *Korsets seier* 23 May 1997, p. 9.

[99] Geir Lie, interview with Benjamin Jensen, dated 8 June 2024. However, the preparatory work for the prison congregation had already been laid during Fall 1990 when young students from the Danish Pentecostal school in Mariager gave their testimonies at a prison meeting and it was decided to start meetings on a regular basis. Else Palma Johannesen, 'Åpne dører i Salta, Argentina', *Korsets seier* 21 June 1991, pp. 10, 17.

[100] Anne Gustavsen, 'Unge vil trenes til å forandre', *Korsets seier* 20 July 2007, p. 19.

version of John Maxwell's *EQUIP* (One Million Leaders Mandate) or *LIDERE* as it is called in Latin America.[101]

The latest Argentina missionaries until now are Rakel Ystebø Alegre and her Argentinian husband Ariel, both with the Tabernaklet, Bergen as sending church in 2023. Rakel will be dean at the newly founded *Universidad Evangélica* in Buenos Aires, with actual commencement in March 2025. Both Rakel and Ariel will be teaching at the faculty.

Missionaries representing the Free Evangelical Assemblies

The first Argentine missionaries sent out by the Free Evangelical Assemblies were Tordis and Daniel Dahl.[102] Daniel had previously pastored both the congregation Eben-Ezer in Brooklyn, U.S. and the Free Evangelical Assembly in Sarpsborg.[103] The couple arrived in Argentina in 1966 and temporarily settled in the city of Rosario.[104] It is interesting to note that on their arrival in Buenos Aires they were met on the dock by Palma and Per A. Pedersen, missionaries from *Pinsebevegelsen*, while in Rosario they were met by Erling Andresen.[105] While they lived in Rosario, they attended the congregation Andresen pastored and where Dahl baptized ten new converts during a baptismal service.[106] As they moved to San Salvador de Jujuy in 1967,

---

[101] Geir Lie, interview with Benjamin Jensen, 8 June 2024. Rebeca and Jorge Romero ran the Bible school in Salta and the itinerant Bible school together with Benjamin Jensen.

[102] Berger Johnsen had in many ways acted independently of the Norwegian *Pinsebevegelsen's* mission, although he had a stronger connection to the Free Evangelical Assemblies than to the *Pinsebevegelsen*. That is why Edvin Andreassen writes in the article 'De Frie Evangeliske Forsamlinger har drevet misjon i 80 år', *Det gode Budskap* 15 March 1990, p. 12: 'In Argentina Berger Johnsen's work was taken over by the *Pinsebevegelsen* when Berger Johnsen withdrew, and *DFEF* did not have missionaries who were ready to go out. The Free Evangelical Assemblies resumed work in Argentina in 1966'.

[103] Bjarne Staalstrøm, 'Nye misjonskandidater for Argentina', *Det gode Budskap* 10 September 1965, pp. 3-4; Tordis and Daniel Dahl, 'Gå derfor ut!' *Det gode Budskap* 10 March 1966, p. 3.

[104] Tordis and Daniel Dahl, 'Familien Dahl vel ankommet til Argentina', *Det gode Budskap* 10 October 1966, p. 3.

[105] Daniel Dahl, 'På reise fra Norge til argentinsk millionby', *Det gode Budskap* 20 October 1966, pp. 3, 7-8.

[106] Daniel Dahl, 'Argentina – dagens aktuelle misjonsfelt', *Det gode Budskap* 1 March 1967, p. 7.

it became natural to work together with Gunnvald and Julie-Marie Opheim, whom as we already know, also represented *Pinsebevegelsen.*[107] In the same year, however, they moved on – this time to the city of Tucumán – where the Free Evangelical Assemblies established their first independent work in Argentina.[108] Before Christmas the following year, they had a baptismal service where 7 new converts were baptized.[109] Soon they were also involved in a weekly radio ministry through the program *Una mirada de fe*, which consisted of both preaching and singing and where a free Bible correspondence course was promoted.[110]

Reidun and Aage Håskjold had felt a missionary call for a long time, and in 1968 they left Norway.[111] In 1971 they wrote home about meetings held in the homes of new converts where people were constantly coming to faith.[112] During that same year, Marit Moen from Salem, Mjøndalen announced her own call to Argentina.[113] However, she did not arrive in Buenos Aires until 1973, and, like the Dahl family, became involved in church related work in Tucumán, as well as in the outpost in Aguilares, about 80 kilometers away.[114] Daniel Dahl was replaced by Berner Solås as pastor in Tucumán[115]

---

[107] Tordis and Daniel Dahl, 'Nytt fra Daniel Dahl i Argentina', *Det gode Budskap* 20 April 1967, p. 3.

[108] Tordis and Daniel Dahl, 'Familien Dahl i Argentina etablerer sin misjons- virksomhet i Tucuman', *Det gode Budskap* 15 February 1968, pp. 3-4.

[109] Tordis and Daniel Dahl, 'Den som tror og blir døpt. Innhøstning i Argentina', *Det gode Budskap* 10 February 1969, p. 3.

[110] Tordis and Daniel Dahl, 'Evangelisk radiomisjon over eteren i Tucuman, Argentina', *Det gode Budskap* 1 July 1969, pp. 9, 12.

[111] 'Åge Håskjold med familie på vei til Argentina', *Det gode Budskap* 10 March 1968, p. 3.

[112] Reidun and Aage Haaskjold, 'Nyheter fra misj. Haaskjold i Argentina', *Det gode Budskap* 1 March 1971, pp. 10-11.

[113] Marit Moen, 'Misjonskandidat for Argentina', *Det gode Budskap* 10 November 1971, pp. 4-5.

[114] Marit Moen, 'Marit Moen vel fremme i Argentina', *Det gode Budskap* 10-20 April 1973, p. 9. She was then to take up pioneer work in the town of La Banda Santiago, just under 200 kilometers from Tucumán. 'Misjonær Marit Moen', *Det gode Budskap* 10 November 1977, p. 8.

[115] It is impressive to read about the married couple Rossana and Víctor Alpaca, who both experienced a Christian conversion through Berner and Olaug's work in Tucumán. Víctor is Peruvian, and in 2010 we read that the couple had moved back to his homeland where they worked as co-pastors in a congregation of 8,000 members in the capital Lima. Leif Frode Svendsen, 'Vunnet for Jesus av de "norske" – i dag vinner de tusener for Jesus', *Det gode Budskap* no. 6 2010, pp. 8-9.

that same year[116] and initiated a pioneering work in Córdoba.[117] Solås was to stay in Tucumán until 1979, when he and his family left for Aguilares, which for a long time had been an outpost to Tucumán despite a distance of almost 90 kilometers.[118] Only in 1990 did they move on to Córdoba to serve the congregation Tordis and Daniel Dahl had founded in 1974.[119]

1976 was the year Turid Sneve from the city of Mandal announced her mission call to Argentina, as she had finished her theological studies at the Ansgar School. Her sending church was Betania, Kristiansand.[120] In 1978 she married the Argentinian Miguel Ardiles, who henceforth worked alongside her in the ministry.[121] As among the missionaries from the *Pinsebevegelsen*, the 1970s reflected a stronger consciousness of the importance of connecting with national collaborators. This applied to both Argentina and Brazil. [122] Symptomatic of this is the fact that Luís Alberto Ledesma from the church in Tucumán was invited as a speaker at the National Convention of the Free Evangelical Assemblies in Karmøy in 1989.[123] He was also to visit the denomination's local churches, and

[116] Daniel Dahl, 'Echeverria, Tucuman, Argentina', *Det gode Budskap* 1 November 1973, p. 5.

[117] Edvin Andreassen, 'Misjonærene Dahl's har leid møtesalong i Cordoba', *Det gode Budskap* 10 May 1974, p. 3. The Solås family was replaced by the Haaskjold family in 1977. Reidun Haaskjold, 'Gleder meg til å komme ut', *Det gode Budskap* 20 January 1977, p. 7.

[118] Berner Solås, 'Jesus lever!' *Det gode Budskap* 20 July 1979, pp. 1, 5. Solås' over forty years of missionary activity in Argentina is described in Einar Vestvik's book *Gud skal ha æren. Olaug og Berner Solås* (Veavågen: Den frie evangeliske forsamling Klippen, 2016).

[119] Einar Vestvik, *Gud skal ha æren,* p. 144. There, Olaug and Berner Solås worked with street children, which contributed to the fact that all the pensioners' societies on Karmøy joined together in a joint effort, together with the local business community, to collect money for the work. Sten Sørensen, 'Pensjonister hjelper gatebarn i Argentina', *Det gode Budskap* 15 April 1991, p. 9.

[120] 'Turid Sneve – ny misjonskandidat', *Det gode Budskap* 20 June 1976, p. 4.

[121] Turid Sneve de Ardiles, 'Bryllup i Argentina', *Det gode Budskap* 10-20 July and 1 August 1978, p. 8. After three years in Norway, where Miguel had worked as a medical doctor, in 1990 the family was again ready to leave for Argentina, where Miguel wanted to start a mobile health service in the area around Tucumán and work among people who could not afford to pay for ordinary healthcare services. 'Miguel E. Ardiles: Misjonslege i Argentina', *Det gode Budskap* 1 February 1990, pp. 10-11.

[122] 'Til Norge etter 4 år i Brasil', *Det gode Budskap* 20 August and 1 September 1979, p. 12.

[123] Edvin Andreassen, 'Besøk fra Argentina til landsmøtet '89', *Det gode Budskap* 1 April 1990, p. 9.

his stay in Norway would extend from July to October.[124] In a similar vein, in 1992, after 26 years of missionary work in Argentina, the first national staff or ministerial conference was held in Tucumán.[125] A description of the visit of Berner Solås and Kjell Arve Tolås to Argentina in 1997 also shows that there were national pastors in a number of cities, in addition to the fact that the directors of the orphanage in Los Sarmientos were Argentines.[126] Unfortunately the orphanage was closed down in 2012.[127]

In spite of the nationalization of the work, some of the Norwegians remained. Among these were Edel and Sverre Vedøy, who built a conference center in Río Ceballo near Córdoba, where a 2-year mission school, *Escuela de Misiones y Plantación de Iglesias* (EMPI), was opened in March 2003.[128]

As we write in 2025, Jan Bjarne and Anita Skrøvje are still in Argentina. Anita is a missionary child, daughter of Olaug and Berner Solås and was born in Argentina. After marrying they left Norway together in January 1993 and spent the first nine years in Tucumán before moving to El Mollar in 2001. They are still overseeing the six congregations in Tucumán, which existed before 1993, in addition to the church they themselves have planted in El Mollar. Daughter Rebeca and husband Cristian Tejera are working alongside them in

---

[124] Edvin Andreassen, 'Evangelist Luis Alberto Ledesma fra Argentina besøker Norge', *Det gode Budskap* 1 July 1989, p. 13.

[125] Sverre Vedøy, 'Historisk dag i Argentina', *Det gode Budskap* 15 April 1993, p. 8.

[126] Kjell Arve Tolås, 'Glimt fra turen til Argentina', *Det gode Budskap* 1 May 1997, pp. 10-12. It was probably not only in Brazil that the role of missionaries gradually changed, where they no longer primarily established churches but rather '[created] a channel of communication between Christians in [the mission field] and Norway, particularly as far as social projects are concerned'. The same was likely true for both Argentina and other Latin American countries where Norwegian missionaries were involved. Geirr Standal, 'Rektor for voksende bibelskole!' *Det gode Budskap* no. 3 2006, pp. 34-35.

[127] Helge Nupen, 'Avvikler barnehjemmet', *Det gode Budskap* no. 2 2012, p. 30.

[128] Kjell Tangen, 'Åpning av Misjonsskole i Cordoba', *Det gode Budskap* 15 May 2003, pp. 36-37. Regardless of this, it is important to point out that missionary commitment is also great in Latin America, and the days when all missions went 'from the West to the rest' are long over. Lie, *Tro og tanke før og nå*, p. 147. In 2007 alone, Argentina had around 200 missionary candidates from the Asam-blea de Dios. Asle Ystebø, '200 misjonærer klare til utreise nå', *Korsets seier* 17 August 2007, pp. 16-17.

leadership positions, while daughter Veronica and husband Gabriel Lazán are youth pastors in a larger congregation in the city of Salta.[129]

---

[129] Geir Lie, interview with Anita and Jan Bjarne Skrøvje, 18 November 2024.

3

BRAZIL

We have already introduced the three Italian Pentecostal ministers Luigi Francescon, Giacomo Lombardi, and Lucia Menna, who left Argentina for São Paulo, Brazil in March 1910. Just a few months later the two Swedes Gunnar Vingren (1879-1933) and Daniel Berg (1884-1963), similarly to the three above, also had some connection with William Durham's congregation in Chicago.

Just a few months before Vingren and Berg's arrival in Brazil, while Berg was pastor of a Baptist church in South Bend, Indiana, a prophetic message was delivered by the Swedish-American Adolf Uldin that Berg should go out as a missionary to Pará, a place neither of them knew the location of.[1] The next day Vingren visited the local library, where he found out with the help of a librarian and an atlas that Pará is in Brazil.

Daniel Berg, together with a number of other Scandinavians, was part of Durham's congregation, and when Berg visited Vingren shortly afterwards, Vingren received a new prophecy in which it appeared that they *both* had missionary calls to Brazil. Durham's congregation assumed responsibility as a sending congregation, which did *not*, however, include financial support.

On November 19, 1910, they arrived in Belém do Pará without knowing anyone. After about six months, they purportedly started ministering in Portuguese, initially in a Baptist church. However, this was not open to preaching about Spirit baptism and speaking in

---

[1] Jan-Åke Alvarsson, 'Frida Vingren', *Reflexões – Uma Perspectiva Pastoral e Ecclesial* 2.1 (Janeiro 2022), p. 66.

tongues, and the two Swedes, together with 16 Brazilians, soon had to leave the assembly.[2] This was the prelude to the Pentecostal denomination As Igrejas Evangélicas Assembleias de Deus, which has around 12 million followers.[3]

In the beginning, 'missionaries came from Sweden and Scandinavians from America'.[4] The first Norwegian Pentecostal missionary, albeit 'sent from Sweden',[5] was Jahn Sørheim, usually referred to in *Korsets seier* as *John* Sørheim, who at least in 1925 worked alongside Swedish missionaries and with a postal address in Rio de Janeiro[6] and later Santos.[7] He originally went out for the Salvation Army in 1924, but was won over to Pentecostal Christianity through his Swedish contacts. His wife Anna (née Johannesson) was also Swedish, and for many years he received his financial support via congregations in Sweden, as well as the *Filadelfiaförsamlingen* in Chicago.[8]

We then have to wait until 1936 before Ragna and Leonard Pettersen's mission call was realized. In one of his books, Leonard claims that he already took a Christian stand as a child. This position was renewed in 1923, and he actively joined the Salvation Army in Arendal. Two years later he was baptized under the auspices of the

---

[2] Jan-Åke Alvarsson, 'Daniel e Sara Berg', *Reflexões – Uma Perspectiva Pastoral e Ecclesial* 2.2 (Outubro 2022), pp. 32-35. 'Two Brazilian sisters, Celina Albuequerque and Maria de Nazaré, were the first to testify that they had [received] the baptism of the Spirit due to the preaching of the brothers. Both belonged to the Baptist congregation in the town where Berg and Vingren made their first [contact], and it culminated with 19 friends [who experienced the power of the Spirit] being expelled from the Baptist church for that reason. The above-mentioned 19 friends together with Vingren and Berg then formed their own congregation on 18 June 1911. This became the first germ of what would later become a gigantic manifestation of God's power: "Assembleia de Deus in Brazil"'. Lars Førland, '5 millioner pinsevenner i Brasil', *Ekko.Korsets seiers utenriks– og misjonsmagasin* August 1986, p. 10.

[3] 'Assemblies of God in Brazil', *https://pt.wikipedia.org/wiki/Assembleias_de_Deus_no_Brasil* [Accessed 4 April 2024].

[4] G. Leonard Pettersen, 'Brasil – Sør-Amerika', *Korsets seier* 2 January 1954, p. 11.

[5] 'Fra Brasilien', *Korsets seier* 7 March 1931, p. 6.

[6] John Sørheim, 'Kjære Korsets Seir's læsere', *Korsets seir* 20 October 1925, p. 7.

[7] John Sørheim, 'Kjære Korsets Seir's læsere', *Korsets seir* 17 March 1928, p. 6.

[8] Arne Dahl, 'Hjem fra Brasilien', *Korsets seier* Christmastime 1939, pp. 821-22. Cf. also Kristian Heggelund, 'Misjonær Jahn Sørheim 50 år', *Korsets seier* 3 December 1949, pp. 604-605, as well as the articles 'Sørheim, Anna' and 'Sørheim, Jahn', in *Norsk misjonsleksikon*. Vol. 3 (Stavanger: Nomi forlag – Runa forlag, 1967), p. 883.

Free Evangelical Assemblies, and in 1926 he joined the local assembly belonging to the *Pinsebevegelsen* at Strømmen. Later he became a member in Filadelfia, Oslo.

In 1933, Leonard was working in Sweden and became aware of Daniel Berg and Jose de Matos, as well as other Swedish Pentecostal missionaries in Brazil. Pettersen soon experienced a specific missionary call, and sent by both the Pentecostal congregation in Arvika, Sweden and the Pentecostal congregation belonging to the *Pinsebevegelsen* in Salen, Ski, in October 1936 he went to Brazil. For many years, Rio de Janeiro became his and Ragna's 'field of work ... and ... starting point for mission, evangelization and church building across large parts of the immense country'.[9] After 4 or 5 months in Porto Alegre, where the Pettersen family assisted the Swedish missionary couple Gustav and Hedvig Nordlund, who had lived there for many years and had a large and vibrant congregation,[10] they settled in the city of Cruz Alta, both to learn Portuguese and to participate in Christian work. After eight months, they relocated to Uruguayana, where a congregation was founded in 1938 with 19 members. As early as 1939, they had built their own church building which accommodated 200 people, and by New Year's 1939-40 the church had grown to 80 members.[11] This congregation was important for the further spread of the Pentecostal movement, not only within Brazil, but also within Uruguay.[12] It is worth noting, as Pettersen writes, that missionaries to Brazil from different nationalities cooperated extensively as they sought to build self-governing and self-sustaining local churches.[13]

---

[9] G. Leonard Pettersen, *Pinse over grensene* (Oslo: Filadelfiaforlaget, 1989), p. 78. 'Our work center in Brazil is Rio de Janeiro, the country's capital. For several reasons, however, the work has branched out to several other states, partly through direct responsibility or also through repeated shorter visits'. G. Leonard Pettersen, 'En del glimt fra misjonsarbeidet i Brasil', *Korsets seier* 17 February 1951, p. 82.

[10] G. Leonard Pettersen, *Blant folkeslag i Sør-Amerika. Misjons- og reiseskildringer* (Oslo: Filadelfiaforlaget, 1947), pp. 25-26.

[11] Pettersen, *Blant folkeslag i Sør-Amerika,* pp. 41-44.

[12] Pettersen, *Pinse over grensene,* p. 82.

[13] Pettersen, *Blant folkeslag i Sør-Amerika,* p. 26. The Norwegian woman Ruth Johansson, whose maiden name was Ingelsrud, traveled to Brazil in 1951. After three years there, she met the Swedish missionary Gustaf Arne Johansson, whom she married in São Paulo. After being on furlough in Norway and Sweden in 1965, they went back to Brazil the following year. In 2017, their son Lars-Gustaf and his Brazilian wife Salma were called to be pastors in Betania, Eidskog; i.e., the mother's

After a year, the Pettersen family moved to Santa Maria, one of the largest cities in the state of Rio Grande do Sul, while their colleague Leonardo Gonçalves took over the work in Uruguayana and served as the congregation's pastor for 50 years. Herbert Nordlund had previously held meetings in Santa Maria where several people had experienced a Christian conversion. A Brazilian evangelist had since taken responsibility for the church, and when the Pettersen family arrived, the congregation had already in-creased to about 250 members. In 1942, a further 90 people were baptized and added to the church. The Pettersen family now received help from Jovino d'Avila as a newly appointed evangelist, while Leonardo Gonçalves worked in the outpost churches before he eventually became the congregation's senior pastor.[14]

Due to the war, in 1943 Leonard Pettersen was assigned to duty in the Norwegian navy in England, while Ragna remained in Brazil.[15] The family had previously moved to Rio de Janeiro, and after two years in England, Leonard was reunited with them.[16] The war was now over, and it felt good to stay in Norway – the family's very first furlough. On August 26, 1945, they left Rio de Janeiro, where Leonard had 'served the congregation for the last few months'.[17] They arrived in Oslo on 18 September.[18] A few months later, in January 1946, the Salen, Ski congregation organized a South America conference. A similar conference was organized in Lillestrøm in the fall of the same year.[19]

In 1946, their furlough was over and they moved to Rio Grande. Together with them traveled Lorentze Thorkildsen, who had previous experience as an evangelist from Norway and had been sent from Filadelfia, Oslo.[20] At least in 1951 she was in Santo André, not

---

home church. 'Avskjedsfest for misjonærene Ruth og Arne Johansson med familie', *Korsets seier* 8 October 1966, p. 9; Anne-Marthe Hop-Hansen, 'Sendte ut misjonær – får pastor i retur', *Korsets seier* 17 February 2017, p. 25.

[14] Pettersen, *Blant folkeslag i Sør-Amerika*, pp. 54-56.

[15] Ragna and G. Leonard Pettersen, 'Hjemme igjen fra Brasil', *Korsets seier* 13 October 1945, pp. 395-96.

[16] Pettersen, *Pinse over grensene*, p. 98.

[17] Pettersen, *Blant folkeslag i Sør-Amerika*, p. 77.

[18] Pettersen, *Blant folkeslag i Sør-Amerika*, p. 80.

[19] Pettersen, *Pinse over grensene*, pp. 102-103. 'Sør Amerika-konferansen', *Korsets seier* 9 March 1946, pp. 157-58.

[20] 'Til Brasil', *Korsets seier* 27 July 1946, p. 481. We do not know whether

far from the port city of Santos, where she ministered in a vibrant congregation under a Brazilian pastor.[21] At about the same time, the two sisters Ruth and Dagny Kjellås announced their mission call to Brazil and received letters of recommendation from the church Sion, Trøgstad.[22]

Shortly thereafter, Ragna and Leonard received a call to the congregation in Rio de Janeiro, as the Swedish Pentecostal missionaries Otto and Adina Nelson had taken up missionary work in another Latin American country. The church had 1,500 members at this time, but experienced further growth in the coming years. Rio now became a natural base for many Scandinavian missionaries, who received assistance before they went on to their own fields of activity.[23] Leonard also had responsibility for a period of time for a congregation of around 1,200 members in the city of Niterói, which is close to Rio de Janeiro.[24]

After the period in Rio de Janeiro was over, the Pettersen family took up a short-term missionary activity in Bolivia. We will return to this matter in the chapter dealing with this country.

In 1948, Olaug and Leif Andersen, from Salem, Oslo, announced a missionary call to Brazil. Leif had joined the *Pinsebevegelsen* in Norway in connection with a personal conversion in 1936, while Olaug already in her early teens had experienced a Christian conversion in a Lutheran context before she became a member of the Salem Pentecostal church in Oslo in 1936.[25] The family first settled in Niterói until they started operations in the state of Paraná,[26] specifically the city of Curitiba at the invitation of the Swedish Pentecostal missionary Simon Lundgren.[27] Later they settled in the town of Londrina where they led a congregation of about 250

Thorkildsen's calling, which she had known about for several years, was actualized through the South American conference at Ski in January 1946.

[21] G. Leonard Pettersen, 'En del glimt fra misjonsarbeidet i Brasil', *Korsets seier* 3 March 1951, p. 105.

[22] 'Til Brasil', *Korsets seier* 1 February 1947, pp. 73-74.

[23] Pettersen, *Pinse over grensene*, p. 110.

[24] Frantz Mangersnes, 'Vel framme i Brasil', *Korsets seier* 20 January 1949, p. 28.

[25] 'Til Brasil', *Korsets seier* 20 June 1948, p. 355-56.

[26] G. Leonard Pettersen, 'En del glimt fra misjonsarbeidet i Brasil', *Korsets seier* 17 February 1951, p. 82.

[27] Leif G. Andersen, 'Parana, Brasil – landet med stor rikdom – og fattigdom', *Korsets seier* 19 April 1952, pp. 193-94.

members.[28] Illness required them to temporarily return to Norway in 1961.[29] They had now been home to Norway twice, so in 1962 they were starting their third missionary term in Brazil.[30] In 1963, they again lived in the city of Curitiba.[31]

In 1948, Frantz Mangersnes also announced his mission call and was sent by the Pentecostal congregation at Haslum in Bærum.[32] Two years later Palma and Per A. Pedersen also announced their missionary calling. After a few months in Rio, they were all sent to the state of Mato Grosso.[33] However, as mentioned in the previous chapter, Palma and Per A. Pedersen, together with their children Evelyn and Cyril, moved to Argentina in 1952 to take responsibility for the work at Embarcación.

In 1954, Berit Eriksen was sent to Brazil, and after a furlough in Norway, she was back in Cambé in September 1960, where she was responsible for the correspondence course Leif Andersen had created three years before.[34] In 1961, *Korsets seier* announced that Jorunn and Lars Førland would be traveling to Brazil during the month of November, sent out by Salem, Lørenskog and Salem, Oslo.[35] In 1963, they were stationed in the 'district of the Paraná River in the border area with Paraguay',[36] more specifically in the

---

[28] Olaug and Leif Andersen, 'Nyttårshilsen fra Parana', *Korsets seier* 22 February 1958, pp. 123-24.

[29] Leif Andersen, 'Hjem fra Parana', *Korsets seier* 14 January 1961, pp. 27-28.

[30] Oddvar Nilsen, 'Til Brasil for tredje gang', *Korsets seier* 5 May 1962, pp. 284-85.

[31] Leif G. Andersen, 'Bibelskole i Paraná', *Korsets seier* 24 August 1963, p. 538.

[32] Gunnerius Tollefsen, 'Misjonsnytt', *Korsets seier* 30 November 1948, p. 611.

[33] Frantz Mangersnes and Per A. Pedersen, 'Fra Brasils innland', *Korsets seier* 11 February 1950, p. 90.

[34] Berit Eriksen, 'Parana, Brasil', *Korsets seier* 11 February 1961. Gerda Lillian Aardalen, who had traveled to Brazil in 1959, had first worked for two and a half years in an evangelical hospital in Londrina in the northern part of Paraná, and then one year with Berit Eriksen in Cambé, where she worked as a nurse and midwife, before she had her first furlough in Norway. Gerda Lillian Aardalen, 'Fra sykearbeidet i Paraná', *Korsets seier* 18 May 1963, p. 313. Leif Andersen writes in the article 'Lokaler brennes i Brasil', *Korsets seier* 16 December 1967, p. 8: 'When I found with several of our young people the Adventists' Bible course per correspondence, I felt pressured to create our own correspondence course. In 1957, it was finished in 18 chapters'.

[35] Leonard Pettersen, 'Nye misjonærer til Brasil', *Korsets seier* 18 November 1961, p. 728.

[36] Jorunn and Lars M. Førland, 'Hilsen fra Parana – Brasil', *Korsets seier* 2 February 1963, p. 77.

town of Cascavel,[37] where the congregation had outposts in 7-8 different locations and where they also broadcast evangelistic radio programs over Cascavel Radio.[38] The Førland family stayed there until they went back to Norway on their first furlough in 1965.[39]As will be noted in the next chapter, they were then to have their field of activity in Paraguay.

In 1962, the Japanese Shigeji Maruyama and his newly married wife Aagot Berge were sent by the congregation Klippen, Sandnes to work among immigrant Japanese in Brazil.[40] Sigrun and Oddmar Byberg were also sent out from the same congregation in January 1964 – she a nurse, while he had worked as an evangelist for several years.[41] During that same time period, Ranveig Annie Edvardsen, trained as a nurse and midwife, was sent from Evangeliesalen, Oslo.[42]

We return to Olaug and Leif Andersen, who went with a vision to assist 'poor people who come to Curitiba to seek medical attention'.[43] They had started with temporary homes for 30 to 40 people gathered under one roof. The Foundation The Evangelical Confederation for Social Assistance also centered its activities around its own mission boat, the *Salem Missionária*, 'for use between the islands down by the Atlantic Ocean'.[44] In addition, a rest home for national ministers called *Oscar Andersen* was established named after Leif's father, former evangelist, who had recently died, as well as radio work and the magazine *Tribuna Pentecostal*.[45] It should also be noted that Aril Edvardsen's Native Evangelist Mission in Sarons Dal started up when Edvardsen responded positively to a notice

---

[37] Berit Eriksen, 'Hilsen fra Parana', *Korsets seier* 4 May 1963, pp. 280-81.

[38] Jorunn and Lars M. Førland, 'Kamp og seier ved Paraná-floden', *Korsets seier* 15 June 1963, pp. 379-80.

[39] Josef Iversen, 'På avskjedsmøter i Brasil', *Korsets seier* 9 October 1965, pp. 13-14.

[40] 'Fra Japan til Brasil som misjonærer', *Korsets seier* 11 August 1962, p. 510. In 1974 they were back in Japan again. 'Misjonen', *Korsets seier* 14 December 1974, p. 10.

[41] 'Nye misjonærer for Brasil', *Korsets seier* Eastertime 1963, p. 222.

[42] 'Til Brasil', *Korsets seier* 16 February 1963, p. 104.

[43] Olaug and Leif Andersen, 'Håpets hospits. En hjelp i nøden', *Korsets seier* 4 December 1971, p. 7.

[44] Olaug and Leif Andersen, 'Håpets hospits', p. 7; Olaug and Leif Andersen, 'Nye landevinninger i Parana', *Korsets seier* 26 January 1972, p. 8.

[45] Leif Andersen, 'Du er i Brasil nå', *Korsets seier* 25 September 1982, p. 5.

Andersen had published in *Korsets Seier* appealing for financial support for national workers in Brazil.[46]

Missionaries sent out by the Free Evangelical Assemblies

The Free Evangelical Assemblies' mission activities in Latin America started in Brazil through evangelist Per Andresen, who experienced a Christian conversion in the congregation Logen in Moss in 1952. It was therefore this congregation which became his sending church.[47] Following a brief period as a pastor in the Eben-Ezer assembly in Brooklyn, NY,[48] he made his way to Brazil in 1962 where he and his wife Alice started a new ministry in Cambará, a small town of around 25,000 inhabitants.[49] Several individuals quickly came to faith, and we read of 8candidates for baptism the following year.[50] Further conversions followed, and Andresen continued as the senior pastor in Cambará and the outposts, although in 1965 he accepted the call as pastor in Curitiba,[51] where, after a youth conference, he was able to baptize over a hundred people.[52] In a New Year's greeting from 1965, Andresen wrote that he visited Cambará every three months.[53] Due to different circumstances such as health challenges, the Andresen family returned to Norway in 1967. The congregation at

---

[46] Anne Christiansen, 'Fyrverkeri i Amazonas', *Korsets seier* 28 November 2014, p. 36.

[47] 'Evangelist Per Andresen til Syd-Amerika', *Det gode Budskap* 2 January 1961, pp. 6-7.

[48] Per Andersen, 'En liten hilsen fra Brooklyn', *Det gode Budskap* 20 September 1961, pp. 217, 222.

[49] Per Andresen, 'Hilsen fra misjonær Per Andresen', *Det gode Budskap* 20 November 1962, p. 270.

[50] Per Andresen, 'Hilsen fra Brasil', *Det gode Budskap* 20 September 1963, p. 202.

[51] Per Andresen, 'Brasil for Kristus', *Det gode Budskap* 10 August 1965, p. 3. However, this does not mean that Andresen became the senior pastor, but that he entered into a cooperative relationship with the local Assembleia de Deus congregation in Curitiba, which since 1962 was led by José Pimentel de Carvalho. Then 'the congregation consisted of approx. 2,500 members with a church in Curitiba, 3 houses of worship in the district and 7-8 outposts'. Seven years later there were '34 small houses of worship on the field with approx. 6,000 members. Each Sunday, a total of approx. 50 meetings', 'Brasil for Kristus', *Det gode Budskap* 1 October 1969, pp. 8-9.

[52] Alice and Per Andresen, 'Brasil kaller', *Det gode Budskap* 10 November 1965, p. 3.

[53] Alice and Per Andresen, 'Nyttårshilsen fra Brasil', *Det gode Budskap* 1 February 1966, p. 3.

this time consisted of 120 baptized believers and was now served by evangelist Nicanor Pereira dos Santos, who was supported financially from Norway.[54] The following year, Per Andresen returned, but due to 'school conditions' this time alone.[55] In 1969, however, the family was again together in Brazil.[56] In 1977, they purchased the river boat *Espeland Betel* in order to more easily evangelize along the great river in the state of Amazonas.[57]

In 1969, May-Lise and Gunnar Standal also left with plans to run their own work in Cambará.[58] We later read that Per Andresen, 'after working relatively isolated' for 2 years in Cambará, was 'offered to cooperate with this evangelical revival movement', that is Assembleia de Deus, which 'has been of mutual benefit'.[59] Andresen was 'responsible for the field in Cambará' until he and his family temporarily returned to Norway in 1973 and Gunnar Standal took over the main responsibility.[60] In 1975, the Andresen family was back

---

[54] 'Feltet i Brasil i trygge hender', *Det gode Budskap* 1 June 1967, p. 8.

[55] Per Andresen, 'Per Andresen reiser til Brasil 20. mai', *Det gode Budskap* 1 May 1968, p. 9.

[56] Alice and Per Andresen, 'Ut til en ny periode i Brasil', *Det gode Budskap* 1 December 1969, pp. 7, 4; Alice and Per Andresen, 'Brasil', *Det gode Budskap* 1 February 1970, p. 8.

[57] Alice and Per Andresen, 'Flodmisjon åpnes i Amazonas', *Det gode Budskap* 10 and 20 August 1977, p. 11. In 1978, we read that they had '15 native evangelists, as well as 4 riverboats who, with their native evangelists, carry out a large evangelistic work'. Per Andresen, 'Hjem fra Brasil', *Det gode Budskap* 20 May 1978, p. 1. In 1979, we read about plans to start a printing company in Curitiba in connection with Andresen going to Brazil on a short trip together with evangelist Raymann Karlsen. Edvind Andreassen, 'Per Andresen til Brasil igjen', *Det gode Budskap* 10 January 1979, pp. 6, 9. During 1985 alone, some 16 million tracts and more than 50,000 books were printed. Rolf Kjeilen, 'På reise i Brasil 1985-4', *Det gode Budskap* 1 November 1985, p. 16.

[58] May-Lise and Gunnar Standal, 'Takk til vennene fra misj. Standal og frue', *Det gode Budskap* 10-20 December 1969, p. 10.

[59] 'Fremstill deg for Gud', *Det gode Budskap* 10 – 20 August 1969, p. 3.

[60] Gunnar Standal, 'Avskjedsmøter og fest på floden i Brasil', *Det gode Budskap* 10-20 February 1973, p. 6. In 1991 we read both about an orphanage and a congregation with a national senior pastor. Olav Fjalestad, 'Det nye barne-hjemmet i Cambara en lysstråle i den sosiale nøden i Brasil', *Det gode Budskap* 15 March 1991, pp. 12-13, 19, 23. In 2005, a separate boys' home was also started, so that the first orphanage had 25 girls and the new orphanage had eight boys. Alice and Per Andresen, 'Barnehjemmet i Cambara', *Det gode Budskap* no 8 2005, p. 39.

in Brazil, this time in the city of Curitiba,[61] while the Standal family soon moved on to the capital, Brasilia.[62]

The Free Evangelical Assemblies had for a long time maintained good contact with the Örebro mission in Sweden, and several of the Free Evangelical Assemblies' mission candidates had attended their Bible school in Sweden.[63] In that respect, it was not unexpected that the Standal family's work in Brazil would 'be carried out in collaboration with the Swedish Örebro mission'.[64] In addition to starting up work in two districts of Brasilia,[65] national workers were sent to the cities of Paracatu, Belo Horizonte, and Vilhena. After a short period of time there were around 60 baptized members in the newly founded congregation in Paracatu.[66] In 1981 the Standal family left for Manaus in the state of Amazonas in northern Brazil.[67] Well

---

[61] Alice and Per Andresen, 'Vel fremme i Brasil', *Det gode Budskap* 10 – 20 February 1975, pp. 8-9.

[62] May-Lise and Gunnar Standal, 'I Brasils hjerte – "Brasilia"', *Det gode Budskap* 10 May 1976, pp. 6-7.

[63] 'Hva er Ørebromisjonen?' *Det gode Budskap* 10 July 1961, p. 159.

[64] 'Misjonærene May-Lise og Gunnar Standal flyttet til Brasils hovedstad, Brasilia', *Det gode Budskap* 10-20 July 1976, p. 6. The fact is that Brazilian law did not allow the establishment of 'unregistered congregations in Brazil following the pattern of the Free Evangelical Assemblies in Norway. Foreign missionaries [had to] have a calling from an established denomination in the country and work according to their guidelines. For Standals, it has therefore become very practical to be able to slip into the Örebro mission's national denomination called [Convenção das Igrejas Batistas Independentes]. In English: Convention of Free Baptist Churches. The congregations are independent and governed according to democratic principles. Extensive joint work is carried out both locally and when missionaries are sent to neighboring countries'. Siman Nordmo, 'Det vokser i Brasil', *Det gode Budskap* 15 August 1981, p. 11. See also the book *Da Suécia ao Brasil. Uma história missionária* , ed., Marciano Kappaun (Campinas, Brazil: Convenção das Igrejas Batistas Independentes – CIBI, 2012). In this, the work of the Örebro Mission in Brazil, initiated by emigrant Swedish Örebro Baptists in 1912, is described, and one chapter is devoted to Norwegian Free Evangelical Assemblies missionaries (pp. 183-98). With the exception of Per Andresen, who worked with Assembleia de Deus, the other Free Evangelical Assemblies missionaries have collaborated with Convenção das Igrejas Batistas Independentes. Bjørn Olsen, '100-års misjonsjubileum i Brasil', *Det gode Budskap* no. 3 2012, p. 31.

[65] The work in Brasilia, after the Standal family moved on, had in 2017 resulted in almost 20 congregations in the area. Oddwin Solvoll, 'Misjonsmøte torsdag', *Det gode Budskap* no. 7 2017, pp. 20-21.

[66] May-Lise and Gunnar Standal, 'Glimt fra misjonsarbeidet i Brasilia', *Det gode Budskap* 10 June 1979, p. 1.

[67] Siman Nordmo, 'Det vokser i Brasil', *Det gode Budskap* 15 August 1981, p. 11. After three years in Manaus, the Standal family temporarily returned to Norway,

over a decade later, there was another move, this time to the city of Recife in north-eastern Brazil.[68] In 1998, there were already several congregations and outposts in these districts, with constant growth and with some of the congregations having national leaders.[69] These churches were also part of the Convenção das Igrejas Batistas Independentes.[70] After completing his theological studies at the Ansgar School in Norway, Geirr Standal became involved here, both as a pastor and Bible school director.[71] The congregations became involved in missionary work early on, and a former pastor couple, Tamilla and Alan Deelo, worked as missionaries in the African country of Guinea-Bissau in 2015, while another family was sent to Spain.[72]

Turid Dahl, who had started as an evangelist in the Free Evangelical Assemblies back in 1977 and for several years had worked as children and youth secretary in the Children and Youth

---

and the work was continued for a period by Ragnhild Kihle. After the Standal family returned to Brazil, they stayed in the Amazon area for about ten years before the congregation in Manaus had a national senior pastor. In 2017, we read that the congregation had sent missionaries to both Peru and Venezuela. Bjørn S. Olsen, 'Eventyret i Amazonas', *Det gode Budskap* no 4 2017, pp. 2-3. We also read that 'in Manaus there have been seven self-sustaining congregations with many outposts'. Oddwin Solvoll, 'Misjonsmøte torsdag', *Det gode Budskap* no. 7 2017, p. 21.

[68] May-Lise and Gunnar Standal, 'Nytt misjonsfelt i Brasil', *Det gode Budskap* 15 January 1992, p. 13. In 2012, we read that May-Lise and Gunnar Standal had jointly established ten congregations in Brazil. Bjørn S. Olsen, 'DFEF har satt fotspor i Brasil', *Det gode Budskap*, p. 33.

[69] May-Lise and Gunnar Standal, 'Framgang og vekst for arbeidet i Recife', *Det gode Budskap* no 14 1998, pp. 18-19. In 2012 we read that there were now 'four sister congregations in the city with their own pastors, a three-year Bible school and a large project for malnourished children'. Oddwin Solvoll, 'Eva og Geirr Standal klare for utreise til Brasil', *Det gode Budskap* no. 2 2012, p. 31. The congregation started in the living room of May-Lise and Gunnar, but due to space requirements they soon had to move the meetings to the garage. Then they rented a school and carried chairs and equipment back and forth. A short kilometer away, they were able to buy land – a sinkhole where 120-150 truckloads of filling material were needed to level it. Today, the congregation Igreja Batista Ebenezer is established there with approx. 350 members'. Oddwin Solvoll, 'Menigheten begynte i stuen', *Det gode Budskap* no. 1 2015, p. 22.

[70] Leif F. Svendsen, 'Geirr Standal står i en rik tjeneste!' *Det gode Budskap* 1 June 2001, pp. 18-20.

[71] 'Misjonærer fra Brasil', *Jesus mitt liv. DFEFs sommerstevne 10.-15. juli 2007 Åkrahallen, Karmøy*, p. 3. Supplementary to *Det gode Budskap* no. 5 2007.

[72] Oddwin Solvoll, 'Misjonsmøte ble frelsesmøte med barnevelsignelse', *Det gode Budskap* no. 1 2015, p. 23.

Council (*BUR*),[73] traveled to Brazil in 2002, and after less than a year had, in collaboration with the Convenção das Igrejas Batistas Independentes, started a congregation in Mogi das Cruzes, a district of São Paulo.[74] Together with her cousin Jakob Langåker, she also bought a property of 52 acres to make the work among the children more efficient: 'Every morning, from Monday to Friday, 45 children aged six to 12 come to the project. The day starts with breakfast and continues with worship, play, arts work, assistance with homework and regular school teaching before ending with a good and nutritious dinner'.[75] Her goal was to take in a hundred children living in the slums.[76]After marrying Karl Stokland in 2006, both returned to Brazil where they continued the work Turid had begun.[77] In 2007, there were 120 children in the age group from 6 to 12 years, in addition to 18 young people.[78]

In 2017, Turid was made an honorary citizen of Mogi das Cruzes, a suburbia town that then had around 400,000 inhabitants.[79] The following year, the main responsibility for the work was handed over to national worker Eliza Maria Silva, as Turid and Karl returned permanently to Norway, although Turid continued with short-term trips to Brazil.[80]

Ragnhild Kihle's more than 40 years of missionary labor in Brazil also deserve attention, which has included the construction of a

---

[73] Knut Østbye, 'Takk, Turid!' *Det gode Budskap* no 1 1998, p. 22.

[74] Turid Dahl, 'Gud har velsignet med sjelers frelse!' *Det gode Budskap* 1 December 2002, pp. 34, 44.

[75] 'Turid og Jakob utvider i Sao Paolo', *Det gode Budskap* no 11 2004, pp. 32-33. The work was named *Árvore da Vida* (Tree of Life).

[76] Leif F. Svendsen, 'Møtesal med plass til 600 stoler', *Det gode Budskap* no 11 2004, p. 33.

[77] 'Turid + Karl = Sant!' *Det gode Budskap* no 2 2006, p. 48.

[78] Leif Frode Svendsen, 'Ingen kan hjelpe alle, men alle kan hjelpe noen', *Det gode Budskap* no 6 2007, pp. 32-33. In 2012, there were approximately 200 children who daily received 'food, help with homework, teaching in practical and theoretical subjects as well as hearing the preaching of the Word of God'. Bjørn S. Olsen, 'DFEF har satt fotspor i Brasil', *Det gode Budskap* no 3 2012, pp. 32-33.

[79] Sten Sørensen, 'Æresborger av Mogi das Cruzes', *Det gode Budskap* no 6 2017, pp. 26-27.

[80] Arne Håkon Hansen, 'Turid Dahl Stokland gir stafettpinnen videre i Brasil', *Det gode Budskap* no. 5 2018, pp. 16-17.

church building and a school in Campina Grande, the location where she has 'laid down most of her work in Brazil'.[81]

After one year at the Salvation Army's College for Officer training and then, besides other responsibilities, seven years as a slum sister, she went out as a salvationist missionary in 1969. After ten years in Brazil, the leadership of the Salvation Army thought that she was not strong enough to continue, and during one of her furloughs they offered her a leadership position within the Salvation Army in Norway. As a matter of fact, she had to either accept this offer or leave the Salvation Army. However, Kihle believed that she had a calling to continue in Brazil and contacted the Free Evangelical Assemblies, which she had known from her youth. She therefore became a Free Evangelical Assemblies missionary in 1981 when she returned to Brazil.[82]

Missionaries sent out from New Life Mission

In addition to the *Pinsebevegelsen* and the Free Evangelical Assemblies, the New Life Mission also became involved in Brazil. The mission organization Maran Ata New Life Mission was founded in 1978, but after a break with the mother congregation Maran Ata, Oslo in 1985, it formalized itself as an independent congregation the following year.[83] Wiggo Abrahamsen, former minister within Maran Ata, was involved in the start-up until in 1987 he moved to São Paulo, Brazil and there founded the organization *Vida Nova* with an emphasis on work among street children. Abrahamsen moved back to Norway in 1994, but the ministry was continued by his mother Janni. She

[81] Bjørn S. Olsen, 'DFEF har satt fotspor i Brasil', *Det gode Budskap* no. 3 2012, p. 33. Kihle came to Brazil for the first time in 1969, initially as a missionary within the Salvation Army, and worked in various places until in 1996 she settled in the city of Campina Grande. Here she had a new school built for 500 children. At the age of 79, Kihle then started constructing the church building, that is to say, not only 'administering the construction process and providing money', but she was daily on the construction site and had 'supervision of the work' in addition to her single-handedly having built the platform and the walls of the baptismal pool. Oddwin Solvoll, 'Misjonær Ragnhild Kihle: Pensjonist og kirkebygger', *Det gode Budskap* no 1 2014, pp. 24-25.
[82] Oddwin Solvoll, 'Misjonær Ragnhild Kihle har skrevet sin selvbiografi', *Det gode Budskap* April 2016, pp. 30-31; Also cf. Ragnhild Kihle, *Mitt livs historie: Kallets tjeneste* (Horten: R. Kihle, 2015).
[83] Geir Lie, 'New Life Mission', in Lie, (ed.), *Norsk pinsekristendom og karismatisk fornyelse*, p. 121.

initiated the construction of two centers, with almost 200 children enrolled there. One of her pronounced goals was to get all the children into school, not least through motivational work aimed at both the children themselves and their parents.[84] The work was discontinued when she returned to Norway in 2012.

---

[84] Tore Bjørn Ringås, 'Jeg kunne ha nøyd meg med å strikke sokker for misjonen', *Korsets seier* 13 February 2004, pp. 12-13.

4

PARAGUAY

The history of the Pentecostal movement in Paraguay has not yet been written, but there is much evidence that Norwegian missionaries were among the first pioneers. The American researcher David Bundy believes that the first impulses came via the Norwegian Pentecostal mission in Bolivia along the border with Paraguay in 1938.

Simultaneously, German, Polish and Russian Pentecostal refugees arrived both during and after the Second World War. These founded small congregations, but persecution from the Catholics created unfavorable conditions for growth. Raymond Stawinski was sent out from the American Assemblies of God in 1945, and shortly afterwards a local church was founded in Asunción.

Similarly, the Church of God also established itself in Paraguay, with initial contacts among German speakers. By 1960, this Pentecostal denomination had a dozen churches in the country. Since then, other Pentecostal denominations have also gained a solid foothold in Paraguay, one example being The Foursquare Church.[1]

In Norwegian sources, however, we read from as early as 1937 that Kaleb Hansen from Lillehammer, even though he was initially sent to Argentina, visited Paraguay: 'I will naturally try to gather the

---

[1] David Dale Bundy, 'Paraguay', in Stanley M. Burgess and Eduard M. van der Maas (eds.), *The New International Dictionary of Pentecostal Charismatic Movements* (Grand Rapids, MI: Zondervan Publishing House, 2002), p. 198. Others have argued that the first two American Assemblies of God missionaries came as early as 1936. Inge Bjørnevoll, 'I Paraguay: Ein misjonseksplosjon!' *Ekko. Korsets seiers utenriks- og misjonsmagasin* February 1988, p. 10.

Paraguayans for meetings here, so that when God gives me what is necessary and when the people start to trust, the banner of salvation shall also be raised here in Monte Sociedad'.[2] Shortly thereafter, Hansen chose to move to the capital, Asunción.[3]

It is probably correct to say that the Pentecostal movement as such came via Swedish missionaries Beda and Gunnar Svensson, who had previously worked in Buenos Aires, Argentina.[4] They held their first public meeting in Asunción on June 1, 1938. The following year, the first Filadelfia congregation was founded, with 15 members. Gunnar Svensson remained the senior pastor of the congregation until his death in 1952 and was then succeeded by his wife. Later, the Swedish missionary Nils Ivan Kastberg took over the role, and during his tenure several outposts were established.[5] One of those who were converted through Kastberg's ministry was the Paraguayan Leonardo Alderete, who for several years was supported financially from Norway as an evangelist before he was called to be the pastor of the Filadelfia congregation in Asunción.[6] In 1972, the church had about 400 members including those belonging to the outposts.[7]

In 1952, Bergljot Nordmoen took up missionary work in Paraguay[8] after having stayed for over a year in Spain,[9] a period which included learning Spanish. After a month in Brazil, she flew to Asunción, but after a short period with Beda Svensson it became

---

[2] Kaleb Hansen, 'Fra Paraguay', *Korsets seier* 23 January 1937, p. 6.

[3] Kaleb Hansen, 'Fra Paraguay', *Korsets seier* 5 March 1938, p. 6.

[4] 'The time has often been long for me when I have walked alone here, so I have tried to get away at least to another country, but now I see in its entirety how great God has arranged this misguided walk of mine here in Paraguay. Missionary Svensson who for approx. 13 years has worked in Buenos Aires, Argentina, has come here now with his family, something I could not imagine in my dreams. […] I was indeed thinking of leaving Paraguay at the end of this year, but if God helps me in some way, after Svensson's arrival, I will try to hold out for another time, at least as long as God wills'. Kaleb Hansen, 'Paraguay', *Korsets seier* 17 September 1938, p. 6.

[5] 'I dag har bevegelsen grupper mange steder i Paraguay', *Korsets seier* 23 January 1971, pp. 6-7.

[6] Lars M. Førland, 'Besøk fra Paraguay', *Korsets seier* 19 August 1972, p. 6.

[7] Lars M. Førland, 'Vi venter himmelsk vårregn', sier paraguayisk pastor', *Korsets seier* 9 September 1972, p. 9.

[8] Anna Strømsrud, 'Radioarbeid på tale i Paraguay', *Korsets seier* 16 February 1972, pp. 1, 8.

[9] Erling Ritse, 'Fra Sør-Amerika', *Korsets seier* 8 November 1952, p. 541.

clear to her that she was to go to the city of Concepción.[10] Due to Catholic opposition, however, she decided instead to initiate a work in Bella Vista, near the Brazilian border, in addition to staying a few months at the mission station in Embarcación, Argentina.[11]

She received assistance from Gunvor Johansen, sent from Filadelfia, Sarpsborg and Ruth Kjellås in 1956 before they started operations in Paso Cadena,[12] which was surrounded by small Indian villages deep in the jungle.[13] They soon received further assistance from Frantz Mangersnes, who had previously worked in both Brazil and Argentina.[14] In 1961, however, Kjellås and Johansen left to go back to Norway, and Bergljot Nordmoen was now the only Norwegian missionary in Paraguay.[15] In 1963, while she was in Norway, she married Olav Norheim, who announced a missionary call to Paraguay the same year after serving as an evangelist and pastor in Norway for around 28 years.[16]

---

[10] Bergljot Nordmoen, 'Hilsen fra Paraguay, Sør-Amerikas hjerte', *Korsets seier* 17 October 1953, pp. 650-51.

[11] Bergljot Nordmoen, 'Opplevelser i Sør-Amerika', *Korsets seier* 9 June 1956, pp. 363-64.

[12] 'In 1958, three single sisters ... came to Paso Cadena and took up work among the Ava Guarani Indians who lived in the area. It all started very simply with reading lessons, nursing care and meetings under a large tree'. Inge Bjørnevoll, 'Høytidsdag da kirken i Paso Cadena ble innviet', *Korsets seier* 7 October 1994, p. 12.

[13] Gunvor Johansen, 'Til Paraguay', *Korsets seier* 7 July 1956, p. 427; Ruth Kjellås, 'En hilsen fra Paso Cadena, Paraguay', *Korsets seier* 6 December 1958, p. 779. Cf. also Gunvor Iversen's independently published booklet *Ut til Paraguay* [n.d.]. Parts of the story have already been documented in Maria Elena Forberg Benitez, *The Norwegian Pentecostal Mission and Indigenous Peoples in the Eastern Border Regions of Paraguay (1952-2015). Disseminating Colonial Worldview and Adapting to Human Rights?* (Master's thesis, The University in Southeast Norway, 2024).

[14] Frantz Mangersnes, 'En hilsen fra Nord-Paraguay', *Korsets seier* 13 June 1959, pp. 377-79. For a more in-depth presentation of Mangersnes, cf. Britt and Birger Sandli, 'En trofast Herrens tjener legger årene inn', *Korsets seier* 15 October 1983, pp. 14-15.

[15] Bergljot Nordmoen, 'Fra Guarani-indianernes land, Paraguay', *Korsets seier* 8 April 1961, pp. 220-21.

[16] Olav Norheim, 'Til Paraguay', *Korsets seier* 7 December 1963, p. 774. It is interesting to read Bergljot's retrospective reflections: 'My thoughts go back to the day when, 14 years ago, I set foot on Paraguayan soil. [...] When I think of the first time here in Paso Cadena, when we had school under a tree in the courtyard, with a few students, and now this past year, when we have had 60 students divided into three classes, and gathered in a magnificent schoolhouse, I must thank my God, who has helped so well. Nursing treatment no longer takes place in the open, but in a magnificent infirmary. Thanks to our friends in Seattle. And now I'm sitting

During Gunvor Johansen's first furlough in Norway, she married Josef Iversen in 1962. The same year both were in Paso Cadena,[17] and the following year in the town of Caacupé.[18] In addition, they started to hold meetings in the town of Ypacaraí.[19] In 1961, Anna Strømsrud announced her missionary call to Paraguay after having served eight years as an evangelist in Northern Norway. She was sent by the Pentecostal congregation in Lårdal, while Eben-Ezer, Dalen in Telemark and the home church Betel, Vallset became financially supporting congregations.[20] We also read about Astrid Myrvold, with partial support from both Seattle, WWA, and the congregation in Sarpsborg, Norway.[21]

In 1966, Ingrid and Knut Stuksrud, living in Lillehammer, announced a missionary call to Paraguay.[22] The steady influx of missionaries to Paraguay made it natural to expand the work, and we read about plans to build a missionary clinic in Atyrá where both Asta Hadland and Gerda Lillian Aardalen were to settle down.[23] Certainly

---

here in our new missionary home, which my husband sawed every single plank and table for, and set up himself in Norwegian style, so now we no longer live in mud huts'. Bergljot Norheim, 'Arbeidet vokser blant indianerne i Paraguay', *Korsets seier* 21 January 1967, p. 12.

[17] 'Det skjer under i Paraguay', *Korsets seier* 5 August 1972, p. 10. Gunvor and Josef Iversen, 'Hilsen fra Paso Cadena, Paraguay', *Korsets seier* 8 September 1962, pp. 571-72. Josef Iversen had previously traveled for about 7 years as an evan-gelist within the Free Evangelical Assemblies. 'Våre misjonærer', *Korsets seier* 7 September 1963, p. 570. In 1967, Gunvor and Josef Iversen were back in Caacupé. Gerda Lillian Aardalen, 'Feltkonferanse i Paraguay', *Korsets seier* 29 July 1967, p. 7. The following year it was decided that they should move to the city of Concepción in northern Paraguay. Lars M. Førland, 'Over til Concepcion', *Korsets seier* 4 May 1968, p. 12.

[18] Berit Eriksen, 'Hilsen fra Parana', *Korsets seier* 4 May 1963, p. 280.

[19] Gunvor and Josef Iversen, 'Hilsen fra Caacupé', *Korsets seier* 24 August 1963, pp. 538-39. Cf. also Anne Gustavsen, 'Ukens portrett: Gunvor Iversen', *Korsets seier* 19 February 1983, pp. 7, 15.

[20] 'Ny misjonær', *Korsets seier* 11 February 1961, p. 91.

[21] Hanne-Berit and Finn Jensen, 'Avskjedsmøter i Paraguay', *Korsets seier* 15 October 1966, p. 6. 'She is from Sarpsborg, sent from Filadelfia, with support from Seattle. She stayed in the United States for five years before coming to Paraguay. She has three years of Bible school in Seattle, and good experience from personal soul-winning work'. Anna Strømsrud, 'Indianere får høre evangeliet for første gang', *Korsets seier* 21 October 1967, p. 12.

[22] 'Nye misjonærer til Paraguay', *Korsets seier* 10 December 1966, p. 7.

[23] Øyvind Hamre and Georg Surland-Hansen, 'Nytt misjonsprosjekt i Paraguay', *Korsets seier* 21 December 1966, p. 12; Gerda Lillian Aardalen, 'Norsk pinsemisjon innregistrert i Paraguay', *Korsets seier* 20 May 1967, p. 12; 'Nytt

for this reason, the Norwegian Pentecostal Mission was registered as a separate legal entity in Paraguay under the name *La Misión Noruega del Movimiento Pentecostal en Paraguay* – shortened to *Misión Norma*. This was because one did not have full freedom of religion in the country and, therefore could not hold open-air meetings, but had to have one's own premises or gather privately to hold meetings. Until then, the mission's properties had been registered under the missionaries' names but were now transferred to *Misión Norma* as the rightful owner.[24] During the actual inauguration of the clinic in Atyrá in 1967, both the chief of police and the mayor participated, as well as the Norwegian ambassador for Argentina, Uruguay, and Paraguay.[25]

In the previous chapter we read about Sigrunn and Oddmar Byberg who had worked in Brazil. In 1965 they came to Paraguay and eventually settled in Ypacaraí, about 30 kilometers from Paraguay's capital Asunción. Jorunn and Lars M. Førland also came there in 1967 after having been in Norway on furlough for one and a half years.[26] They took responsibility for building an orphanage[27] in addition to 'overseeing the evangelical work there'.[28] Thus the orphanage had 'contributed to forming the foundation for the church'.[29]

misjonsprosjekt i Paraguay', *Korsets seier* 21 December 1966, p. 12. The mission station was a fact the following year. Gerda Lillian Aardalen and Asta Hadland, 'Ny misjonsstasjon åpnet i Atyra, Paraguay', *Korsets seier* 21 June 1967, p. 5. When Hadland returned to Norway on furlough in 1968, she was temporarily replaced by Lisbeth Jensen, who was a missionary in Chile. Asta Hadland, 'Åpen dør for Guds ord i Atyra, Paraguay', *Korsets seier* 2 October 1968, p. 8.

[24] Gerda Lillian Aardalen , 'Norsk pinsemisjon innregistrert i Paraguay', *Korsets seier* 20 May 1967, p. 12.

[25] Lars M. Førland, 'Misjonshistorie skrevet i Paraguay', *Korsets seier* 13 January 1968, p. 1.

[26] Lars M. Førland, 'Ypacarai – et sted med mange muligheter', *Korsets seier* 28 June 1967, p. 3; Jorunn and Lars M. Førland, 'Salem, Lørenskog, har Paraguay som ytterste utpost og gir evangeliet og sosial hjelp til de nødlidende', *Korsets seier* 4 October 1967, pp. 5, 8.

[27] Jorunn and Lars M. Førland, 'I dag er Angel en annen gutt', *Korsets seier* 28 June 1969, p. 12. Around 1990, the orphanage, *Hogar Norma*, became more geared towards children with physical and mental challenges. Hanne, Jorunn and Lars M. Førland, 'Flest glade og lyse dager på Hogar Norma', *Korsets seier* 9 November 1990, p. 9.

[28] Oddvar Nilsen, 'Paraguay et av våre nyere misjonsfelt', *Korsets seier* 21 January 1970, p. 4.

[29] Kjell Larring, 'Jorunn og Lars Førland ble feiret. Misjonærer i 40 år', *Korsets seier* Christmastime 2001, p. 31.

In 1967, Anna Strømsrud moved north to the border with Brazil to create a new mission field among the indigenous people having in mind a mission station, church, and a boarding school. In the early days, she worked alongside Astrid Myrvold, and their initial main base was the town of Pedro Juan Caballero.[30] Strømsrud was greatly involved in the allocation of approximately 10,000 acres of land approximately 100 kilometers from the city so that the indigenous people could live safely there without risking a forced break-up in the future. This was partly due to the fact that many foreigners had bought up large areas of land, and as landowners they were not interested in having indigenous people on their properties. The latter had thus been forced to 'settle deep in the jungle to find peace,' which made contact difficult for the missionaries.[31] With support from NORAD, a 'clinic, an administration building, a sawmill, and some houses' were built.[32] School activities were also initiated. For a period Eva Sagen (later Figueredo) labored alongside Strømsrud.[33] In 1975 Strømsrud received The Paraguayan Ministry of Defense's medal of merit for her work among the indigenous people in the Eben Ezer colony.[34]

From the 1970s, there has been a steady influx of missionaries to Paraguay. Inge and Inger Johanne Bjørnevoll arrived in December

---

[30] Anna Strømsrud, 'Indianere får høre evangeliet for første gang', *Korsets seier* 21 October 1967, p. 12.

[31] Oddvar Schjølberg, *Med Bibel og moped i Paraguyays jungel. Et møte med pioner-misjonæren Anna fra Løten* (Oslo: Ibra Media Norge, 2008), p. 121.

[32] Hans Svartdahl, 'Agronom på Eben-Ezer, Paraguay', *Korsets seier* 8 September 1976, p. 2. 'When the hospital was inaugurated, it was the first hospital for indigenous people in Paraguay. It was together with two sister residences and other housing, financed by NORAD, and missionary Gunvor Westgård was to be the hospital's manager. Alongside her, she was assisted by nurse Anne Lise Jorud and agronomist Ole Johannes Jorud. The hospital had both a maternity ward, a polio clinic and its own dentist's office'. Schjølberg, *Med Bibel og moped i Paraguays jungel*, p. 144. Westgård and Jorud were replaced by Brit-Lajla and Rudolf Leif Larsen in 1978. Eva and Candido Figueredo worked actively at the station in the period 1979-96, while Gunvor Westgård, Henny Marie Rasmussen and Margarita Bogado were there in the first main part of the 1980s. Schjølberg, *Med Bibel og moped i Paraguays jungel*, p. 149.

[33] Oddvar Schølberg, *Med Bibel og moped i Paraguays jungel*, p. 120.

[34] 'KS i samtale med Anna Strømsrud om fortjenestemedalje og det daglige slit for en misjonær', *Korsets seier* 23 April 1975, pp. 5, 15.

1970,[35] while Knut and Kitty Asplund were sent out in 1973.[36] In the same year Rigmor and Thorleif Overhalden arrived. Thorleif was a school instructor and was to teach the Norwegian missionaries' children at the newly founded Norwegian school.[37] During the same period, they began to systematically buy time on several local radio stations.[38] In 1972, the Filadelfia congregation in Encarnación was also formally founded with around 160 members, spread over 20 different locations. Until then, the group had been under Filadelfia, Asunción.[39]

An initiative by IBRA radio in 1979 regarding closer co-operation between the Norwegian and Swedish radio missions in Paraguay brought about a greater degree of coordination; one of these endeavors was a new radio program that was started in 1980 by Swedish IBRA in collaboration with the Norwegian Pentecostal Mission's *Centro Evangélico Filadelfia* in Caacupé, where the technical work was carried out. At this time, Swedish IBRA had the financial responsibility for three weekly programs and Norwegian IBRA for four.[40]

---

[35] 'Vel framkomne i Paraguay', *Korsets seier* 9 January 1971, p. 9.

[36] Erling Andreassen and Hans Svartdahl, 'Nye misjonærer til Paraguay', *Korsets seier* 21 February 1973, p. 8.

[37] 'Thorleif Overhalden med familie til Paraguay', *Korsets seier* 21 July 1973, p. 2. 'Finally, this long-awaited school of ours in Paraguay has started. For several years, the missionary mothers taught their own children at the kitchen table or wherever they could. Some of the Norwegian children tried their hand at the Paraguayan school, with the result that they forgot their own mother tongue and gained little knowledge of their actual homeland's geography and history. [...] At the field conference in Paso Cadena in 1971, it was decided to send an application to the Ministry [of Education] in Norway. The paper mill was started, and with the help of skilled and eager people, the school plans were finally adopted. In July 1973, the Overhalden family left Norway, and in August the school opened in the former clinic in Atyra'. Ingrid Stuksrud, 'Norsk skole på misjonsmarken', *Korsets seier* 23 February 1974, p. 8. The school was moved to Tartagal, Argentina in 1989. 'Ny norsk skole i Argentina', *Korsets seier* 17 November 1989, p. 9. After just one year, the school moved back to Paraguay before it was discontinued half a year later, and the Norwegian missionary chil-dren were instead home schooled while also interacting digitally with teachers in Norway. Geir Lie, interview with Benjamin Jensen, 8 June 2024. The former clinic has also served as a Bible school in addition to as a rehabilitation center for drug addicts. Gerda Lillian Aardalen, 'Sterkt gjensyn med Juan som hun reddet fra døden', *Korsets seier* 27 January 2006, p. 15.

[38] Oddmar Byberg, 'Radioarbeidet i Paraguay', *Korsets seier* 25 May 1974, p. 31.

[39] Inge Bjørnevoll, 'Merkedagar for pinserørsla i Paraguay', *Korsets seier* 27 September 1972, p. 12.

[40] Inge Bjørnevoll, 'Skandinavisk IBRA-samarbeid i Paraguay', *Korsets seier* 17 May 1980, p. 10.

After completing her agronomist training in Norway, Anna Strømsrud returned to Paraguay in 1981. She soon felt led to take up a pioneer work in the indigenous colony of Fortuna, a few kilometers from the village of Curuguaty. A primary school with room for 450 pupils, a secondary school and a high school were opened here, as well as a church.[41] Strømsrud returned permanently to Norway in 2001, but the work continued by national staff, in addition to other Norwegian missionaries – such as Anne Lise and Ole Johannes Jorud, Gunvor Westgård and Brit-Lajla and Rudolf Leif Larsen.[42]

'The missionary work in Paraguay is characterized more and more by the nationals taking over where Norwegian missionaries have previously been in charge',[43] we read from 1987. 'We Norwegians have probably many times made decisions over the heads of the nationals,' stated Lars Førland self-critically. It was nonetheless believed that there was still a need for Norwegian missionaries in the country, not least in pioneering fields among the poor in the countryside.[44] This is confirmed by a letter signed by both Norwegian missionaries and national leaders requesting that additional

---

[41] From 1986 we read: 'For many years the primary school was held in small cabins, but they gradually began to deteriorate. Anna Strømsrud was therefore eager to have a building constructed for both the primary school and the recently started colegio (junior high school). She had no large grants to rely on, but faithful missionary friends in Norway who gave, and the result has become a modern school with four classrooms and an office'. Rudolf Leif Larsen, 'Innvielse av skole i Curuguaty, Paraguay', *Korsets seier* 17 January 1986, p. 7.

[42] Schjølberg, *Med Bibel og moped i Paraguays jungel*, p. 169 ff. Rudolf Larsen has collected a lot of material from the period in Paraguay on the website 'Brit-Lajla og Rudolf's side' – *https://www.pymisjon.com/Guarani/larsen_bs.htm.* [Accessed 28 November 2024].

[43] Jostein Janøy, 'Nasjonaliseringen går videre i Paraguay', *Korsets seier* 27 February 1987, p. 5.

[44] Janøy, 'Nasjonaliseringen går videre i Paraguay', p. 5. Respect for the nationals was expressed in several ways, not least reflected through Rudolf Leif Larsen, who in addition to Spanish had also learned to communicate in Guarani. In Paso Cadena, where he and his wife Brit-Lajla had been working for several years, a national worker was the administrative manager at the station, Maxemino Velásquez, in addition to another Paraguayan being Director of the school, which at this time had 150 students. Hans Svartdahl, 'Nasjonale overtar oppgaver i Paraguay', *Korsets seier* 21 August 1987, p. 8; Lars M. Førland, 'Paraguay informerer', *Korsets seier* 30 October 1987, p. 4. In Oddvar Johansen's article 'Antall misjonærer på rekordlavt nivå', *Korsets seier* 27 October 2006, p. 17 we read: 'Not too many years ago there were over 90 missionaries from Norwegian Pentecostal churches in Latin America. Today there are 18, as well as some who commute between Norway and this continent in various projects'.

Norwegian missionaries be sent to Paraguay.[45] Consider the attitude of Leo Alderete, who was already in full-time ministry as an evangelist when he was as young as 22 years old and later oversaw the construction work for the Norwegian Pentecostal mission where the clinic in Atyrá was built (later converted into a rehabilitation center for drug addicts) as well as the orphanage in Ypacaraí. Later Alderete pastored various congregations, and at the age of 50 he expressed great gratitude to Norwegian Pentecostal missionaries. Still, it was important to recognize that times were changing: pioneer missions where foreign missionaries led the work were no longer relevant. New missionaries should join a local, national congregation, being an extension of the church ministerially, and submit to its leadership.[46]

A relevant example of the nationalization of the work can be seen when in 1989 an itinerant Bible school between the various churches was started with embedded church praxis.[47] The school was named the *Instituto Teológico Filadelfia ITF*[48] and was started by Margarita Müller and Aina Delgado in Atyrá. To a large extent, it became a meeting point for the three independent Filadelfia groups, that is, the missionary work of the Norwegian, Swedish, and Danish largest Pentecostal denomination respectively.[49] The school was eventually moved to Asunción and was given a permanent location there, while mobile Bible schools continued as a complementary addition. In

---

[45] Reinert O. Innvær, 'Paraguay kaller på hjelp', *Korsets seier* 6 May 1988, p. 20.

[46] Lars M. Førland, 'Misjonærenes plass i den nasjonale bevegelsen', Mission supplement entitled *Paraguay*, p. 2 published together with *Korsets seier* on 22 May 1998. Inge Bjørnevoll writes in 'En misjonerende livsstil, hva er det?' *Misjons-magasinet*. Theme: Stewardship. *Et temamagasin for De Norske Pinsemenigheters Ytremisjon*, p. 8: 'Previously it was common to send health workers and teachers, agronomists and construction experts to the mission fields. They were to improve living conditions at the same time as they ministered God's Word. Today, in most cases, it is different. Where the missionaries arrive, usually there already are skilled ministers, professional personnel and vibrant congregations: the missionaries no longer automatically become the big leaders but must enter as part of a collaboration under national leaders. The pioneer lifestyle has been replaced by teamwork. The nationals, with their language and cultural knowledge, spread the Christian message better than we foreigners do'. (Supplement to *Korsets seier* 18 May 2007.)

[47] Kjellaug Palma Sjølund, 'Ambulerende bibelskole', *Korsets seier* 17 March 1989, p. 13.

[48] Anna Strømsrud, 'Bibelskolestart i Paraguay', *Korsets seier* 28 April 1989, p. 1.

[49] Besides, 'the new indigenous congregations ... also have the common name Filadelfia'. 'Paraguay', *Korsets seier* 12 March 1999, p. 11.

1998, Fabian Daniluk and his wife Beatriz were the leaders of the two-year Bible Institute. They had assumed this responsibility several years earlier. By 1998, around 120 students had completed their education, and 20 students attended the Institute that year. Around 10-15 of the former students were at this time engaged full-time as either pastors or evangelists, while others had other types of leadership responsibilities in their respective congregations.[50]

A further example of the independence of the work can be seen through the Textbook Project, initiated by indigenous people who wanted their culture to be expressed in the schoolbooks. They read onto cassette tape personal considerations about their own culture, which were later written and published in the books. By 2005, there were 26 books which, in addition to text, also included photographs and drawings.[51] Inge Bjørnevoll points out the importance of 'supporting and encouraging and perhaps opening the way where the national staff have not succeeded', for example 'among oppressed people groups and indigenous peoples'.[52] He criticizes an elitist way of thinking where missionaries may have led the work as 'kings of the Hills,' without giving the people an ownership to their own future plans.[53]

Kjellaug Palma Sjølund still works in Paraguay. She first arrived in 1969 and since 2011 has been ministering in Lambaré, one of the larger cities in the country. The congregation became an independent legal entity in 2015, and Sjølund is pastoring the assembly.[54]

---

[50] Lars M. Førland, 'Framtiden blir sådd i Paraguay', *Korsets seier* 16 October 1998, p. 15.

[51] Inge Bjørnevoll, 'En misjonerende livsstil, hva er det?', p. 9. What Bjørnevoll modestly omitted in this article was that he himself 'created the Guarani Indians' first textbook based on their own culture and history'. Almidio Aquino, linguist and Bible translator, who with the support of PYM has translated the New Testament into Guarani, writes further: 'Until 2005, 26 textbooks and a trilingual Dictionary were produced. From 2006, the same type of work started among the Mbya and Acheindians'. Almidio Aquino, 'William Carey og vi', *Korsets seier* 5 October 2012, p. 30.

[52] Inge Bjørnevoll, 'En misjonerende livsstil, hva er det?', p. 8.

[53] Inge Bjørnevoll, 'En misjonerende livsstil, hva er det?', p. 8.

[54] Geir Lie, interview with Kjellaug Palma Sjølund, dated 21 November 2024.

5

CHILE

The founder of the Pentecostal movement in Chile was the North American Methodist minister Willis C. Hoover Kirk (1856-1936). He first founded a Methodist church in the area around Iquique but quickly moved to Valparaíso where he pastored a Methodist congregation beginning in 1902. Five years later somebody sent him the booklet *The Baptism of the Holy Ghost and Fire*, written by Minnie Abrams, who actually was a friend of his wife. In 1909, Hoover experienced his personal Pentecost, and the Methodist church in Valparaíso, as well as two other congregations led by Hoover's former colleagues, followed him in his Pentecostal quest.

Hoover was forced to break with the Methodist Church, and in 1910 he founded the *Iglesia Metodista Pentecostal*, one of the very few Pentecostal denominations that practice infant baptism. However, the newly established denomination soon experienced its own schisms, resulting in the two separatist denominations *Iglesia del Señor* and *Iglesia Evangélica de los Hermanos Pentecostales*. In 1933 there was another split, and now it was Hoover himself who had to leave the newly established denomination and instead founded *the Iglesia Evangélica Pentecostal*. Quite a few Pentecostal denominations are represented in Chile, and one of these, the *Iglesia Pentecostal de Chile*, became a member of the World Council of Churches in 1962.[1]

Nils Gunstad (1877-1949) was the first Norwegian Pentecostal missionary in Chile. He initially traveled out for the Scandinavian Alliance Mission and arrived in Chile in 1903. Gunstad relocated

---

[1] Lie, *Tro og tanke før og nå*, pp. 177-78.

several times, probably first settling in Valdivia in the north. From 1906 onwards he was living in Ancud on the Chiloé island. There had been a Christian and Missionary Alliance presence in Chiloé since 1904, and this was probably the reason why Nils and his first wife Marie chose to settle there. The Gunstads joined CMA after six months in Chile.

Around 1909, Nils and Marie became Pentecostals, however. The following year, Marie wrote a lengthy article for *Det gode Budskab* about the beginnings of the Pentecostal movement in Chile, in Hoover's Methodist church in Valparaíso. Marie refers to two 'humble sisters, who in the power of the Spirit went about in all places where there were open doors'. Their visit made 'a deep impression' on her.[2]

Several years earlier, Marie had experienced 'the grace of sanctification, received a pure heart, and a new power over everything that was profane and sinful', but by reading letters and magazines that mentioned the baptism of the Spirit, a longing was created within her, and on July 6, 1910, she received her personal Pentecost.[3]

In 1913 the Gunstads received reinforcements from Norway through Kirsti Melbostad , who, like Nils and Marie, had settled in Ancud.[4] We are also acquainted with another Norwegian, Emil Jakobsen, who had recently arrived in 1914.[5] During this period, the Gunstads thought about constructing a church building and wrote that T.B. Barratt had promised to accept money on their behalf in Norway and forward it to them.[6] It is uncertain exactly when, but at least in 1916, they were part of what had now become a Oneness organization in the United States; i.e., the Pentecostal Assemblies of the World. Consequently, the Gunstads were among the first pioneers of the Oneness Pentecostal tradition in Chile.[7]

---

[2] Marie Gunstad, 'Hvorledes pinseilden kom til Chile!' *Det gode Budskab* 15 July 1910, p. 54.

[3] Marie Gunstad, 'Fra Sydamerika', *Det gode Budskab* 1 October 1910, p. 73.

[4] Kirsti Melbostad, 'Fra Chile', *Det gode Budskab* 1 August 1913, p. 60.

[5] Marie Gunstad, 'Syd-Amerika', *Korsets seir* 1 April 1914, p. 54.

[6] Nils and Marie Gunstad, 'Fra missionærerne Gunstad.' *Det gode Budskab* 1 December 1913, pp. 90-91; 'Syd-Amerika', *Korsets seir* November 15, 1913, pp. 174-75.

[7] Eugenio Domínguez, *Noruega a Chile: En el nombre de Jesús. Biografía del misionero noruego Nils Gunstad (1877-1949)*. Kindle edition available from Amazon. Still in 1915, however, Marie Gunstad felt 'one with God's people in the Spirit', which at

Gunstad wrote home to his family in Norway stating that he was actively involved in ministry work in various denominations, even though he was allegedly a universalist and preached 'the doctrine of the restoration of all things'.[8] Nonetheless, he preached regularly in the Methodist Church in the town of Pitrufquén, where he was also part of the congregation's church choir.[9] He had moved there in 1923. This suggests that Gunstad was eclectic in nature, as the combination of universalism and Oneness Pentecostalism has hardly occurred either before or since.

Despite being Oneness, the Gunstads had a good relationship with Trinitarian Christians, and on Marie's death in 1926 both the local Baptist minister and the Anglican vicar made their church buildings available for the funeral. Ten ministers were present, as well as many female missionaries from different denominations, and in addition to Nils himself, two Anglican vicars, two Baptist pastors and a Methodist minister spoke.[10]

The first two missionaries sent out to Chile through the Norwegian *Pinsebevegelsen* were Karin and Hardy Wilhelm Moss-

---

least included the readers of *Korsets seir*. Marie Gunstad, 'S. Amerika', *Korsets seir* 1 May 1915, pp. 68-69. Probably in 1916 Marie Gunstad had also written an article in the magazine *Missionæren*, 'about the restoration of all things', which had apparently been misunderstood, and she therefore felt the need to state that she did not have the same understanding of doctrine as Jehovah's Witnesses. Marie Gunstad, 'Fra Huillinco', *Det gode Budskab* 1 June 1916, pp. 42-43.

[8] Halvor Western, 'Fra Jevnaker til Chile – historien om misjonæren Nils Gunstad', *Årbok for Hadeland*, Vol. 40 (2007), pp. 66-67. It is also universalism, 'the doctrine of everyone's salvation', which Barratt in 1916 states as the reason why Marie and Nils Gunstad's application for financial support has been rejected: 'It is regrettable as we loved these friends very much, but it is impossible to support a teaching that we believe is unbiblical'. 'Norges Frie Evangeliske Missionsforbund', *Korsets seir* 1 February 1916, p. 21. Barratt may have misunderstood here, since in another context he identifies this teaching from America with the 'new light', which often refers to the so-called 'New Issue', which had nothing to do with the doctrine of *apokatàstasis*, but exclusively referred to Oneness Pentecostalism. In that case, this is neither the first nor the last time Barratt is inaccurate in his renderings. Most famous, perhaps, are his many references to Albert Benjamin Simpson in the United States, whom Barratt consistently names *Adna* Simpson. 'Alles frelse', *Korsets seir* 15 August 1916, pp. 122-23. Later that year, however, Barratt rightly identifies the new 'light' with Oneness Pentecostalism. 'Det "nye lys" saakaldet paa retur', *Korsets seir* 15 October 1916, p. 159.

[9] Nils Gunstad, letter to Sofie, dated 22 June 1934. Norwegian Pentecostal Historical Archives, *NPA-PA/Gunstad, Nils og Marie/D/L0001*.

[10] Nils Gunstad, 'Fra Syd-Amerika', *Det gode Budskab* no 2 February 1926, p. 1.

berg.[11] More specifically they were sent out by the church Salen, Halden. In 1946 they had announced their mission call, and the following year they arrived. Hardy believed that his call to Latin America had been latent within him since his school days when the family had 'visits at home by the now deceased br. Berger N. Johnsen from Argentina'.[12] Hardy envisioned a close collaboration with the Swedish missionaries Fanny and Albin Gustavsson, who had left Argentina in favor of Chile in 1938.[13]

In 1948, Karin and Hardy wrote from Lautaro, where they lived together with the Swedish Pentecostal missionaries Evert and Märta Larsson, who after 14 years of ministerial work in Latin America were about to return to Sweden. The congregation in Lautaro had until recently had over 100 members, but the approximately 20 who lived in the town of Osorna had just established a congregation there. Karin and Hardy were therefore to be pastors for the approximately 80 members of Lautaro.[14] After about a year, at the end of January 1950, however, there was a move to the city of Concepción. In February, the congregation Asamblea de Dios de Concepción was founded with nine members.[15]

They quickly started translating into Spanish the British Pentecostal leader Howard Carter's Bible correspondence course, which was also used in Filadelfia, Oslo under the name *Brevskolen*.[16] This Spanish-language Bible course was also promoted when Karin

---

[11] Karin Mossberg presents everyday descriptions from Chile in the book *Ved foten av Andesfjellene* (Oslo: Filadelfiaforlaget, 1962).

[12] 'Til Chile, – Sør Amerika', *Korsets seier* 28 December 1946, pp. 831-32.

[13] The Gustavsson couple thus became the founders of the *Iglesia Asamblea de Dios Autónoma de Chile*, which the missionaries from the Norwegian *Pinse-bevegelsen* chose to work within. This Chilean Pentecostal denomination published the magazine *El Clamor* from 1953 to 1989, which has later been deposited at the Flower Pentecostal Heritage Center in Springfield, Missouri. Unfortunately, I did not have the opportunity to consult this material, which would undoubtedly have provided additional relevant information.

[14] Hardy and Karin Mossberg, 'Hilsen fra Chile', *Korsets seier* 20 June 1948, p. 356.

[15] Karin and Hardy Mossberg, 'Hilsen fra Chile', *Korsets Seier* 19 August 1950, p. 520. The congregations which had been built up by Norwegian and Swedish Pentecostal missionaries and which eventually were to have Chilean pastors, were often called free Pentecostal congregations since, as appears in note 13, they were identified as *Asambleas de Dios Autónomas*. Thor J. Thoresen, 'De frie pinsemenigheter i Chile', *Korsets seier* 18 December 1968, p. 5.

[16] Karin and Hardy Mossberg, 'Hilsen fra Chile', *Korsets Seier* 1 September 1950, p. 419.

and Hardy visited congregations in Argentina, Brazil, and Uruguay respectively in 1952.[17]

Early on, Hardy saw the importance of evangelism via evangelical radio programs, which were eventually broadcast from various stations – as many as nine in 1964.[18] Many of the listeners wrote letters to the missionaries, who in the follow-up work sent literary sections of the Bible, tracts and educational courses.[19] Also, Hardy became involved in distributing Christian literature to sailors who were docked at the port of Concepción, including Norwegians.[20] The ministerial work seems to have had a steady flow, and in 1962 there were 'over 60 meetings and Sunday school lessons a month'.[21] It was often an initial ministry towards children which later resulted in general outpost activities.

In 1961, Gerd and Tom Bye announced their mission call to Chile. Tom had previously worked for 11 years as a Pentecostal evangelist in Southern, Western and Northern Norway.[22] The couple was sent out by Filadelfia, Kristiansand in 1962.[23] They worked alongside Karin and Hardy Mossberg in Concepción until 1966 when they

---

[17] Hardy Mossberg, 'På langreise i Syd-Amerika', *Korsets seier* 5-12 July 1952, pp. 335-36.

[18] 'Tusener lytter til evangeliske radioprogram i Chile', *Korsets seier* 17 October 1964, p. 23.

[19] 'Japan, Thailand, Argentina og Chile får støtte til misjon', *Korsets seier* 13 January 1971, pp. 4-5. 'South America in particular has proven to be an open door for IBRA radio. There, at an early stage, various excellent radio stations were contacted. Regular IBRA programs are sent from these. Radio La Cruz del Sur in Bolivia is one such station. From there, there is a 15-minute program every Thursday. In the same country, daily IBRA programs are also broadcast, namely over Radio Nacional in Cochabamba. There is a native who is in charge of the radio work. In Chile, one covers the entire northern part of the country with the shortwave broadcasts that are sent every Sunday from Radio Riquelme in Coquimbo. In countries such as Paraguay, Uruguay and Argentina, IBRA has also participated in the radio mission, and in these countries the work will be intensified. If we move over to Puerto Rico in the Antilles, we will find there both medium wave broadcasts and UKW broadcasts, the latter in the city of San Juan. IBRA participates here', Erik Martinsson, 'Intens IBRA-aktivitet på misjonsfeltene', *Korsets seier* 3 March 1962, p. 131.

[20] Karin and Hardy Mossberg, 'Til Chile på ny', *Korsets seier* 2 July 1955, pp. 426-27.

[21] Karin and Hardy Mossberg, 'Guds ord har framgang i Chile', *Korsets seier* 20 January 1962, pp. 44-45.

[22] Gerd and Tom Bye, 'Til Chile', *Korsets seier* 2 December 1961, p. 763; Georg Surland-Hansen, 'Anbefaling', *Korsets seier* 2 December 1961, p. 763.

[23] 'Våre misjonærer', *Korsets seier* 12 October 1963, p. 652.

moved 600 kilometers north, to Llolleo[24] where in the same year they had a congregation of 30 members in addition to having started a small orphanage.[25] Also that year, nursing student Lisbeth Jensen from Salen, Halden felt a missionary call to Chile.[26] Thor J. Thoresen did the same, and received a missionary recommendation from the same church in Halden.[27] And in 1966 or 1967, Signe Hauge arrived in Chile.[28]

Despite Lisbeth Jensen's call to Chile, she stayed for a year and a half in Paraguay, as documented in the previous chapter, but then traveled to Concepción, Chile before moving to the small town of Lautaro.[29] In 1971, as will be seen in chapter 6, Lisbeth married Cuban missionary Mario Fumero and moved to Honduras.[30] During this same period, we read that the Mossberg couple planned to return permanently to Norway.[31] This took place in 1970, when Christian Romo from Chile became the new pastor in Concepción.[32]

A few years later, new missionaries arrived – first Liv Haddal, who had previously worked for several years as an evangelist in Norway,[33] and then Else Ekornaas, sent out from Salem, Oslo.[34] During this period, we are informed that the Thoresen family had

---

[24] Gerd Bye, 'Ny misjonsstasjon med barnehjem i Chile', *Korsets seier* 19 February 1966, p. 7.

[25] Gerd Bye, 'Dagligliv hos misjonærene i Chile', *Korsets seier* 23 July 1966, p. 12.

[26] 'Nye misjonærer', *Korsets seier* 1 January 1966, p. 4.

[27] 'Ut med evangeliet', *Korsets seier* 14 December 1966, p. 16. Still, he did not leave Norway until 1968. Thor J. Thoresen, 'Blant incaindianernes ætlinger', *Korsets seier* 16 October 1968, p. 4. Thoresen married Elbjørg Aase when she came out as a missionary to Chile in 1969. 'Fra Bergen til Chile', *Korsets seier* 31 May 1969, p. 3.

[28] Signe Hauge and Lisbeth Jensen, 'Misjonærene møter store behov i Chile', *Korsets seier* 11 March 1967, p. 12.

[29] Signe Hauge, 'Han ville ha flere i tale den kvelden', *Korsets seier* 24 June 1970, p. 5.

[30] Thor J. Thoresen, *Talende tårn* (Oslo: Filadelfiaforlaget 1980), p. 80.

[31] Lisbeth Jensen, '"Hjemme igjen" i Chile', *Korsets seier* 14 February 1970, p. 9.

[32] Liv Haddal, 'Da Gud møtte menigheten i Concepcion', *Korsets seier* 27 September 1975, p. 6. Typical for the 1970s in several of the Latin American countries was that national workers took over more and more of the preaching responsibility, and in 1976 the 26-year-old Chilean Luís Humberto Marques became an evangelist, with financial support from, among others, the Pentecostal church Salen in Halden. 'Ny menighetsarbeider i Chile', *Korsets seier* 31 January 1976, p. 11.

[33] 'Ny misjonær til Chile', *Korsets seier* 22 November 1972, p. 5.

[34] Else Ekornaas, 'Mitt møte med vennene i Concepcion', *Korsets seier* 12 February 1975, p. 11.

settled in the small town of Villa Alemana.[35] Else Ekornaas also moved there, and a local church was quickly planted.[36] In this small town, a wine seller called Claudio Navarro became the first convert through Else's ministerial work in 1975. They were later married, and Claudio quickly became engaged as an evangelist in addition to running a Christian bookstore. [37] As national workers assumed pastorates in the different churches, the missionaries' responsibilities became more geared towards Bible teaching and social work.[38] In 1993, the church in Villa Alemana had almost 250 baptized members. They also ran a Bible school and a home for poor children.[39]

The Free Evangelical Assemblies have not had any missions work in Chile, if we overlook the fact that one of the daughters of minister Daniel and his wife Signe Nilsen was married to the Swedish missionary Berndt Hörstrand, 'so that she too got to minister in Chile'.[40]

[35] Thor Johnny Thoresen, 'Barnearbeidet – åpen dør til hjemmene', *Korsets seier* 13 August 1975, p. 2.

[36] Else Ekornaas, Eldbjørg and Thor Johnny Thoresen, 'Første dåpshandling i V. Alemana Chile', *Korsets seier* 31 December 1975, p. 9.

[37] 'Kommentarer', *Korsets seier* 3 May 1978, pp. 7, 15; Andreas Viumdal, 'Førstegrøden som ble pastor', *Korsets seier* 18 June 2004, pp. 16-17. After several years at a Bible school in Chile, Claudio has ministered both as an evangelist, pastor and church planter. In several congregations, he is considered to be an apostle, and Claudio has overseen these churches also while living in Norway.

[38] '5 minutter med Liv Haddal', *Korsets seier* 3 May 1978, p. 11.

[39] Mary and Jakob Ekornaas, 'Guds verk går fram i Chile', *Korsets seier* 18 June 1993, p. 12.

[40] 'Misjonærkontakt med Chile', *Det gode Budskap* 1 August 1969, pp. 10-11.

6

BOLIVIA AND PERU

In an earlier chapter, we described parts of G. Leonard and Ragna Pettersen's missionary work in Brazil and referred to the fact that after finishing their stay in Rio de Janeiro, they went on to Bolivia, more precisely La Paz. This occurred in 1953, but resulted in just a brief stay before, due to health challenges in connection with the climate in Bolivia, they returned to Norway.[1] Prior to this, but still in 1953, Leonard wrote that the congregation he served in Rio de Janeiro, Brazil was about to send out its first evangelist to Bolivia.[2] However, nothing seems to have come of this, and when Leonard and Ragna arrived in La Paz on 13 February 1953, Bolivia was 'a completely new mission field for Norwegian Pentecostals'.[3]

Still, *Swedish* Pentecostals had already done missionary work 'among isolated Indian tribes' for about 20 years but 'with extremely meager results'. The same was true of North American Pentecostal

---

[1] Pettersen, *Pinse over grensene*, p. 114; David D. Bundy, 'Missões Pentecostais no Brasil. O Caso do norueguês G. Leonard Pettersen', *Reflexões – Uma Perspectiva Pastoral e Ecclesial* 2.2 (Outubro 2022), p. 72; Kjell Ruud, '30 år i Herrens tjeneste', *Korsets seier* 1 September 1956, p. 533.

[2] G. Leonard Pettersen, 'Rio de Janeiro, Brasil', *Korsets seier* 10 January 1953, p. 28.

[3] G. Leonard Pettersen, 'Bolivia', *Korsets seier* 11 April 1953, p. 234. The Pettersen family only stayed a few months in Bolivia and made plans to return to Norway already in June 1953. Gunnerius Tollefsen, 'Misjonsnytt', *Korsets seier* 2 May 1953, p. 283.

missionaries, and Leonard suggested that the total number of Pentecostals in Bolivia hardly exceeded 300 people.[4]

Five years later, however, missionary work was taken up 'at the Beni River'.[5] Here, to the village of Gonzalo Moreno, Erling and Marita Andreassen arrived at the turn of the year 1958-59.[6] Erling had made 'the final decision to serve the jungle Indians on the rivers in Bolivia' in 1956,[7] after 'finishing education at the helmsman's and skipper's school' while attending Örebro Missions school,[8] and upon arrival the small riverboat *Embajador* became their first 'house'. Eventually they were able to build up their own mission station. A school and a hospital were also started, and after eight years about a fifth of the village's inhabitants had become Christians.[9] In 1961, Ada Bjørstad announced *her* mission call to Bolivia. In the autumn of 1959, she had attended Bible school in Filadelfia, Oslo and then

---

[4] G. Leonard Pettersen, 'Bolivia', *Korsets seier* 11 April 1953, pp. 234-35. 'At the beginning of the year 1921, the first Scandinavian Pentecostal missionaries came to Bolivia', writes Gunn Elisabeth Lie in 'Misjonærsamling i Cochabamba', *Korsets seier* 6 March 1987, p. 16. Detailed descriptions of the initiation of Swedish Pentecostal missionary work in the country when Gustaf Flood together with Ruth and Kristian Nielsén crossed the border from Argentina to Bolivia in May 1921 can be found in Jan-Åke Alvarsson's book *La historia de la misión sueca libre en Bolivia. Una iniciativa nórdica pentecostal para evangelizar a los pueblos de Bolivia* (Uppsala: Uppsala University, 2021), pp. 48 ff. In 1923, the American Pentecostal minister Thomas Anderson also came to Bolivia. He worked independently but was appointed as a Foursquare mis-sionary in 1928. Nathaniel M. Van Cleave, *The Vine and the Branches. A History of the International Church of the Foursquare Gospel* (Los Angeles, CA: International Church of the Foursquare Gospel, 1992), pp. 100-101.

[5] Erling Andreassen, 'Store muligheter og store behov i Bolivia', *Korsets seier* 22 April 1972, p. 4.

[6] Kari Opsahl, 'Jesu befaling er å lære dem', *Korsets seier* 6 May 1972, p. 7. 'It started in 1957', says Roger [Samuelsen]. Erling Andreassen had arrived in Bolivia and had started learning Spanish up in the highlands when he met a Wycliffe missionary. [...] Erling came to the Wycliffe mission's jungle base in northern Bolivia. [...] The Wycliffe missionaries told us that a small rural community just across the river had been designated as the provincial capital of the Pando district. [...] Can't you and your wife settle down there? asked the Wycliffe missionaries'. Andres Küng, 'Norsk pinsemisjon i Bolivia', *Korsets seier* 16 March 1977, pp. 6-7.

[7] Erling Andreassen, 'Flodmisjonen i Bolivia får støtte fra Hvaler', *Korsets seier* 30 June 1971, p. 5.

[8] Ivar Trannum, 'Ung styrmann fra Hvaler med sin svenskfødte hustru pionermisjonær i Bolivia', *Korsets seier* 27 May 1961, pp. 336-37.

[9] 'Da floden var misjonsstasjon', *Korsets seier* 28 August 1971, p. 7. In addition to his helmsman's and skipper's exam Erling had completed studies at the missions school in Örebro, Sweden. 'Til Sør-Amerika', *Korsets seier* 10 November 1956, pp. 697-98.

followed up with language training.[10] She arrived in Bolivia in 1961, around the same time that Ella Ritse changed mission fields from Argentina to Bolivia.[11] In 1963, Bjørstad wrote excitedly that they had been able to buy the neighboring plot and thus also would be able to offer boarding school for the children who lived 'far up the river and also deep in the jungle'.[12] In 1963, there were 56 school children from first to fifth grade, and 24 of these were in the boarding school.[13] While on furlough in Norway, Ada married Jan Olsen from Ski, and they traveled out together in 1965.[14]

In 1963, Liv and Ivar Aas announced *their* mission call to Bolivia. Ivar had worked as a school teacher for several years in Northern Norway, and they were sent out from the Pentecostal congregation in Gjøvik, where Liv was from, although she now belonged to Salem, Oslo, while Ivar was a member in Filadelfia, Oslo.[15] The following year, Asta Hadland, who belonged to the Pentecostal church in Egersund, also announced her mission call after having been working for many years as a nurse and midwife.[16] So did Helge and Greta Stø, he with a recommendation from his home church in Flekkefjord[17]

---

[10] 'Ny misjonær', *Korsets seier* 25 February 1961, pp. 110-11.

[11] Ada Bjørstad, 'Hilsen fra Bolivia', *Korsets seier* 11 November 1961, pp. 715-16. Due to illness, however, Ritse returned to Norway in 1962. Ada Bjørstad, 'Jungelnytt fra Brasil', *Korsets seier* 11 May 1963, p. 296.

[12] Ada Bjørstad, 'Jungelnytt fra Bolivia', *Korsets seier* 11 May 1963, p. 296.

[13] 'The school started [in 1962] with 27 pupils, the second year 56, the third year 101 and this school year we have 140 pupils'. Erling Andreassen, 'Det bygges skole i Bolivia, men...' *Korsets seier* 21 August 1965, p. 13. 'A 22-year-old missionary sits one day and teaches a Bolivian woman the art of reading. In the middle of the spell, the woman suddenly stands up and begins to cry and pray to God. Then she exclaims: "Couldn't you start school for my children, Sister Ada? They do go to the state's small school, but the teacher has punished them so cruelly now since I became an evangelical. They don't get any education anymore"'. Solveig Samuelsen, '"Pinsevennenes evangeliske grunnskole" i Gonzalo Moreno, Bolivia fyller 15 år', *Korsets seier* 13 April 1977, p. 11.

[14] Morgan Kornmo, 'Til Bolivia', *Korsets seier* 20 March 1965, p. 6. He and Ada would later take the surname Bjørfjell.

[15] 'Til Bolivia', *Korsets seier* 7 September 1963, pp. 567-68; Norvald Sundal, 'Nye misjonærer til Bolivia', *Korsets seier* 6 May 1964, pp. 201-202. The Aas couple stayed two years in Gonzalo Moreno and then moved, due to the 'corroding effect of the jungle climate on health' to Cochabamba, where they 'besides their evangelical work [could] be of great help to the Norwegian missionaries in the counties of Pando and Beni'. Helge Stø, 'Avskjed og velkomst i Gonzalo Moreno, Bolivia', *Korsets seier* 11-15 January 1967, p. 7.

[16] 'Til Bolivia', *Korsets seier* 7 March 1964, pp. 156-57.

[17] 'Til Bolivia', *Korsets seier* 18 April 1964, p. 213.

and she with a recommendation from her home church in Sion, Vikna.[18]And in 1965, Gerda Aardalen arrived after working in Brazil since 1959.[19] During the same year, Bjørg Tolleshaug announced that she had a missionary call to Bolivia, and was recommended by her home congregation in Alta, [20] while Kari Opsahl from Zion, Stavanger and Borgny Mølland from Filadelfia, Kristiansand did the same in 1966.[21]

Two miles from Gonzalo Moreno is the jungle town of Riberalta, a hub in this part of the country with slightly less than 20,000 inhabitants. Ada and Jan Olsen established themselves there in 1966, after several people had experienced Christian conversions during a campaign there the year before.[22] Five years later, the congregation already had 100 members.[23]A few years further down the road, the congregations in Gonzalo Moreno and Riberalta were 'viable, ... with their own pastors, 6 evangelists working full-time on rivers and smaller places'. [24] In addition, one had a 'primary school with boarding opportunities, an infirmary, Bible and vocational courses and youth camps'.[25]

Berit and Torstein Tørre were sent out from Tabernaklet, Skien in 1968.[26]After some time in Gonzalo Moreno, they moved to Riberalta

---

[18] 'Til Bolivia', *Korsets seier* 26 September 1964, p. 627.

[19] Gerda Lillian Aardalen, 'Flodmisjonen i Pando, Bolivia', *Korsets seier* 6 March 1965, pp. 11-12.

[20] 'Til Bolivia', *Korsets seier* 11 December 1965, p. 9.

[21] 'Ny misjonær til Bolivia', *Korsets seier* 23 March 1966, p. 2; 'Ny misjonær til Bolivia', *Korsets seier* 10 September 1966, p. 4.

[22] Marita and Erling Andreassen, 'Arbeidet ved Benifloden vokser både i bredde og dybde', *Korsets seier* Eastertime 1967, p. 20.

[23] Kari Opsahl, 'Jesu befaling er å lære dem', *Korsets seier* 6 May 1972, p. 7; Berit and Torstein Tørre, 'Misjonsarbeidet i Bolivia: Folkeskolen åpnet vei', *Korsets seier* 24 March 1971, p. 3.

[24] Andreassen, 'Store muligheter og store behov i Bolivia', p. 4.

[25] Andreassen, 'Store muligheter og store behov i Bolivia', p. 4. In 1976, the primary school had 140 pupils, including 30 boarding pupils. However, the mission's clinic had been closed down the same year as there were no nurses. Solveig Samuelsen, 'Feltkonferanse for PYMs misjonærer i Bolivia', *Korsets seier* 24 November 1976, pp. 9, 15. However, the school was planned to gradually close down in 1971 as they did not want to be in competition with the state school. This was not what society at large wanted, though, and 'from 1972 the mission took over all primary school education from 1st to 5th grade, while the state took responsibility for the upper secondary school'. Solveig Samuelsen, '"Pinsevennenes evangeliske grunnskole" i Gonzalo Moreno, Bolivia fyller 15 år', *Korsets seier* 13 April 1977, p. 11.

[26] 'Nye misjonærer til Bolivia', *Korsets seier* 26 October 1968, p. 7.

where they replaced Ada and Jan Olsen.[27] Mention should also be made of Helge Adolfsen who arrived in 1968, while Eva Marie Steiner and Berit Stø arrived the following year. Eva Marie and Helge were married in Gonzalo Moreno in 1971. The Swedish missionaries Birgitta and Börje Green, who were both teachers, also worked in Gonzalo Moreno after Liv and Ivar Aas traveled home and until Solveig and Roger Samuelsen came out in 1971. Then the Green family traveled on to Villa Montes, the Swedish mission field in southern Bolivia.

Roger Samuelsen had the main responsibility for the primary school in Gonzalo Moreno until 1978, interrupted by a furlough in Norway between the two periods there. Then the mission gradually withdrew from responsibility for the school, until it was completely handed over to the authorities in 1981. Most of the Norwegian missionaries began their work in Gonzalo Moreno, although several of them eventually continued elsewhere. This applies to Gunn Elisabeth Lie and Ingrid and Reidar Vatne who arrived in 1974, Finn and Reidun Røine in 1977 and Oddvar and Laila Bauge in 1979.

In 1976 Eva Marie and Helge Adolfsen moved to Rurrenabaque, a small town with around 3,000 inhabitants located at the end of the Beni River. Together with pastor Alberto Cartagena, who also moved with his family from Gonzalo Moreno, they started a mission work there. Jaime Sainz took over the pastorate in Gonzalo Moreno after having ministered for several years as an evangelist and church leader in various places along the Beni River. The churches of Riberalta and Gonzalo Moreno continued to send evangelists to the villages upriver, while the congregation in Rurrenabaque worked in the immediate area and the villages downriver.[28]

In January 1977, Cartagena and Adolfsen started a 30-minute radio program that ran every morning, *La luz y la vida*.[29]

---

[27] Börje Green, 'Ung misjonærstab i Bolivia', *Korsets seier* 7 October 1970, p. 6.

[28] Eva Marie and Helge Adolfsen, 'Høytidsdager i Rurrenabaque', *Korsets seier* 27 November 1976, p. 6. Later, Laila and Oddvar Bauge joined the congregation, which in 1991 had around 600 members and 'a dozen or so outposts'. The church still had a national senior pastor, as Oddvar mainly wanted to support and encourage. Nils-Erik Bergman, 'Vi trives i jungelen', *Ekko. Korsets seiers utenriks- og misjonsmagasin* February 1991, p. 13.

[29] Helge Adolfsen, 'Radiomisjonen når millioner av lyttere i Sør Amerika', *Korsets seier* 4 May 1977, pp. 8-9.

It is typical of the 1970s in most Latin American countries that the work was consolidated to a greater extent and national ministers were drawn into the work more than in previous years. As Berit and Torstein Tørre prepared for a new missionary period in Bolivia, they stated 'that their task in the future [would] be to stand next to the national believers as advisers, so that the natives themselves [could] run their congregations'.[30] We see the same tendency in the work that sprung from Rurrenabaque, where national evangelists were ministering in neighboring villages.[31] Helge Adolfsen therefore wrote in 1978, with reference not only to Bolivia, but to South America as a whole:

> I would say that if there is anything we need in today's South America, it is Spirit-filled missionaries who are deeply rooted in God's word, and who can help teach and help the national witnesses. This is where we have our biggest task at this moment. Now many people may think that I am against social work, but I am not. I am for social work where it is required to reach the people with the gospel. But one must be clear that missionary work in today's South America is completely different from what it was 20 years ago.[32]

Adolfsen further argued that when working in new fields, one should choose 'centrally located places' and let the newly founded congregation 'evangelize the surrounding areas'. To be successful in missionary work, the missionary had to be willing to 'play second fiddle': if not, one had 'nothing to do as a missionary in today's South America'. This willingness included the ability to 'admit to our

---

30 O.L., 'Berit og Torstein Tørre til ny periode i Bolivia', *Korsets seier* 30 July 1977, p. 2.

31 Helge Adolfsen, 'Menighetsdannelse og utvidelse av arbeidet fra Rurrena-baque', *Korsets seier* 14 September 1977, p. 7.

32 Helge Adolfsen, 'Våre muligheter for misjon i Sør-Amerika i dag', *Korsets seier* 22 July 1978, p. 13. In the same chronicle, Adolfsen writes: 'When it comes to groundbreaking work, we have to be willing to go to new places, even if it means that we have to leave a well-established work and start over with the same problems as before. When a congregation is independent, we missionaries must be ready to go to new places. Let's not get stuck. We must not wait too long to hand over the responsibility to the nationals, but rather let's do it too quickly'.

[national] colleagues when we have done wrong and be humble enough to ask their forgiveness'.[33]

However, there was still a need for foreign assistance. In 1980 we read that Jan Olsen, who had taken the surname Bjørfjell, after finishing a radio production course in London was to 'coordinate the radio work for Assamblea [*sic!*] de Dios throughout Bolivia, while at the same time [he was to] be IBRA Radio's contact person' in the country. Since 1966, Bjørfjell had been engaged in radio work similar to Helge Adolfsen, but now together with a national worker, since the goal 'as with all missionary work [was] to make oneself redundant'. They wanted through good Bible teaching to '[contribute to] unifying the various Pentecostal denominations and missions in Bolivia', preferably by 'being involved in creating a national Pentecostal movement in Bolivia'.[34] In the meantime, the Norwegian and Finnish Pentecostal missionaries in Bolivia had joined the Swedish ones in their legal entity. They carried out extensive work in several locations in the country and not least 'Norwegian missionaries [replaced] Swedish ones and vice versa'.[35] In that connection, writes *Korsets seier*, Helge Adolfsen, as chairman of the Swedish-Norwegian Pentecost mission in 1980, had been granted a certificate of honor from the Bolivian Minister of Education, 'as a gesture of gratitude' on behalf of the government.[36]

In 1979, it was decided to open a 2-year Bible school, *Instituto Bíblico Pentecostal*, and in February of the following year the first 2-months course commenced. Finn Jensen, a former Argentine missionary, became the school's principal.[37] About 20 students

---

[33] Helge Adolfsen, 'Våre muligheter for misjon i Sør-Amerika i dag', *Korsets seier* 22 July 1978, p. 13.

[34] Jan-Kristian Viumdal, 'Hele Bolivia skal dekkes med kristne radioprogram!' *Korsets seier* 17 May 1980, p. 6.

[35] Erling Andreassen and Börje Green, 'Store behov i Bolivia-arbeidet', *Korsets seier* 14 February 1981, p. 13. In 1982 we read that the Finns were also included in a joint annual conference. Solveig Samuelsen, 'Årskonferanse for nordiske pinsemisjonærer i Bolivia', *Korsets seier* 20 February 1982, p. 9.

[36] Erling Andreassen and Börje Green, 'Store behov i Bolivia-arbeidet', *Korsets seier* 14 February 1981, p. 13. In 1985, the *Nordisk Misjon* in Bolivia (which consisted of the *Nordisk Pinse Misjon*, the *Norske Misjonsallianse* and the *Norsk Luthersk Misjonssamband*) received Bolivia's highest order, *El Condor de los Andes*. Erling Andreassen, '"El Condor de los Andes" til nordisk misjon i Bolivia', *Det gode Budskap* 15 October 1985, p. 10.

[37] Claes Waern, 'Bibelskolen i Bolivia har en positiv utvikling', *Korsets seier* 3 June

participated, and at the end of the course all expressed an interest in continuing the next course when it would be starting in August. The teaching staff consisted of both Norwegian and Swedish Pentecostal missionaries.[38] In 1988, the school had around 70 students in addition to about 100 who studied by correspondence. Most of the approximately 100 students who had completed their entire education had pastoral or other leadership duties in Bolivian congregations.[39]

In 1978, the evangelical school *Buenas Nuevas* (Good News) was opened in a very poor area of Cochabamba. Ivar Aas was responsible for designing the primary school section, and Börje Green was headmaster in the start-up of the school while the Aas family was in Norway. In the first school year there were around 400 students with around 1,000 the following year. When Ivar Aas returned, he became headmaster, but in 1980 he was succeeded by Roger Samuelsen. At that time, the school had about 1,200 students from pre-school up to and including 9th grade, and a gradual expansion up to and including 12th grade was planned. The school followed Bolivia's curriculum, but in addition there were Bible lessons, devotions, camps etc. Not all the teachers were Christians, but all had to support the school's values. Most of the staff were paid by the Bolivian state, but the Mission paid the salaries for the Bible teachers and the administrative staff. A Brazilian missionary family started a local church in the area, while at the same time they were responsible for a large Sunday school with several hundred participants in the aula of the *Buenas Nuevas* school. Solveig and Roger Samuelsen also became involved in this church, and much of the membership growth in the congregation came from *Buenas Nueva's* classes.[40]

1981, p. 12. The Bible school was later subordinated to the Bolivian pastors' conference, and in 1992 the number of students had grown to 200 people if we count the ambulatory Bible schools in other congregations 'with the same study plan and teaching material as in Cochabamba'. It is also interesting to note that the number of Pentecostals had increased from 5,000 to 50,000 in Bolivia in the twelve years since the Bible school in Cochabamba started in 1980. 'Bibelskolene viktige i Bolivia', *Ekko. Bilag til Korsets seier* May 1992, pp. 10-11.

[38] Hanne-Berit and Finn Jensen, 'Bibelskolen i Cochabamba, Bolivia', *Korsets seier* 25 June 1980, p. 8.

[39] Erling Andreassen, 'Innvielse av bibelskolen i Cochabamba, Bolivia', *Korsets seier* 14 October 1988, p. 28.

[40] Claes Waern and Solveig Samuelsen, 'SIDA satser 5 millioner på skole-

Together with Bolivian professionals, Roger Samuelsen was responsible for developing new curricula in collaboration with the Ministry of Education. In Bolivia, it was completely new that one could get practical vocational training at the same time as completing high school. That all programs should be open to both boys and girls was also new thinking. When the school year started in 1983, there were a total of around 1,600 students. Roger Samuelsen had the main responsibility for the school until 1987, except for one year when the family was on furlough in Norway. He was also the project manager for a large school that was built in a poor area of Santa Cruz, following the same concept as *Buenas Nuevas* in Cochabamba. When the primary school section was completed in 1987, a Swedish couple took responsibility for the school's management and further development.

In 1978-79, the *Pinsebevegelsen's* Foreign Mission in Norway (PYM) was asked to 'do something for the many orphans and abandoned children in Cochabamba', and in connection with the TV campaign *Aksjon Håp* in 1982, money was allocated to a children's village a short distance away from the city centre.[41]

From 1971 to 1981 Erling and Marita Andreassen worked in Norway, but from 1981 they were in Cochabamba where *Villa Infantil Nueva Esperanza*, which is the children's *New Hope* village, was inaugurated in 1986.[42] It was constructed according to the same principle as SOS Children's Villages with family units that could have up to 12 children in each house. In the *New Hope* village Erling and Marita became managers, in addition to Erling becoming the

---

prosjekt i Bolivia', *Korsets seier* 11 July 1981, p. 8; Jan-Aage Torp, '"Gode nyheter" i fattigkvarteret', *Korsets seier* 26 January 1983, p. 12; Solveig Samuelsen, input and corrections to an earlier version of this book manuscript.

[41] 'Pinsevennenes Ytre Misjons prosjekter ved Aksjon Håp', *Korsets seier* 25 June 1980, p. 8.

[42] 'It was the Bolivian authorities who advised Swedish and Norwegian Pentecostals to take up work for the many children who were abandoned or orphaned. A survey from 1979 showed that many children spent the night on the street in parks, at the railway station or in cemeteries. Many revolutions and a lot of political unrest led to several postponements, but with support from NORAD and the TV campaign *Aksjon Håp*, the children's village became a reality'. Geir Magnus Nyborg, 'Tragedier møtes med kjærlighet', *Ekko. Korsets seiers utenriks- og misjonsmagasin* February 1988, p. 12. In this sense, it is more than ironic that the Bolivian authorities would later introduce a new law with a prison sentence of five to 12 years for open evangelism. 'Evangelisering forbudt i Bolivia', *Korsets seier* 26 January 2018, p. 35.

Norwegian consul in Bolivia.[43] When Marion and Frank Stensland were sent out to Bolivia, however, they quickly discovered that something was wrong. Sexual abuse was uncovered, and in 2001 Marion and Frank became the new managers during a transitional period. The children's village is still functioning with financial assistance from sponsors and local churches. Betania, Tønsberg has the main responsibility, and a resource group of enthusiastic individuals supports the national board and the staff workers.[44]

Despite the fact that the national workers became increasingly valued on equal terms with the Norwegian missionaries, some of the Norwegians continued as senior pastors. Eva and Helge Adolfsen had moved on to La Paz in 1993 where they built up a large congregation, *Vida Nueva*. Here Helge was the senior pastor for many years.[45] Several local churches, daycare centers and schools grew out of the *Vida Nueva* congregation and the *Doxa* foundation. An evangelical university, *UNIDOXA*, also functioned for a few years.[46]

After about 10 years in Norway, Roger and Solveig Samuelsen received a request from Filadelfia, Stockholm and *Pingstmissionens Utvecklingssamarbete* (PMU) to help for a year at *Buenas Nuevas* in Santa Cruz, in the period 1997-98. The school now had around 2,000 students in addition to a daycare center with 75 children. Sweden provided the finances for the Samuelsens, but everything was channeled through their sending congregation, Salen in Halden. Their main task was to assist in the process of nationalization. A

---

[43] Kjell Hagen, *Marit og Erling Andreassen: På spesialoppdrag i jungelen* (Oslo: Filadel-fiaforlaget 1994), pp. 159-60.

[44] Anne Gustavsen, 'De uskyldige ofrene er vår største smerte', *Korsets seier* 30 November 2001, pp. 10-11; Solveig Samuelsen, input and corrections to an earlier version of this book manuscript.

[45] In just a five-month period, almost 70 people had been baptized. Solveig Samuelsen, 'Levende menighet i vekst i La Paz', *Korsets seier* 30 September 1994, p. 12.

[46] Eva and Helge Adolfsen saw early on the need to strengthen the level of teaching in addition to prioritizing social work, and they started the foundation Doxa, which in 2012 had 'ten day centers for children from one year and up, and ten schools from first grade up to upper secondary'. Kjell Hagen, 'Startet nytt universitet i Bolivia', *Korsets seier* 13 January 2012, p. 22. And after three years of waiting, the Bolivian Ministry of Education also approved the university *UNIDOXA*. As Eva and Helge Adolfsen put it: 'Our vision is to provide Bolivian children with an education throughout their upbringing, including higher education, the university is a further development of this'. Hagen, 'Startet nytt universitet i Bolivia', p 22.

national board was formed for the school with representatives from several congregations in the area. One of the representatives was a pastor who also taught at the large evangelical university in the city. It turned out that this man had once been a student at the small boarding school in Gonzalo Moreno! Although the mission station there has long since closed down, one can still see the fruits of the work. All over Bolivia one can meet people who have experienced Christian conversion through the mission's work and who are now carrying on the work themselves.[47]

The organization *Fundación para Educación y Servicio* or *FES* (Foundation for Education and Services) was founded in 2003 to take care of many of the functions of the *Nordisk Pinsemisjon* when it was decided to discontinue it. After some adaptations in the first years, *FES* today functions as an umbrella organization for four legal entities: (1) *Asamblea de Dios Boliviana*: Pentecostal churches started by Brazilian missionaries in Bolivia. There are more than 1,200 congregations with over 20,000 members; (2) *Iglesia Evangélica Nacional – Asamblea de Dios*: Pentecostal congregations that are the fruit of Norwegian-started missionary work along the Beni River from Riberalta to Rurrenabaque. Altogether, there are several thousand members; (3) *Iglesia Evangélica Pentecostal* is the fruit of Swedish-initiated work from Quillacollo. It currently works in four counties in Bolivia, has 80 congregations and more than 5,000 members; (4) *Universidad Evangélica Boliviana*, the Evangelical University which was founded by an American missionary in Santa Cruz in 1980. This now has more than 3,000 students.

FES organizes a pastoral conference in Cochabamba every year. Over 200 pastors and staff gather here for seminars and edification. This helps to create unity between the congregations and organizations that are part of *FES*. There are several congregations and fellowships with roots in the *Nordisk Pinse Misjon* that have chosen to stand outside *FES*.[48]

---

[47] Solveig and Roger Samuelsen, 'Tilbake til Bolivia igjen', *Korsets seier* 9 January 1998, p. 11. By mistake, it says 1997 on this issue of *Korsets seier*. Solveig Samuelsen, input and corrections to an earlier version of this book manuscript.

[48] Solveig Samuelsen, input and corrections to an earlier version of this book manuscript. It will often be difficult to agree with oneself about what should be included and what should be left out in such a brief introductory book as this one. An in-depth study of the Norwegian Pentecostal missionary work would need to

Peru

The Pentecostal movement in Peru seems to have had its beginning in 1911 through missionaries Howard W. and Clara Cragin, who tried to establish a ministerial work in Callao. In 1922, two missionary couples representing the Assemblies of God arrived, J.R. Hurlburt and wife whose name is unknown, as well as Forrest and Ethel Barker. The Hurlburts founded a congregation in Callao that same year. Churches were also founded in Huancayo, Callejón, and Carás. In 1925 reinforcements were received through the American missionary couple Leif and Florence Erickson. Three years later, Ruth Couchman and Olga Pritt also arrived, both of whom represented the Assemblies of God.

The 1940s and 50s were characterized by numerical growth but also by splits as several Pentecostal denominations were established.[49] In addition to a relatively steady influx of American Pentecostal missionaries, there were also emissaries from neighboring Chile. The *Swedish* Pentecostal missionary Per Anderås also came via Chile in 1955. The following year he and his wife Britta founded the *Casa de Oración* assembly in Tarma about 240 kilometers east of Lima. In 1962, additional Swedish Pentecostal missionaries are said to have arrived in Tarma, namely Ingeborg 'Bojan' and Lennart Lindgren, and the work expanded.[50]

---

give detailed attention to Ingrid Vatne's involvement with PYM's school project in Bolivia. The same applies to the Tørre family's work in Oruro and the orphanage in Cochabamba. Such a study should also provide insights into the missionary service of pilots Finn Røine and Jan Smidsrød (both stationed in Riberalta), as well as Vegard Tørre (stationed in Cochabamba). Solveig Samuelsen has also, rightly, called for attention to all these matters in her input and corrections to an earlier version of this book manuscript. And still, it must be admitted that neither *Korsets seier* nor *Det gode Budskap* gives a complete or balanced perspective of Norwegian Pentecostal missionary work in other contries, and that what has been included in these two periodicals seems a bit random. Not all missionaries have been equally concerned with documen-ting their own missionary activities. Personal interviews are therefore necessary as supplementary source material in addition to investigating whether relevant correspondence or diary entries can be located.

[49] David D. Bundy, 'Peru', in Burgess and van der Maas (eds.), *New International Dictionary of Pentecostal Charismatic Movements*, pp. 198-200.

[50] John Agersten, 'Peru – inkaindianernes land', *Korsets seier* 21 December 1966, p. 7; Lennart Lindgren, 'En missionärsson berättar om sin kallelse', *Evangelii Härold* 27 July 1961, pp. 6-7; Evy Norrmann, interview with missionary Len-nart Lindgren, 30 October 1996. Available as pdf from the Institute for Pentecostal

Gro and John Agersten from Salem, Oslo announced a mission call – preferably to Peru, although they '[found] it practical and according to God's guidance to begin in Argentina, starting from the Norwegian Pentecostal mission there'.[51] Yet by November, it turned out to be Peru after all, a country which at this time was an 'unknown mission field for Norwegian Pentecostals'.[52] While still living in Norway they had been corresponding with Lennart Lindgren, and it was natural to start their missionary work alongside them in the city of Tarma, while Brita and Per Anderås had moved on to the provincial capital Huancayo.[53]

Even before leaving Norway, Agersten felt the call to work among indigenous people in unreached areas. After 2 years in Tarma, they moved north to Bagua and from there further east to the jungle areas along the Marañón River in the province of Alto Amazonas, where the gospel had not previously been preached. Wycliffe Bible Translators had missionaries in two villages in this area, where there were also several indigenous tribes.

In Yurimaguas, Agersten built the boat *El Sembrador* with furnishings that allowed a whole family to live in the boat for quite some time. In October 1969 they initiated a several months' trip along the Marañón distributing tracts, helping the sick and preaching the gospel while simultaneously praying for God's wisdom regarding where to take up permanent missionary work. They felt God's guidance to settle down in a village called Tigre Playa, where several conversions took place within a short time and a Sunday school was started with over 60 children and young people attending.[54]

In 1972 came Alice and Rudolf Wilhelm, who after having completed missionary work in Honduras had spent two years in Norway.[55] In the summer of 1971, Liv Haug came to Tigre Playa, where Edith Aateigen had already arrived at the end of 1970. After

---

Studies in Sweden. Cf. also John Agersten, 'Blant indianere og mestizer i Peru's jungel', *https://peru.agersten.com/category/category8/* [Accessed 25 October 2024].

[51] 'Nye misjonærer', *Korsets seier* 26 June 1965, p. 11.

[52] Gro and John Agersten, 'Peru venter', *Korsets seier* 20 November 1965, p. 19.

[53] Gro and John Agersten, 'På høyfjell og i jungelen forkynnes evangeliet', *Korsets seier* 8 July 1967, p. 16.

[54] Gro and John Agersten, 'På høyfjell og i jungelen forkynnes evangeliet', *Korsets seier* 23 May 1970, p. 7.

[55] John Agersten, 'En nyfrelst vitnet – og landsbyen bad om besøk av misjonærene', *Korsets seier* Eastertime 1973, p. 2.

the Agerstens left for Norway on furlough during Spring 1971, Aateigen continued the work in Tigre Playa assisted by Christina Pålsson from Sweden, until Liv Haug arrived. In 1972, the Agerstens returned to Tigre Playa, while Aateigen and Haug took up missionary work in Pampa Silva/Puerto Libre in the Perené Valley, where in 1973 there was a small congregation with membership just below 30.[56] A mission station was built, with the assistance of Liv's father, Håkon Haug.[57] Håkon had been the senior pastor in Filadelfia, Kristiansand since 1966 and had spent a couple of months in Peru since July 1975 until the three-story mission building in Puerto Libre en Pampa Silva in the Perené valley was completed.

In October of the same year, Håkon was back again, this time with NORAD-support to build a factory for juice production so that poor indigenous people would not have to transport home-cultivated fruit to Lima to sell it there – and probably at a lower price than the transportation would cost them. This time Håkon stayed until April 1976.[58]

In May 1981, he and his wife Ruth made their third visit to Peru, this time until January 1982. With NORAD's support, work was now begun to build a bridge over the Perené river as a substitute to the old cableway 'with a gondola made of dark planks' that the children had to cross to get to school: 'Just as it was, accidents happened, the gondola could fall down, and several children had drowned in the

---

[56] Edith Aateigen and Liv Haug, 'Glimt fra Peru, kontrastenes land', *Korsets seier* 29 May 1974, p. 5. The village of Puerto Libre had been founded in 1961 as the first settlement in the Perené valley of indigenous peoples from the mountains. During a land reform in 1969, the land in the Perené valley was distributed between indigenous peoples from the jungle and mountains, respectively, and by Liv Haug's arrival in 1988, due to indigenous peoples who had moved from the mountains, there were 88 villages in the Perené valley. Harald Mydland, (ed.), *Liv Margrethe Haug - misjonær og samfunnsbygger blant urbefolkningen i Peru* (Kjeller: Hermon forlag, 2021), pp. 50-51.

[57] M.S., 'Hjem fra Peru', *Korsets seier* 12 November 1975, p. 11. While Håkon Haug was a Pentecostal pastor in Filadelfia, Kristiansand, that is, the con-gregation that had sent out Edith Aateigen and Liv Haug to Peru, it was via Olav Strømme (priest in the Church of Norway and who after his death in 1976 had Strømme Foundation named after him) money was granted for missionary housing for Aateigen and Liv Haug. Liv and Håkon went out in July 1975, and Håkon built an entire mission station with a multi-story building with a floor area of around 150 square metres.

[58] Fredrik Schjander, *I samtale med Håkon Haug: Mitt liv i tjeneste* (Oslo: Filadelfiaforlaget, 1988), pp. 57-92.

rough river water'.[59] The project was completed, largely with the help of voluntary efforts by both Håkon and Liv, as well as the local population.

Liv had been elected mayor in 1981 as the three districts of Puerto Libre, Pampa Silva and Santa Ana chose to merge into one city under the name Villa Perené in 1977.[60] During the mayor's term, Liv initiated plans for each and every village to have its own school, and three years later 17 schools were built while the authorities provided teachers.[61] In 1986 Liv was also 'granted Peru's highest award – the Order of the Sun with the rank of commander'.[62] During these years, several hundred people came to faith and were baptized.[63]

Liv also succeeded in building a larger school library/literature center, as well as a radio channel, Radio Filadelfia, which enabled the production of radio programs that were listened to in over 40 villages around Villa Perené.[64] And that was not all: in 1991, a technical vocational school was inaugurated for young people who had finished upper secondary school and could not afford to move to the capital to continue their education – 'the three-year technical college, IST, started with car mechanics, secretaries and agriculture courses, and the one-year vocational school CEO, with a carpentry course, car mechanics, sewing and assistant nursing courses'.[65] In addition to this, Liv initiated a 5-year teacher training course.[66] In 1996, Perené also received status as its own district – with responsibility for just under 200 villages, of which Villa Perené became the district capital. This meant that the district received its own budget from the state and in that way could continue to improve social conditions in the Perené valley. This was the same year that Liv was elected municipal

---

[59] Schjander, *I samtale med Håkon Haug*, p. 82.

[60] Schjander, *I samtale med Håkon Haug*, p. 108. The bridge was '121 meters long, 3.60 meters wide and with a permissible axle pressure of 36 tonnes'. Arvid Møller, *Liv Haug. Norsk misjonær, ordfører og anleggsbas i Amazonas-jungelen* (Oslo: J.W. Cappelens Forlag A/S, 1987), p. 57.

[61] Møller, *Liv Haug*, p. 67.

[62] Møller, *Liv Haug*, p. 187. In Norway, in 2005 Liv was appointed Knight of the First Class by King Harald V. Mydland, *Liv Margrethe Haug*, p. 154.

[63] Mydland, *Liv Margrethe Haug*, p. 79.

[64] Mydland, *Liv Margrethe Haug*, pp. 106-107.

[65] Mydland, *Liv Margrethe Haug*, p. 124.

[66] Mydland, *Liv Margrethe Haug*, p. 132.

mayor.[67] Due to re-election in 1999, she remained mayor until 2002.[68] In the period 2007-2010, she was again elected mayor, this time in the province of Chanchamayo.[69]

When Liv came to Peru in 1971, she was registered in the *Iglesias Pentecostales Autónomas del Centro*, AIPA, which was founded by Swedish Pentecostals. In 2006, however, the churches within Perené registered their own religious organization, the *Iglesia Evangélica Filadelfia*, FILA. The congregations today have Peruvian pastors.[70]

Liv Haug's pioneering endeavors in Peru are well documented through books and national television coverage. However, as we have already seen, Gro and John Agersten were the first pioneer missionaries sent out from Norway. In 1973, the river boat *Alli Shungo* (The Good Heart) was purchased. Both this river boat and a speed boat were in constant use in the years that followed to reach the villages along the Marañón with the Gospel. From the very beginning, work was carried out among the sick, who came in increasing numbers to the missionaries at Tigre Playa for help. Gradually, congregations and outposts were established. Bible weeks for leaders and co-workers were held twice a year in Tigre Playa, combined with local Bible days in the villages. Eva and Wilhelm soon assumed the main responsibility working with the sick when Gro Agersten, who was a teacher by profession, started the Norwegian school beginning with 2 pupils in 1972 and increasing to 5 during the 1970s. In 1974, Vigdis Flatland came from Rjukan and helped with the school for a period of around two years.

In the autumn of 1978, the Wilhelm family returned to work in the jungle after a year in Norway. Together with them came teacher Martha de Jong from Alta. The Wilhelms now had Filadelfia, Alta as their sending church, just like Martha. She and Gro Agersten shared

---

[67] When Liv Haug was elected mayor in the Perené valley, the Norwegian *PYM* protested because this allegedly contradicted their mission regulations, 'which state that a missionary cannot participate in political work,' which in turn implied that she would 'be laid off as a missionary during the period she [was] mayor, which [would signify] that she [would] lose NORAD's support during that same period'. Then it should also be added that the sending church, Filadelfia, Kristiansand, '[disputed] PYM's interpretation of the regulations and [rejected] the proposal for layoffs'. Anne Gustavsen, 'Blir ordfører i Perene-dalen. Liv Haug permitteres som misjonær', *Korsets seier* 23 February 1996, p. 5.

[68] Mydland, *Liv Margrethe Haug*, p. 144.

[69] Mydland, *Liv Margrethe Haug*, pp. 174-75.

[70] Mydland, *Liv Margrethe Haug*, p. 168.

the work at the school for the first couple of years she was there. When the Agerstens went on furlough to Norway, Martha had the main responsibility for the remaining 3 pupils until 1982 when she and Wilhelm traveled to Norway.

At the turn of the year 1974, a formal relationship was established with Wycliffe Bible Translators involving daily radio contact and fuel storage for their small aircraft which operated in the area where the Norwegian missionaries worked. This contract turned into mutual help and joy in the work and lasted until Wycliffe Bible Translators ended their work in the jungle in 1999. Their center was located at Pucallpa, 800 kilometers as the crow flies from Tigre Playa. Ågot Bergli, sent from the Pentecostal church in Mo i Rana, for many years worked as a linguist for Wycliffe Bible Translators in Peru starting in the 1980s.

The missionaries Oddbjørg and Gunnar Vervik visited Tigre Playa for the first time in 1974. They worked in Puerto Libre together with Liv Haug from the time they arrived in Peru the year before and were there until 1975. In 1977 they returned to Peru and served in the river mission out of Tigre Playa a year before they replaced and later collaborated with the Swedish missionaries Anita and Göran Olsson in the town of Chulucanas in the county of Piura in Northern Peru. In 1981, the Verviks returned to Tigre Playa and worked in the area until, due to sickness, they returned to Norway in 1983. Missionary Øyvor Skjennum visited Tigre Playa on a Bible week in 1979. She worked for a period at Villa Perené together with Liv Haug.

In August 1983, the Wilhelms returned to Tigre Playa together with teacher Birgitte Krogtoft from Lofoten, later married to David Lindgren, son of the Swedish missionaries Lindgren. Birgitte worked for many years in Spain after her marriage to David.

In January 1984, the Agerstens returned to the jungle after 3 years on furlough in Norway. In May of the same year, the Wilhelm family moved down the Marañón to Industrial /San Lorenzo to reinforce and expand the work in the eastern part of the field. Birgitte Krogtoft moved with them and continued the Norwegian school there. She was in Peru until the summer of 1986. The Wilhelm family worked from Industrial until they left for Norway for good in 2006. By then, several new congregations and outposts had been established in that area in addition to those that had been founded from Tigre Playa. The Wilhelms also carried out extensive work among the many sick and poor, eventually in close collaboration with the municipal health center in San Lorenzo.

The Agerstens moved west from Marañón to Saramiriza, which had grown into a larger village since the Peruvian oil company established a center there in the latter part of the 1970s. The place was among the many visited in previous years and had a group of believers. Soon the congregation in Saramiriza was established and, like the churches at Tigre Playa, San Lorenzo and Industrial with outposts, it was registered as part of the *Asociación Iglesias Pentecostales Autónomas* (AIPA) which was founded by Swedish and Norwegian missionaries in 1967. The health work was strengthened in 1986 when nurse Bodil and her husband Manolo Suárez came to Saramiriza sent by a Pentecostal congregation in Sweden and with financial support from PMU. They returned to Sweden in 1990.

María and Isidro Villavicencio from Lima were installed as pastors of the church in Saramiriza from 1991 to 1994. They had previously worked in the area as evangelists together with local evangelists and outpost leaders. Villavicencio was later pastor for a few years in the congregation Lindgren founded in Lima. In the following years, the congregation in Saramiriza had pastors from the Swedish missionaries' work in the Piura county and local pastors.

In 1990, the Health Center in Saramiriza was completed and inaugurated. This project received support from NORAD in collaboration with the Peruvian health authorities for construction and operation during the first years. The authorities later applied for an extension of the Health Center. This was granted and the facility was completed and inaugurated in June 1999. The Agerstens were project managers for the Health Center project parts 1 and 2.[71]

While the Agerstens were in Norway on furlough from 1992, Morgan and Lourdes Førland worked in Saramiriza, Peru starting New Years 1993.[72] The Agerstens returned to Peru in 1994, and since over 70% of Latin Americans lived in cities, they now wanted to alternate between Peruvian cities and, as before, the jungle.[73] They chose to settle in Piura, a city in the northwestern part of the country,

---

[71] Gro and John Agersten, email to the author dated 19 November 2024 and with supplementary information for the unfinished manuscript as it then existed.

[72] 'Peru: Flodevangelisering og bibelmaraton', *Misjonsbilag,* p. 10 as a supplementary to *Korsets seier* on 14 May 1993.

[73] 'Gro og John Agersten tilbake i Peru', *Korsets seier* 6 January 1995, p. 18.

where they began with evangelistic radio broadcasts on various stations.[74] This work was carried out in collaboration with pastors in the area where the Swedish missionaries Anita and Göran Olsson had founded churches as an extension of the congregation in Chulucanas. In a suburb named Ignacio Merino in Piura, a church was founded and a building for church services was purchased in 1999. Lourdes and Morgan Førland were in Ignacio Merino, Piura from 2000 to 2003. The current pastor in Saramiriza (2025), William Tocto, was for several years pastor in Ignacio Merino but had occasionally visited the Saramiriza church and its outposts together with a group of young people.

Despite the urban focus, the 32 churches and outposts around Saramiriza kept growing, and in 1996 alone, with over 100 new believers being baptized, the congregations counted by then a total of 880 active members.[75]

There are no exact statistics concerning the number of churches and outposts and members after 1996. During the 1990s, a few other denominations and missions entered the area through Peruvian evangelists. Some of the congregations and outposts in both the eastern and western part of the area, started by the Norwegian Pentecostal mission, have passed to either the Peruvian *Asamblea de Dios* or MEPI (*Misión Evangelica Pentecostal Internacional*). Members having moved out from the jungle have started a congregation in the city of Yurimaguas, while others minister as evangelists and pastors in other Pentecostal denominations, such as in the cities of Iquitos and Nauta. A youth from Tigre Playa is even a pastor in Belo Horizonte, Brazil.[76]

Maran Ata sends out missionaries

Not only *Pinsebevegelsen*, but also *Maran Ata*, another Pentecostal denomination originating in Norway, has had a missionary involvement in Peru. *Maran Ata's* involvement was initiated through Kolbjørn Granseth (b. 1929), who together with his family left for Peru in 1967. They settled in Arequipa and became involved in radio

[74] Oddvar Johansen, 'Evangeliet må videre fra jungelen til storbyen', *Korsets seier* 2 February 1996, p. 20.
[75] Gro and John Agersten, 'Misjonsrapport fra Peru: Dåpsmøter og nye kirker', *Korsets seier* 11 April 1997, p. 9.
[76] Gro and John Agersten, email to the author dated 19 November 2024.

evangelism in addition to providing opportunities for itinerant evangelists.

Due to problems with residence permits, the Granseth family had to temporarily leave Peru and worked in Spain, El Salvador, and Bolivia. However, they returned to Peru in 1996 where they settled in Nazca while another Norwegian couple, Solfrid and Erling Eriksen, sent out from Maran Ata, Oslo in 1970, settled in Tacna.[77]

---

[77] Ole Bjørn Saltnes, *Som et stormvær. En bok om Maran Ata vekkelsen* (Tofte: Misjon Europa Forlag, 2017), p. 215.

7

MEXICO, CENTRAL AMERICA, AND THE CARIBBEAN

Mexico

The revival among Pentecostals in Azusa Street, Los Angeles had a rapid impact among Latin Americans, and then mainly among Mexicans. In fact, it was a Mexican believer who first specifically claimed to have had an encounter with the Spirit of God in the premises at 312 Azusa Street after the Pentecostals had secured a lease there. This occurred one day before the Pentecostals had their first service there in April 1906.[1]

Although it is natural to imagine that several of the Mexican believers who had experienced their personal Pentecost during the services in Azusa Street in 1906 then returned to their homeland to further the movement, this has so far not been documented. In 1914, however, a Oneness church was founded in Villa Aldama in the state of Chihuahua, Mexico, which in turn formed the prelude to the Oneness denomination *Iglesia Apostólica*.[2] Similarly, the first church of the Trinitarian stream, the *Iglesia de Dios* (Church of God), was

---

[1] Gastón Espinoza, 'The Holy Ghost is here on Earth? The Latino Contributions to the Azusa Street Revival', *Enrichment* Spring 2006, p. 119. Cf. also Gastón Espinoza, *Latino Pentecostals in America: Faith and Politics in Action* (Cambridge, MA: Harvard University Press, 2014), pp. 35-36.
[2] Philip Wingeler-Rayo, 'A Third Phase of Christianity: Reflections on One Hundred Years of Pentecostalism in Mexico', in Vinson Synan, Amos Yong and Miguel Álvarez (eds.), *Global Renewal Christianity: Spirit Empowered Movements. Past, Present, and Future*. Vol 2: *Latin America* (Lake Mary, FL: Creation House, 2016), pp. 7-10.

formed in Mexico in 1932.[3] In fact, it was a Scandinavian, H. A. Johnson, who allegedly belonged to T.B. Barratt's group in Oslo, who is said to have been evangelizing in Mexico as early as 1911 and 1912.[4] If this history is correct, he was still not the first one to preach the Pentecostal message in Mexico. The credit for this must possibly be attributed to the husband of American healing minister Carrie Judd Montgomery. George is said to have received his personal Pentecost around 1908, perhaps even a little earlier, and was spreading Christian literature in the mining town of Nacozari. A missionary named George Thomas also worked in Nacozari from 1911 onwards.[5]

Few Norwegian missionaries have been sent to Mexico, and perhaps the first ones, possibly after H.A. Johnson, were Marika and Kari Ranta, with the Filadelfia congregation in Oslo as their sending church in 1997. Despite her American upbringing, Kari has a Finnish background. The couple worked as Wycliffe missionaries and translated the Bible into Native American tribal languages. Marika had previously been sent by Filadelfia, Oslo as a short-term missionary to Peru, and that is how she came to know the Wycliffe Bible Translators.[6]

In 2009, Sara and Torbjørn Tande left for Monterrey, Mexico to work with orphans under the auspices of the organization Back2Back Ministries and Youth with a Mission. The couple still works there. Sara Jensen has done the same. From 2019 to 2024, she worked at a youth home and, in addition was responsible for aftercare for young people who either had a foster home background or had lived in a youth home.[7]

Oslo Kristne Senter with branches Mexico
The church Oslo Kristne Senter (OKS) is also represented in Mexico. It all started with Norunn (Norwegian) and Miguel Inzunza

---

[3] Wingeler-Rayo, 'A Third Phase of Christianity', pp. 10-11; Lie, *Tro og tanke*, p. 173.

[4] Allan H. Anderson, 'Primeras misiones pentecostales en América Latina', *Hechos: Una Perspectiva Pneumatológica* 4.1 (2022), p. 6.

[5] Luisa Jeter de Walker, *Siembra y cosecha. Las Asambleas de Dios de México y Centroamérica*. Vol. 1 (Deerfield, FL: Editorial Vida, 1990), p. 16.

[6] Oddvar Johansen, 'Lever for å gi stammefolk i Mexico Guds ord', *Korsets seier* 22 October 1999, p. 12.

[7] Geir Lie, interview with Sara Jensen, 7 November 2024. Back2Back Ministries started in 1998 as they wanted to be a supporter of existing work among children and young people in need.

(Mexican), who, after attending Oslo Kristne Senter's Bible school in the period 2005-2006, returned to Miguel's home country where the congregation Centro Cristiano Campiña in the city of Culiacán became a formal part of the OKS family in 2006. The church changed its name to OKS Iglesia Campiña in 2016. Then, the congregation OKS Iglesia Guadalajara in the city of Guadalajara was established in 2023 with Nacho and Paulina Huizar as senior pastors. Previous to this, in 2021, they had started a house group in Guadalajara.[8]

Guatemala

As early as 1908, Pentecostal Christianity was introduced in Guatemala by and through Amos and Effie Bradley, American missionaries who received their personal Pentecost in San Jerónimo.[9] In the year 2000, the newly married couple Elisabeth and Roberto Sandli from Norway traveled to Guatemala, which they had visited the year before in connection with a seven-week honeymoon to Nicaragua.

PYM was already involved in Guatemala through a five-year project partly related to school construction and partly to training in agriculture. The schools were to be built in collaboration with local Pentecostal congregations, which in turn would be responsible for further operation. Elisabeth and Roberto were to be project assistants and work together with Britt and Birger Sandli, who led the projects.[10]

Honduras

Mario Eduardo Fumero was born in Cuba to Spanish parents and is also briefly mentioned during this chapter's review of Cuba. When Fidel Castro 'seized the power in 1959, Mario soon became the captain of military youth groups in the name of the revolution, [but] eventually he distanced himself from the turn towards Marxist-

---

[8] 'Mexico', *https://oks.no/mexico/* [Accessed 24 October 2024].
[9] Allan H. Anderson, 'Primeras misiones pentecostales en América Latina', *Hechos: Una Perspectiva Pneumatológica* 4.1 (2022), p. 6.
[10] Elisabeth and Roberto Sandli, 'Nye misjonærer til Guatemala', *Korsets seier* 14 April 2000, p. 28.

Leninism'.[11] He fled to the United States in 1960, where the following year he experienced a Christian conversion while attending a revival campaign with Billy Graham. In 1964, Mario went to Honduras, where for several months each year he was involved in evangelism, not least through radio missions. During a visit to Chile in 1970, he was introduced to Lisbeth Jensen, who had worked as a missionary there since 1966 (apart from a year and a half in Paraguay). They married in Norway in 1971 and settled in the Honduran capital Tegucigalpa.[12]

Even before the marriage between Lisbeth and Mario, in 1966, Eva and Rudolf Wilhelm announced *their* calling to Honduras. Rudolf was Swiss but had worked as an evangelist in Norway for about 5 years and before that he had also lived in Sweden for a few years. Incidentally, it was via Swedish friends that the call to Honduras became actual. The couple received a recommendation from their home church in Balsfjord.[13] They traveled to Honduras in 1966 to work together with the Swedish missionaries Stina and Hans Alsbo who had arrived in 1964. Eventually other Swedish missionaries also came to work in San Pedro and La Lima.[14] In 1969 we read that they had started a church in San Pedro Sula and were also engaged in radio work, as well as had plans for both an orphanage and reading education.[15] The orphanage became a fact at least as early as 1970, and close to 400 people were present when the church building in San Pedro and the orphanage in La Lima were formally inaugurated.[16] The stay in Honduras was nevertheless relatively short-lived, as after

[11] Solveig Samuelsen, 'Lisbeth og Mario Fumero', unpublished manuscript, September 2024.

[12] Trygve Lie, 'Cubaneren Mario Fumero til Norge', *Korsets seier* 26 June 1971, p. 12; Lisbeth and Mario Fumero, 'Også Honduras-misjonærer satser på radiomisjon', *Korsets seier* 14 June 1972, p. 4; Solveig Samuelsen, 'Internasjonal familie fra Halden til Honduras', *Korsets seier* 12 November 1975, p. 11. The first Pentecostal approach towards Honduras which I am personally aware of, was through evangelist Adam Brandt in 1918. Walker, *Siembra y cosecha*, p. 150.

[13] 'Misjonærer til Honduras', *Korsets seier* 2 February 1966, p. 4.

[14] Gro and John Agersten, email to the author dated 19 November 2024.

[15] Eva and Rudolf Wilhelm, 'Det bygges i Honduras', *Korsets seier* 16 August 1969, p. 6. In retrospect, Helge Adolfsen claimed 'that 60-70% of our congregations [in Bolivia] are an indirect result of the radio work', Oddvar Johansen, 'Helge Adolfsen på IBRA-seminar', *Korsets seier* 4 October 1985, p. 19.

[16] Eva and Rudolf Wilhelm, 'Høytidsdager i Honduras', *Korsets seier* 28 January 1970, p. 5.

the end of 1970 they returned to Norway where Rudolf became the pastor in Smyrna, Kirkenes until leaving for Peru in the fall of 1972.[17] Lisbeth and Mario, however, continued in Honduras, and in 1978 we read that the congregation numbered around 200 members, most of whom were young students.[18] Three years later, they worked within nine different Honduran congregations.[19] Solveig Samuelsen writes:

> In addition to church work, they engaged in various types of relief aid. There were orphanages, daycare centers, literacy training, schools, help for disadvantaged families and single mothers, as well as a rehabilitation center for alcoholics and drug addicts. Radio and TV were also used to teach and encourage people to improve their own life situation. They worked according to the principle of 'helping somebody to learn how to help themselves', and they were good at getting others on board and training them to take responsibility. Eventually, over 100 national young people were organized into 'The Christian Love Brigade'. Teams from the Brigade still travel around to many towns and villages to help where there is a need.[20]

Much of this work continued when the family left in 1982 to work as missionaries in Spain.[21] However, they returned to Honduras again in the period 1994-98, until Lisbeth again relocated to Spain while Mario continued to live in Honduras.[22] He became one of several coordinators for the relief work in connection with Hurricane Mitch's catastrophic destruction in October 1998. Both *PYM* and *Korsets Seier* were active participants in collecting 'food, medicine, clothing and equipment' for both Honduras and neighboring Nicaragua.[23] Mario still works and lives in Honduras.

---

[17] Gro and John Agersten, email to the author dated 19 November 2024.

[18] Peder Westgård, 'Effektivt radioarbeid i Honduras', *Korsets seier* 7 January 1978, p. 1.

[19] 'Misjonærer hilser', *Korsets seier* 10 January 1981, p. 14.

[20] Solveig Samuelsen, 'Lisbeth og Mario Fumero', unpublished manuscript, September 2024.

[21] Lisbeth and Mario Fumero, 'Avskjed med Honduras etter 11 rike år', *Korsets seier* 8 December 1982, pp. 12, 15.

[22] After serving 40 years as a missionary, Lisbeth was awarded the King's Merit Medal in silver in 2006. Solveig Samuelsen, 'Med misjon som livsstil', *Korsets seier* 22 September 2006, p. 30.

[23] Oddvar Johansen, 'Herre! Forbarm deg over vårt lidende folk', *Korsets seier* Christmastime 1998, pp. 20-21.

Nicaragua

PYM's investment in Nicaragua had its immediate background in an inquiry from the *Asambleas de Dios* in the country in 1989 with a request for financial assistance in connection with a powerful hurricane that had caused great destruction the year before. A desire was also expressed to receive foreign missionaries, not least with a view to getting help with the training of people working in children's ministries, as well as contributing as Bible school instructors and church planters. Both Miriam and Tor Inge Andersen, who had worked as missionaries in the Perené Valley in Peru since 1985, became interested in this new mission field.[24] Moreover, the country already had more than 400 *Asambleas de Dios* congregations and a total membership of 60,000 people, and had experienced a 40% increase in congregations since 1979. The first American missionaries, Andersen wrote, had arrived in the country as early as in 1912, but because of the tense political situation due to counter-revolutionary groups' opposition to the Sandinista government in Nicaragua, there were no longer any missionaries left.[25]

By 1990, Hanne Miriam and Tor Inge, together with their children, had arrived in Nicaragua, where they settled in the city of San Marcos, around 40 kilometers from the capital Managua.[26] By early 1993, the San Marcos congregation had more than doubled, with 54 baptized members and 50-70 regular attendees.[27]

In 1991, it was decided that Birger Sandli, who together with his family had worked for two periods in Argentina, would become 'project manager for PYM's involvement [in Nicaragua], which included administrative assignments in agriculture, health care,

---

[24] Anne Gustavsen, 'Nicaragua – PYMs nye misjonsfelt', *Korsets seier* 27 October 1989, p. 5. Tor Inge had also spent six months in Peru in 1984. 'Hanne Miriam and Tor Inge Andersen i Perus jungel', *Ekko. Korsets seiers utenriks- og misjonsmagasin* November 1986, p. 3.

[25] Tor Inge Andersen, 'Pinsebevegelsen i Nicaragua: En bevegelse i framgang', *Korsets seier* 27 October 1989, p. 5. However, it may seem that the first Pentecostal missionary to Nicaragua, indeed to Latin America as such, was Edward Barnes, who arrived as early as 1907 and stayed in the country until 1917. Anderson, 'Primeras misiones pentecostales en América Latina', p. 10.

[26] Tor Inge and Hanne Miriam Andersen, 'Vekkelseskampanje og menighets-bygging i Nicaragua', *Ekko* November 1990, p. 16.

[27] 'Nicaragua: Menigheten mer enn fordoblet', *Misjonsbilag*, p. 10 as a supplement to *Korsets seier* 14 May 1993.

schools and house building'. This was due to the fact that Sandli's two previous visits to Nicaragua had given him a 'very good entry into the central Pentecostal movement in the country, and [he had therefore] agreed to a request from the movement's leadership to travel within the country on a national basis to inspire and help the many small congregations outside in the districts'.[28]

In 1995, Hanne Miriam and Tor Inge were ready to return to Nicaragua, this time with the aim of founding a church in the town of Jinotepe, about ten kilometers from San Marcos, where the congregation was already financially self-supporting.[29] The Andersen family remained in Jinotepe until 1998.[30]

Cuba

Despite relatively many notices about Cuba in *Korsets seier*, no Norwegian missionaries have been sent there. Lisbeth J. Fumero, whose husband Mario is Cuban, has nonetheless visited Cuba on several occasions and has had contact with both churches and individual Christians. In 1998, she had already visited the country six times. One of her motives was to provide financial support to pastors.[31]

Similarly, Gro and John Agersten, former missionaries to Peru, lived in Cuba from 2003 to 2006 where they, as representatives of the Swedish organization Erikshjälpen (Eriks Development Partner), worked as project managers with the main focus on improving conditions for people with physical disabilities. They lived in Sancti Spiritus where they repaired and improved three buildings for these

---

[28] Svenn-Olav Larsen, 'Misjonær Birger Sandli m/familie til Nicaragua', *Korsets seier* 8 February 1991, p. 16. *Korsets Seier* had already in 1987 dedicated almost an entire page to Nicaragua. 'Unge søker Gud i det urolige Nicaragua', *Korsets Seier* 6 November 1987, p. 5.

[29] Oddvar Johansen, 'Vår oppgave er menighetsbygging', *Korsets seier* 13 January 1995, p. 21.

[30] Lasse Rosten, 'Vekst og behov i Nicaragua', *Korsets seier* 28 October 2005, pp. 12-13. In addition, they founded a congregation in St. Teresa. Altogether, the three congregations had a membership of several hundred people. Tor Inge Andersen, 'Støtte til nicaraguanske menigheter', *Korsets seier* 12 March 2010, p. 20.

[31] Lisbeth J. Fumero, 'Et besøk på Cuba', *Korsets seier* 9 October 1998, p. 15. It may seem like J.M. Shidens was the first Pentecostal missionary who arrived in Cuba in 1913. Anderson, 'Primeras misiones pentecostales en América Latina', p. 11.

children and young people and also provided interior equipment. Several commercial kitchens for the distribution of meals to primary schools and special schools were renovated and given new equipment. This also applied to the children's hospital in Sancti Spiritus. The Agerstens also com-pleted three village schools and started work on a fourth school. At weekends they visited evangelical churches, where they were given permission to testify in the services. They also provided financial support to pastors and their families, particularly by improving their housing conditions.[32]

The publisher New Life Ministries Norway demonstrates an indirect approach to ministry in Cuba by sending Spanish-language translations of Manga books for children and young people to them.

Puerto Rico

Pentecostal Christianity appears to have arrived in Puerto Rico through Juan León Lugo around 1915. He had experienced a Christian conversion in Hawaii in 1907 and joined a Spanish-speaking congregation there before temporarily moving to California and founding a Spanish-speaking congregation in the city of San Jose.[33] The *Norwegian* contribution to Pentecostalism on the island, on the other hand, is largely centered around Sally Olsen (1912-2006). She was born in Bergen, but after her father died when she was 5 years old, she spent the next six or seven childhood years on Andøya in northern Norway.[34] Little is known of her childhood except that she was put to look after goats. At the age of 12, she was allowed to live with her mother again, and five years later the reunited family immigrated to the United States,[35] where Sally experienced a Christian conversion. After one year at the Swedish-American Joseph Mattson-Bozé's church Bible school in Chicago, in 1952 she traveled to Puerto Rico.[36] Here she was drawn towards the church La Roca in Santurce on the outskirts of the city of San Juan, where Frank Hernández was pastor. Here she also met 4-year-old Carmencita,

[32] Geir Lie, interview with Gro and John Agersten, 29 October 2024.
[33] Anderson, 'Primeras misiones pentecostales en América Latina', p. 11.
[34] Max Manus, *Sally Olsen: Fangenes engel i Puerto Rico* (Oslo: Luther forlag, 5th. ed. 1986), p. 14.
[35] Egil Mentzen, *Jubileumsboken om Sarons Rose og Sally Olsen – 'Fangenes engel' på Puerto Rico … men Gud ga vekst* (Oslo: Nye Luther Forlag, 1987), pp. 28-29.
[36] *https://www.maran-ata.no/sally-olsen/* [Accessed 22 March 2024].

who constantly not only wanted to sit next to her at the meetings but also wanted her to be her new mum. Sally probably had an encounter with her own painful childhood and finally agreed to take care of the little girl, since her parents had abandoned her and she only received sporadic care from neighbors.

Sally now had to find family-friendly housing in Río Piedras, San Juan, but sure enough, it was not long before an ever-increasing number of orphaned or abandoned children forced her to move once again. Together with an ever-growing flock of children, she now acquired a house in the suburb of Guaynabo, which became the base for her Rose of Sharon Foundation.[37] During the war hero and author Max Manus' visit in 1975, her orphanage had around 80 children of various ages,[38] and twelve years later, Rose of Sharon had five buildings on the property 'with room for more than 60 children besides school premises and office for the administration' in addition to a suitable kitchen, dining room, laundry and emergency storage.[39]

Egil Mentzen came to Puerto Rico in 1975 and replaced Sally Olsen in running the orphanage.[40] In addition, Rose of Sharon has held meetings in various prisons in San Juan, where many of the prisoners have experienced Christian conversion and had their lives restored. The Rose of Sharon organization has also dis-tributed Bibles and supported churches and evangelists financially.[41] In order to strengthen the newly converted prisoners in their faith, a correspondence course was created in the mid-1970s where the basic truths of the Bible were explained in 10 study booklets. The correspondence course also became popular in several congregations in Puerto Rico and was even ordered from Spain and various Latin American countries.[42] A radio studio was also built, and from there evangelical programs were produced that reached not only the whole of Puerto Rico but several of the island nations of the Caribbean.[43]

Rose of Sharon has always defined itself as an independent and interdenominational missions project. Since Sally Olsen's visit to Norway in 1963 the work has nonetheless had close ties to the Maran

---

[37] Mentzen, *Jubileumsboken*, pp. 9-15.
[38] Manus, *Sally Olsen*, p. 107.
[39] Mentzen, *Jubileumsboken*, p. 16.
[40] Mentzen, *Jubileumsboken*, p. 50.
[41] Mentzen, *Jubileumsboken*, pp. 85-86.
[42] Mentzen, *Jubileumsboken*, pp. 99-108.
[43] Mentzen, *Jubileumsboken*, p. 123.

Ata denomination, even though Rose of Sharon has had its independent missions office in Oslo.[44] It expanded its operations to include more Latin American countries, but this expanded operation no longer exists. The work is now led by Karin Skau Colón, who came to Puerto Rico in 1967.[45] While the orphanage no longer exists, a prison mission continues in addition to a Christian private school.[46]

---

[44] Mentzen, *Jubileumsboken*, pp. 143-50. Sally Olsen visited Maran Ata, Oslo for the first time already back in 1961. Saltnes, *Som et stormvær,* p. 59.

[45] Mentzen, *Jubileumsboken*, p. 156.

[46] Geir Lie, phone convesation with Ole Bjørn Saltnes, 28 October 2024.

8

BEYOND LATIN AMERICA

Alaska

I choose to include a presentation of Gustav and Laura Nyseter's work among Eskimos in this book. Alaska belongs to the United States, and since Gustav and Laura Nyseter chose to settle on the Little Diomede Island in the middle of the Bering Strait and this island is a part of Alaska, I stand for this choice.

Gustav had had a Christian conversion in 1907, but from childhood had experienced a pull towards missions. After his conversion, he was deliberately called 'even to the ends of the earth'.[1] Together with Laura, whom he had met in Northern Norway, in 1921 he moved to Alaska where two years later he was contacted by the Swedish missionary Nils Fredrik Höijer (1857-1925) with a request to 'accompany him ... over to Siberia and preach Christ to the Eskimos there'.[2] 66-year-old Höijer had been ministering for about 40 years in Russia, the Caucasus and Central Asia.

Gustav and Laura now made the Little Diomede Island their base, but Gustav made several trips to the Big Diomede Island 4 kilometers away, which was part of Russia. The Eskimos also often crossed from one island to the other, which made it possible to preach to them

---

[1] Gustav Nyseter, *Jordens ytterste ender. En virkelighetsskildring fra et mangeårig ophold i Beringstredet* (Kvinesdal: Kvina Trykk, 1976), p. 7.
[2] Nyseter, *Jordens ytterste ender*, p. 31.

with the help of an interpreter. However, Laura died in 1930 and Gustav then returned to Norway.[3]

Trinidad

Kåre Wilhelmsen (1922-83),[4] with a former missionary back-ground from India where he had married the American Jean Mitchell (1913-84) in 1949, had left India in 1953. While they were living in Los Angeles, they heard about the need for missionaries in Trinidad. The island nation in the Caribbean seemed ideal considering the many Indians who lived there, and both Kåre and Jean spoke fluent Hindi.

In 1954 they initiated a work under the auspices of the Open Bible Standard Mission in the city of San Fernando.[5] The following year they received assistance from the Norwegian couple Spencer and Klara Jones, who, like Jean and Kåre, had previously worked as missionaries in India. Spencer and Klara stayed in Trinidad until 1957.[6] In addition to church planting, a Bible school was also started

---

[3] The Norwegian-American couple Oskar Brune (Brown) from Stranda in Sunnmøre and Ella Rølvaag fom Dønna in Nordland, Northern Norway seems to have continued the work of the Nyseters in Alaska according to Torbjørn Greipland, 'Kaldt til kulden', *Dagen* 5 January 2020. *https://www.dagen.no/korsets-seier/kalt-til-kulden/910688* [Accessed 23 November 2024]. Cf. also Agnes Rodli, *Strait gate. A norse saga: Mission to the Diomede islands in the 1920's* (Enumclaw, WA: WinePress Publishing, 1999).

[4] 'Wilhelmsen, Kåre', *Norsk Misjonsleksikon*. Vol. 3 (Stavanger: Nomi forlag – Runa forlag, 1967), p. 1069. Jean Wilhelmsen authored *Trails through Trinidad* (Los Angeles, CA: The Go Ye Fellowship, 2nd pr., 1973), which contains six testimonies from Trinidad.

[5] Robert Bryant Mitchell and Marietta Mitchell Smith, *Jennie and the Song of the Meadowlark* (Weaverville, CA: Isaiah Sixty One, 1988), pp. 103, 137-41. Open Bible Churches (formerly Open Bible Standard Churhes), with headquarters in Des Moines, Iowa is the result of a merger of the two former Pentecostal groups The Bible Standard Conference (a splinter group of the Apostolic Faith, with headquarters in Portland, Oregon) and The Open Bible Evangelistic Association (a breakaway group of The Foursquare church).

[6] Spencer's father, with an identical name, was British and had worked as a medical missionary in China. He married Agnes Marie Iversen in 1915. She had been a pioneer missionary within the Alliance mission in China since 1911. Their son, Spencer Norman Jones (1916-85), had met Klara Ellen Hansen (1922-99) while he was working as an evangelist in Gudbrandsdalen. They were married in 1946. After Spencer had studied tropical medicine in London in 1945, they went out as missionaries and Spencer had the main responsibility at the Chopda mission station in India. After Spencer and Klara returned to Norway, in 1963 Spencer took the philological *embedseksamen* (which includes a master's degree) at the University

to equip national co-workers. Spencer Jones led the Bible school during 1955-57. Kåre and Jean left Trinidad in 1960, but the work has continued under national leaders.[7]

In 1996, Torkel Pedersen also left for Trinidad with his wife Kathleen, who was born there. They received support from both the Evangeliesenteret and the Tabernaklet, Bergen and have been particularly engaged in drug rehabilitation work.

of Oslo. Geir Lie, interview with John Yngvar Jones, dated 11 November 2024; 'Jones, Klara Ellen' and 'Jones, Spencer Norman', in *Norsk Misjonsleksikon*. Vol. 2 (Stavanger: Nomi forlag – Runa forlag, 1966), p. 461.

[7] 'Tribute to our founders', Brochure, published by Open Bible Church in San Fernando, Trinidad [n.d.]. For further information concerning the work in Trinidad, cf. Robert Bryant Mitchell, *Heritage & Harvest. The History of International Ministries of Open Bible Standard Churches* (Des Moines, IA: Open Bible Publishers, 1995), pp. 248-77 and Andy Homer, *Praise & Promise: A History of the Open Bible Standard Churches of Trinidad and Tobago* (Des Moines, IA: Open Bible Publishers, 2004).

Bibliography

'5 minutter med Liv Haddal', *Korsets seier* 3 May 1978, p. 11.

Aardalen, Gerda Lillian, 'Feltkonferanse i Paraguay', *Korsets seier* 29 July 1967, p. 7.

—'Flodmisjonen i Pando, Bolivia', *Korsets seier* 6 March 1965, pp. 11-12.

—'Fra arbeidet i Nord-Parana, Brasil', *Korsets seier* 29 August 1959, pp. 555-56.

—'Fra sykearbeidet i Paraná', *Korsets seier* 18 May 1963, p. 313.

—'Norsk pinsemisjon innregistrert i Paraguay', *Korsets seier* 20 May 1967, p. 12.

—'Sterkt gjensyn med Juan som hun reddet fra døden', *Korsets seier* 27 January 2006, p. 15.

Aardalen, Gerda Lillian, and Asta Hadland, 'Ny misjonsstasjon åpnet i Atyra, Paraguay', *Korsets seier* 21 June 1967, p. 5.

Aateigen, Edith, and Liv Haug, 'Glimt fra Peru, kontrastenes land'. *Korsets seier* 29 May 1974, p. 5.

Adolfsen, Eva Marie, and Helge Adolfsen, 'Høytidsdager i Rurrenabaque'. *Korsets seier* 27 November 1976, p. 6.

Adolfsen, Helge, 'Menighetsdannelse og utvidelse av arbeidet fra Rurrenabaque', *Korsets seier* 14 September 1977, p. 7.

—'Radiomisjonen når millioner av lyttere i Sør Amerika', *Korsets seier* 4 May 1977 pp. 8-9.

—'Våre muligheter for misjon i Sør-Amerika i dag', *Korsets seier* 22 July 1978, p. 13.

'Åge Håskjold med familie på vei til Argentina', *Det gode Budskap* 10 March 1968, p. 3.

Agersten, Gro, and John Agersten, 'Blant indianere og meztiser i Peru's jungel'. *https://peru.agersten.com/author/johnagersten-com/* [Accessed 23 November 2024].

—Email to the author dated 19 November 2024 and with supplementary information for the unfinished manuscript as it then existed.

—'Langs floden med evangeliet'. *Korsets seier* 23 May 1970, p. 7.

—'Misjonsrapport fra Peru: Dåpsmøter og nye kirker', *Korsets seier* 11 April 1997, p. 9.

—'Peru venter', *Korsets seier* 20 November 1965, p. 19.

—'På høyfjell og i jungelen forkynnes evangeliet', *Korsets seier* 8 July 1967, p. 16.

Agersten, John, 'En nyfrelst vitnet – og landsbyen bad om besøk av misjonærene', *Korsets seier* Eastertime 1973, p. 2.

—'Peru – inkaindianernes land', *Korsets seier* 21 December 1966, p. 7.

Alegre, Rakel Ystebø, *La misión pentecostal en Embarcación. Conversiones y cambios socio-culturales entre los indígenas afectados por la misión de Berger Johnsen (1916-1945)* (Master's tesis, Universidad Nacional de San Martín, Buenos Aires, Argentina, 2010).

—*The Pentecostal Apologetics of T. B. Barratt: Defining and Defending the Faith 1906-1909* (PhD thesis, Regent University School of Divinity, Virginia Beach, Virginia, 2019).

'Alles frelse', *Korsets seir* 15 August 1916, pp. 122-23.

Alvarsson, Jan-Åke, 'Daniel e Sara Berg', *Reflexões – Uma Perspectiva Pastoral e Eclesial* 2.2 (Outubro 2022), pp. 29-62.

—'Frida Vingren', *Reflexões – Uma Perspectiva Pastoral e Eclesial* 2.1 (Enero 2022), pp. 63-105.

—*La historia de la misión sueca libre en Bolivia. Una iniciativa nórdica pentecostal para evangelizar a los pueblos de Bolivia* (Uppsala: Uppsala Universitet, 2021).

Andersen, Leif G. 'Bibelskole i Paraná', *Korsets seier* 24 August 1963, p. 538.

—'Du er i Brasil nå', *Korsets seier* 25 September 1982, p. 5.

—'Hjem fra Parana', *Korsets seier* 14 January 1961, p. 27-28.

—'Lokaler brennes i Brasil', *Korsets seier* 16 December 1967, p. 8.

—'Parana, Brasil – landet med stor rikdom – og fattigdom', *Korsets seier* 19 April 1952, pp. 193-94.

Andersen, Olaug, and Leif Andersen, 'Håpets hospits. En hjelp i nøden', *Korsets seier* 4 December 1971, p. 7.

—'Nye landevinninger i Parana', *Korsets seier* 26 January 1972, p. 8.

—'Nyttårshilsen fra Parana', *Korsets seier* 22 February 1958, pp. 123-24.

Andersen, Per. 'En liten hilsen fra Brooklyn', *Det gode Budskap* 20 September 1961, pp. 217, 222.

Andersen, Tor Inge. 'Pinsebevegelsen i Nicaragua: En bevegelse i framgang', *Korsets seier* 27 October 1989, p. 5.

—'Støtte til nicaraguanske menigheter', *Korsets seier* 12 March 2010, p. 20.

Andersen, Tor Inge, and Hanne Miriam Andersen, 'Vekkelses-kampanje og menighetsbygging i Nicaragua', *Ekko* November 1990, p. 16.

Anderson, Allan H., 'Primeras misiones pentecostales en América Latina', *Hechos: Una Perspectiva Pneumatológica* 4.1 (2022), pp. 3-25.

Anderson, Robert Mapes, *Vision of the Disinherited: The Making of American Pentecostalism* (New York: Oxford University Press, 1979).

Andreassen, Edvin. 'Besøk fra Argentina til landsmøtet '89', *Det gode Budskap* 1 April 1990, p. 9.

—'De Frie Evangeliske Forsamlinger har drevet misjon i 80 år', *Det gode Budskap* 15 March 1990, pp. 12-13, 21.

—'Evangelist Luis Alberto Ledesma fra Argentina besøker Norge', *Det gode Budskap* 1 July 1989, p. 13.

—'Per Andresen til Brasil igjen', *Det gode Budskap* 10 January 1979, pp. 6, 9.

—'Misjonærene Dahl's har leid møtesalong i Cordoba', *Det gode Budskap* May 1974, p. 3.

Andreassen, Erling, 'Det bygges skole i Bolivia, men...', *Korsets seier* 21 August 1965, p. 13.

—'"El Condor de los Andes" til nordisk misjon i Bolivia', *Det gode Budskap* 15 October 1985, p. 10.

—'Flodmisjonen i Bolivia får støtte fra Hvaler', *Korsets seier* 30 June 1971, p. 5.

—'Innvielse av bibelskolen i Cochabamba, Bolivia', *Korsets seier* 14 October 1988, p. 28.

—'Store muligheter og store behov i Bolivia', *Korsets seier* 22 April 1972, pp. 4, 7.

Andreassen, Erling, and Börje Green, 'Store behov i Bolivia-arbeidet', *Korsets seier* 14 February 1981, p. 13.

Andreassen, Erling, and Hans Svartdahl, 'Nye misjonærer til Paraguay'. Korsets seier 21 February 1973 p. 8.

Andreassen, Marita, and Erling Andreassen, 'Arbeidet ved Benifloden vokser både i bredde og dybde', *Korsets seier* Eastertime 1967, p. 20.

Andresen, Alice, and Per Andresen, 'Barnehjemmet iCambara', *Det gode Budskap* no. 8 2005, p. 39.

—'Brasil', *Det gode Budskap* 1 February 1970, p. 8.

—'Brasil kaller', *Det gode Budskap* 10 November 1965, p. 3.

—'Flodmisjon åpnes i Amazonas', *Det gode Budskap* 10 and 20 August 1977, p. 11.

—'Nyttårshilsen fra Brasil', *Det gode Budskap* 1 February 1966, p. 3.

—'Ut til en ny periode i Brasil', *Det gode Budskap* 1 December 1969 pp. 7, 4.

—'Vel fremme i Brasil', *Det gode Budskap* 10 – 20 February 1975, pp. 8-9.

Andresen, Alvina, and Erling Andresen, 'Arbeidet i Argentina går fram', *Korsets seier* 10 September 1966, p. 7.

—'Argentina', *Korsets seier* 18 April 1931, p. 5.

—'Argentina', *Korsets seier* 24 September 1938, p. 6.

—'Argentina', *Korsets seier* 25 February 1939, pp. 122-23.

—'Argentina', *Korsets seier* 24 June 1939, pp. 403-404.

—'Fra Argentina', *Korsets seier* 14 January 1933, p. 6.

—'Hilsen fra misjonær Erling Andresen og hustru', *Korsets seier* 26 January 1946, pp. 63-64.

—'Mer om vekkelsen i Buenos Aires', *Korsets seier* 12 March 1955, pp. 162-63.

—'Misjonsarbeidet bærer frukt i Argentina', *Korsets seier* 11 July 1959, p. 444.

—'Pinsevekkelsen i Argentina', *Korsets seier* 7 December 1929, p. 7.

—'Vekkelse i Buenos Aires', *Korsets seier* 24 – 31 July 1954, p. 475.

Andresen, Erling, *Blandt indianere og katolikker i Argentina* (Oslo: Filadelfiaforlaget, [n.d.]).

—'Ut til "Argentina"', *Korsets seir* 20 April 1925, p. 3.

Andresen, Per, 'Brasil for Kristus', *Det gode Budskap* 10 August 1965, p. 3.

—'Hilsen fra Brasil', *Det gode Budskap* 20 September 1963, p. 202.

—'Hilsen fra misjonær Per Andresen', *Det gode Budskap* 20 November 1962, p. 270.

—'Hjem fra Brasil', *Det gode Budskap* 20 May 1978, p. 1.

—'Per Andresen reiser til Brasil 20. mai', *Det gode Budskap* 1 May 1968, p. 9.

Aquino, Almidio, 'William Carey og vi', *Korsets seier* 5 October 2012, p. 30.

Ardiles, Turid Sneve, 'Bryllup i Argentina', *Det gode Budskap* 10-20 July and 1 August 1978, p. 8.

'Argentinabesøk i norske menigheter', *Korsets seier* 10 March 1989, p. 5.

'Assembleias de Deus no Brasil'.

https://pt.wikipedia.org/wiki/Assembleias_de_Deus_no_Brasil [Accessed 4 April 2024].

'Avskjedsfest for Hanne Berit Johansen', *Korsets seier* 24 October 1964, p. 678.

'Avskjedsfest for misjonærene Ruth og Arne Johansson med familie', *Korsets seier* 8 October 1966, p. 9.

Barratt, Laura, *Minner* (Oslo: Filadelfiaforlaget, 1946).

Barratt, Thomas Ball, *Erindringer* (Oslo: Filadelfiaforlaget, 1941).

Barratt, Thomas Ball, *When the fire fell and an outline of my life* (Oslo: Privately published, 1927).

'Benjamin O. Jensen ønsket velkommen hjem etter første periode i Argentina', *Korsets seier* 4 November 1988, p. 16.

Bergman, Nils-Erik. 'Vi trives i jungelen', *Ekko. Korsets seiers utenriks- og misjonsmagasin* February 1991, p. 13.

Berntzen, Rakel E., and Kristin B. Karlsen, 'En verden av mulig-heter', *M2 Misjonsmagasinet* no. 2 2013, pp. 16-19. Supplement to *Korsets seier* 17 May 2013.

'Bibelskolene viktige i Bolivia', *Ekko*. Bilag til *Korsets seier* May 1992, pp. 10-11.

Bjørnevoll, Inge. 'Bruno Müller til minne', *Korsets seier* 18 January 1978, p. 14.

—'En misjonerende livsstil, hva er det?' *Misjonsmagasinet.* Theme: *Stewardship.* Et temamagasin for De Norske Pinsemenigheters Ytremisjon, pp. 8-9 (Supplement to *Korsets seier* 18 May 2007).

—'Høytidsdag da kirken i Paso Cadena ble innviet', *Korsets seier* 7 October 1994, p. 12.

—'I Paraguay: Ein misjonseksplosjon!' *Ekko. Korsets seiers utenriks- og misjonsmagasin* February 1988, p. 10.

—'Merkedagar for pinserørsla i Paraguay', *Korsets seier* 27 September 1972, p. 12.

—'Skandinavisk IBRA-samarbeid i Paraguay', *Korsets seier* 17 May 1980, p. 10.

Bjørstad, Ada, 'Hilsen fra Bolivia', *Korsets seier* 11 November 1961, pp. 715-16.

—Bjørstad, Ada, 'Jungelnytt fra Bolivia', *Korsets seier* 11 May 1963, pp. 296-97.

Bloch-Hoell, Nils Egede, *Pinsebevegelsen. En undersøkelse av pinse-bevegelsens tilblivelse, utvikling og særpreg med særlig henblikk på bevegelsens utforming i Norge* (Oslo: Universitetsforlaget, 1956).

'Brasil for Kristus', *Det gode Budskap* 1 October 1969, pp. 8-9.

'Brit-Lajla og Rudolf's side', *https://www.pymisjon.com/Guarani/ larsen_hs.htm.* [Accessed 23 November 2024].

Bullen, Vidar, and Ranveig A. Edvardsen, 'Stor dag for indianerne i Ing. Juarez, Argentina', *Korsets seier* 18 January 1991, pp. 1, 5.

Bundy, David Dale, 'Missões Pentecostais no Brasil. O Caso do noruegûes G. Leonard Pettersen', *Reflexões – Uma Perspectiva Pastoral e Eclesial* 2.2 (Outubro 2022), pp. 63-75.

Bundy, David Dale, 'Paraguay', in Stanley M. Burgess and Eduard M. van der Maas (eds.), *The New International Dictionary of Pentecostal Charismatic Movements. Revised and expanded edition* (Grand Rapids, MI: Zondervan Publishing House, 2002).

Bundy, David Dale, *Visions of Apostolic Mission: Scandinavian Pente-costal Mission to 1935* (PhD thesis, Uppsala Universitet, 2009).

Burgess, Stanley M. Burgess, and Eduard M. van der Maas (eds.), *The New International Dictionary of Pentecostal Charismatic Movements. Revised and expanded edition* (Grand Rapids, MI: Zondervan Publishing House, 2002).

Byberg, Oddmar, 'Radioarbeidet i Paraguay', *Korsets seier* 25 May 1974, p. 31.

Bye, Gerd, 'Dagligliv hos misjonærene i Chile', *Korsets seier* 23 July 1966, p. 12.

—'Ny misjonsstasjon med barnehjem i Chile', *Korsets seier* 19 February 1966, p. 7.

Bye, Gerd, and Tom Bye, 'Til Chile', *Korsets seier* 2 December 1961, p. 763.

Christiansen, Anne, 'Fyrverkeri i Amazonas', *Korsets seier* 28 November 2014, p. 36.

Cloumann, Jørgen, 'Fattige indianere vil misjonere blant unådde', *Korsets seier* 16 January 2009, p. 22.

Coletti, Joseph, 'Francescon, Luigi', in Stanley M. Burgess and Eduard M. van der Maas (eds.), *The New International Dictionary of Pentecostal Charismatic Movements. Revised and expanded edition* (Grand Rapids, MI: Zondervan Publishing House, 2002).

Dahl, Arne, 'Hjem fra Brasilien', *Korsets seier* Christmastime 1939, pp. 821-22.

Dahl, Daniel, 'Argentina - dagens aktuelle misjonsfelt', *Det gode Budskap* 1 March 1967, p. 7.

—'Echeverria, Tucuman, Argentina', *Det gode Budskap* 1 November 1973, p. 5.

—'På reise fra Norge til argentinsk millionby', *Det gode Budskap* 20 October 1966, pp. 3, 7-8.

Dahl, Tordis, and Daniel Dahl, 'Den som tror og blir døpt. Innhøstning i Argentina', *Det gode Budskap* 10 February 1969, p. 3.

—'Evangelisk radiomisjon over eteren i Tucuman, Argentina', *Det gode Budskap* 1 July 1969, pp. 9, 12.

—'Familien Dahl i Argentina etablerer sin misjonsvirksomhet i Tucuman', *Det gode Budskap* 15 February 1968, pp. 3-4.

—'Familien Dahl vel ankommet til Argentina', *Det gode Budskap* 10 October 1966, p. 3.

—'Gå derfor ut!', *Det gode Budskap* 10 March 1966, p. 3.

—'Nytt fra Daniel Dahl i Argentina', *Det gode Budskap* 20 April 1967, p. 3.

Dahl, Turid. 'Gud har velsignet med sjelers frelse!', *Det gode Bud-skap* 1 December 2002, pp. 34, 44.

'Det "nye lys" saakaldet paa retur', *Korsets seir* 15 October 1916, p. 159.

'Det skjer under i Paraguay', *Korsets seier* 5 August 1972, p. 10.

Domínguez, Eugenio, *Noruega a Chile: En el nombre de Jesús. Biografía del misionero noruego Nils Gunstad (1877-1949)*. Kindle version.

Dragland, Signora, 'Argentina', *Korsets seier* Christmastime 1931, p. 12.

Edvardsen, Ranveig Annie. 'Takk til Per Talaasen', *Korsets seier* 26 April 1972, p. 4.

Ekornaas, Else, 'Mitt møte med vennene i Concepcion', *Korsets seier* 12 February 1975, p. 11.

Ekornaas, Else, Eldbjørg and Thor Johnny Thoresen, 'Første dåpshandling i V. Alemana Chile', *Korsets seier* 31 December 1975, p. 9.

Ekornaas, Mar,y and Jakob Ekornaas, 'Guds verk går fram i Chile', *Korsets seier* 18 June 1993, p. 12.

Eriksen, Berit, 'Hilsen fra Parana', *Korsets seier* 4 May 1963, pp. 280-81.

—'Parana, Brasil', *Korsets seier* 11 February 1961.

Eriksen, Roar, '"Norsk' kirkevekst i Argentina', *Korsets seier* 26 August 2016, p. 35.

Eriksen, Solfrid, and Roar Eriksen, '10-årsjubileum i Argentina', *Korsets seier* 3 April 1987, p. 14.

—'Begivenhetsrike år i Laboulaye, Argentina' *Korsets seier* 7 February 1976, p. 5.

—'Framgang for Guds Ord i Laboulaye, Argentina', *Korsets seier* 12 November 1980, p. 10.

—'Guds ord forvandler', *Korsets seier* 1973 p. 9.

—'Nye misjonærer møter Argentina', *Korsets seier* 4 November 1970, p. 4.

Espinoza, Gastón, *Latino Pentecostals in America: Faith and Politics in Action* (Cambridge, MA: Harvard University Press, 2014).

Espinoza, Gastón, 'The Holy Ghost is here on Earth? The Latino Contributions to the Azusa Street Revival', *Enrichment* Spring 2006, p. 119.

'Evangelisering forbudt i Bolivia', *Korsets seier* 26 January 2018, p. 35.

'Evangelist Per Andresen til Syd-Amerika', *Det gode Budskap* 2 January 1961, pp. 6-7.

Faupel, David William, *The Everlasting Gospel. The Significance of Eschatology in the Development of Pentecostal Thought* (Sheffield: Sheffield Academic Press, 1996).

'Feltet i Brasil i trygge hender', *Det gode Budskap* 1 June 1967, p. 8.

Fjalestad, Olav, 'Det nye barnehjemmeti Cambara en lysstråle i den sosiale nøden i Brasil', *Det gode Budskap* 15 March 1991, pp. 12-13, 19, 23.

'Følgende misjonærer', *Korsets seier* 16 May 1931, p. 5.

Forberg Benitez, Maria Elena, *The Norwegian Pentecostal Mis-sion and Indigenous Peoples in the Eastern Border Regions of Paraguay (1952-2015). Disseminating Colonial Worldview and Adapting to Human Rights?* (Master's thesis, The University in Southeast Norway, 2024).

Førland, Aina, 'Jeg er verdens heldigste, for jeg treffer mamma og pappa hver helg!', *Korsets seier* 12 October 1983, p. 7.

Førland, Hanne, Jorunn and Lars M. Førland, 'Flest glade og lyse dager på Hogar Norma', *Korsets seier* 9 November 1990, p. 9.

Førland, Jorunn, and Lars M. Førland, '5 millioner pinsevenner i Brasil', *Ekko. Korsets seier utenriks- og misjonsmagasin* August 1986, pp. 10-11.

—'Hilsen fra Parana – Brasil', *Korsets seier* 2 February 1963, p. 77.

—'I dag er Angel en annen gutt', *Korsets seier* 28 June 1969, p. 12.

—'Kamp og seier ved Paraná-floden', *Korsets seier* 15 June1963, pp. 379-80.

—'Salem, Lørenskog, har Paraguay som ytterste utpost og gir evangeliet og sosial hjelp til de nødlidende', *Korsets seier* 4 October 1967, pp. 5, 8.

Førland, Lars M., 'Besøk fra Paraguay', *Korsets seier* 19 August 1972, p. 6.

—'Framtiden blir sådd i Paraguay', *Korsets seier* 16 October 1998, p. 15.

—'Misjonshistorie skrevet i Paraguay', *Korsets seier* 13 January 1968, p. 1.

—'Misjonærenes plass i den nasjonale bevegelsen', Mission supplement entitled *Paraguay* p. 2 published together with *Korsets seier* 22 May 1998.

—'Over til Concepcion', *Korsets seier* 4 May 1968, p. 12.

—'Paraguay informerer', *Korsets seier* 30 October 1987, p. 4.

—'"Vi venter himmelsk vårregn", sier paraguayisk pastor', *Korsets seier* 9 September 1972, p. 9.

—'Ypacarai – et sted med mange muligheter', *Korsets seier* 28 June 1967, pp. 3, 8.

Forsberg, Bengt Samuel, *Svensk Pingstmission i Argentina* (Huddinge: Missions-Institutet-PMU, 2000).

'Fra Argentina', *Korsets seier* 30 August 1930, pp. 6-7.

'Fra Brasilien', *Korsets seier* 7 March 1931, p. 6.

'Fra fjern og nær', *Korsets seier* 30 October 1926, pp. 2-3.

'Fra Japan til Brasil som misjonærer', *Korsets seier* 11 August 1962, p. 510.

'Fremstill deg for Gud', *Det gode Budskap* 10 – 20 August 1969, p. 3.

Froholt, Asbjørn, *De Frie Evangeliske Forsamlingers misjon. 75 år. Et jubileumsskrift* (Moss: Elias forlag, 1985).

Froholt, Asbjørn, *Erik Andersen Nordquelle. Mannen som med god grunn kunne vært kalt pinsebevegelsens 'mor' og den frie bvangeliske bevegelsens 'far' i Norge: En biografi* (Moss: Eget forlag, 1981).

Froholt, Asbjørn, 'Iversen, Gustav', in Geir Lie (ed.), *Norsk pinse-kristendom og karismatisk fornyelse. Ettbinds oppslagsverk* (Oslo: Refleks-Publishing, 2nd. ed., 2008), p. 78.

Fumero, Lisbeth, and Mario Fumero, 'Avskjed med Honduras etter 11 rike år', *Korsets seier* 8 December 1982, pp. 12, 15.

—'Også Honduras-misjonærer satser på radiomisjon', *Korsets seier* 14 June 1972, p. 4.

Fumero, Lisbeth J., 'Et besøk på Cuba', *Korsets seier* 9 October 1998, p. 15.

Gjerlaug, Lars Christian, 'PYM vil høre fra misjonærbarna', *Korsets seier* 22 June 2007, pp. 2-3.

Gjervoldstad, Ole Mats, 'Misjonærbarn og internatbarn'. *Korsets seier* 3 August 2007, p. 17.

Goff, Jr., James, R., *Fields White Unto Harvest: Charles F. Parham and The Missionary Origins of Pentecostalism* (Fayetteville, AR: The Univer-sity of Arkansas Press, 1988).

Green, Börje, 'Ung misjonærstab i Bolivia', *Korsets seier* 7 October 1970, p. 6.

Greipland, Torbjørn, 'Kaldt til kulden', *Dagen* 5 January 2020. *https://www.dagen.no/korsets-seier/kalt-til-kulden/910688* [Accessed 23 November 2024].

Griffin, Kathleen M., *Luz en Sudamérica: Los primeros pentecostales en Gualeguaychú, Entre Ríos, 1910-1917* (PhD thesis, Instituto Univer-sitario ISEDET, Buenos Aires, Argentina, 2014).

Grønvold, Sigurd, 'Argentina', *Det gode Budskab* 15 April 1928, p. 7.

—'Misjon Evangelia', *Det gode Budskab* 15 February 1932, p. 3.

'Gro og John Agersten tilbake i Peru', *Korsets seier* 6 January 1995, p. 18.

Gunnarson, Thorstein, *Dommedagsventing: Millennismen og dens innslag i norsk kristendom* (Bergen: A/S Lunde & Cos Forlag, 1928).

Gunstad, Marie, 'Fra Huillinco', *Det gode Budskab* 1 June 1916, pp. 42-43.

—'Fra Sydamerika', *Det gode Budskab* 1 October 1910, p. 73.

—'Hvorledes pinseilden kom til Chile!', *Det gode Budskab* 15 July 1910, pp. 53-54.

—'S. Amerika', *Korsets seir* 1 May 1915, pp. 68-69.

—'Syd-Amerika', *Korsets seir* 1 April 1914 p. 54.

Gunstad, Nils, 'Fra Syd-Amerika', *Det gode Budskab* no. 2 February 1926, p. 1.

Gunstad, Nils and Marie, 'Fra missionærerne Gunstad', *Det gode Budskab* 1 December 1913, pp. 90-91.

Gustavsen, Anne, 'Blir ordfører i Perenedalen. Liv Haug per-mitteres som misjonær', *Korsets seier* 23 February 1996, p. 5.

—'De uskyldige ofrene er vår største smerte', *Korsets seier* 30 November 2001, pp. 10-11.

—'Nicaragua – PYMs nye misjonsfelt', *Korsets seier* 27 October 1989, p. 5.

—'Pinsemisjonen', *Korsets seier* 29 September 2017, p. 4.

—'PYM-avtale med Gå Ut-senteret', *Korsets seier* 4 April 2008, p. 23.

—'Ukens portrett: Gunvor Iversen' *Korsets seier* 19 February 1983, pp. 7, 15.

—'Unge vil trenes til å forandre', *Korsets seier* 20 July 2007, p. 19.

Gylthe, Ruth, *Frie fanger: Blant fanger og uteliggere på Puerto Rico* (Kvinesdal: Logos forlag, 1992).

Haaskjold, Reidun, 'Gleder meg til å komme ut', *Det gode Budskap* 20 January 1977, p. 7.

Haaskjold, Reidun, and Aage Haaskjold, 'Nyheter fra misj. Haaskjold i Argentina', *Det gode Budskap* 1 March 1971, pp. 10-11.

Haddal, Liv, 'Da Gud møtte menigheten i Concepcion', *Korsets seier* 27 September 1975, p. 6.

Hadland, Asta, 'Åpen dør for Guds ord i Atyra, Paraguay', *Korsets seier* 2 October 1968, p. 8.

Hagen, Kjell, *Marit og Erling Andreassen: På spesialoppdrag i jungelen* (Oslo: Filadelfiaforlaget 1994).

—'Startet nytt universitet i Bolivia', *Korsets seier* 13 January 2012 p. 22.

Hamre, Øyvind, and Georg Surland-Hansen, 'Nytt misjons-prosjekt i Paraguay', *Korsets seier* 21 December 1966, p. 12.

'Hanne Miriam and Tor Inge Andersen i Perus jungel', *Ekko. Korsets seiers utenriks- og misjonsmagasin* November 1986, p. 3.

Hansen, Arne Håkon, 'Turid Dahl Stokland gir stafettpinnen videre i Brasil', *Det gode Budskap* no. 5 2018, pp. 16-17.

Hansen, Kaleb, 'Argentina', *Korsets seier* 2 November 1935, p. 6.

—'Berger Johnsen – misjonær i 25 år', *Korsets seier* 14 September 1935, p. 5.

—'Fra Argentina', *Korsets seier* 17 August 1935, p. 5.

—'Fra Paraguay', *Korsets seier* 23 January 1937, p. 6.

—'Fra Paraguay', *Korsets seier* 5 March 1938, p. 6.

—'Paraguay', *Korsets seier* 17 September 1938, p. 6.

Haug, Håkon, 'Unge misjonærer til Argentina', *Korsets seier* 5 February 1972, p. 12.

Hauge, Signe, 'Han ville ha flere i tale den kvelden', *Korsets seier* 24 June 1970, p. 5.

Hauge, Signe, and Lisbeth Jensen, 'Misjonærene møter store behov i Chile', *Korsets seier* 11 March 1967, p. 12.

Haugstøl, Kjetil, 'Med evangeliet til indianerne i Argentinas skoger', *Korsets seier* 24 October 1970, p. 7.

Heggelund, Kristian, 'Misjonær Jahn Sørheim 50 år', *Korsets seier* 3 December 1949, pp. 604-605.

Herrera, Lazaro, and Ivar Vingren, 'Argentinske predikanter sier sin mening om Ortiz', *Korsets seier* 25 June 1977, p. 12.

'Hjelp indianerne med lokalbygg i Tartagal!', *Korsets seier* 4 August 1973, p. 6.

'Hjem etter første periode i Argentina', *Korsets seier* 5 January 1974, p. 2.

Homer, Andy, *Praise & Promise: A History of the Open Bible Standard Churches of Trinidad and Tobago* (Des Moines, IA: Open Bible Publishers, 2004).

Hop-Hansen, Ane-Marthe, 'Sendte ut misjonær – får pastor i retur', *Korsets seier* 17 February 2017, p. 25.

'Hva er Ørebromisjonen?', *Det gode Budskap* 10 July 1961, p. 159.

'I dag har bevegelsen grupper mange steder i Paraguay', *Korsets seier* 23 January 1971, pp. 6-7.

Innvær, Reinert O., 'Paraguay kaller på hjelp', *Korsets seier* 6 May 1988, p. 20.

Iversen, Gunvor, and Josef Iversen, 'Hilsen fra Caacupé', *Korsets seier* 24 August 1963, pp. 538-39.

—'Hilsen fra Paso Cadena, Paraguay', *Korsets seier* 8 September 1962, pp. 571-72.

Iversen, Gustav, 'Fra Argentina', *Det gode Budskap* 20 May 1953, p. 115.

Iversen, Josef, 'Gud gjør under i Paraguay', *Korsets seier* 23 March 1977, p. 16.

—'På avskjedsmøter i Brasil', *Korsets seier* 9 October 1965, pp. 13-14.

Iversen, Paul, 'Misjonsrøsten. En epoke i DFEF's misjons-historie', *Det gode Budskap* 11-15 June 1984, pp. 20-21.

Janøy, Jostein, 'Nasjonaliseringen går videre i Paraguay', *Korsets seier* 27 February 1987, p. 5.

'Japan, Thailand, Argentina og Chile får støtte til misjon', *Korsets seier* 13 January 1971, pp. 4-5.

Jensen, Finn, 'Festdager i Embarcacion', *Korsets seier* 10 September 1969, p. 5.

—'Til Argentina', *Korsets seier* 9 June 1962, p. 359.

Jensen, Hanne-Berit, *Minner fra et helt liv* (Privately published, 2016).

Jensen, Hanne-Berit, and Finn Jensen, 'Avskjedsmøter i Paraguay', *Korsets seier* 15 October 1966, p. 6.

—'Bibelskolen i Cochabamba, Bolivia', *Korsets seier* 25 June 1980, p. 8.

—'Frelsesmøter og dåp i Argentina', *Korsets seier* 27 July 1968, p. 12.

—'Menighet dannet i Oran, Argentina', *Korsets seier* 17 November 1976, pp. 1, 15.

—'Nye framstøt i Argentina', *Korsets seier* 12 March 1966, p. 12.

—'Nytt virke i Argentina', *Korsets seier* 28 December 1974, p. 6.

Jensen, Lisbeth, '"Hjemme igjen" i Chile', *Korsets seier* 14 February 1970, p. 9.

Johannesen, Else Palma, 'Nasjonal ledelse av menigheten i San Pedro', *Korsets seier* 7 May 1993, p. 15.

—'Åpne dører i Salta, Argentina', *Korsets seier* 21 June 1991, pp. 10, 17.

Johansen, Gunvor, 'Til Paraguay', *Korsets seier* 7 July 1956, p. 427.

Johansen, Oddvar, 'Antall misjonærer på rekordlavt nivå', *Korsets seier* 27 October 2006, p. 17.

—'Evangeliet må videre fra jungelen til storbyen', *Korsets seier* 2 February 1996, p. 20.

—'Helge Adolfsen på IBRA-seminar', *Korsets seier* 4 October 1985, p. 19.

—'Herre! Forbarm deg over vårt lidende folk', *Korsets seier* Christmastime 1998, pp. 20-21.

—'Ja til ny struktur i PYM', *Korsets seier* Christmastime 1996, p. 3.

—'Latin-Amerikakonferansen i Heddal med oppsiktsvekkende klar tale', *Korsets seier* 25 April 1997, p. 6.

—'Lever for å gi stammefolk i Mexico Guds ord', *Korsets seier* 22 October 1999, p. 12.

—'Vår oppgave er menighetsbygging', *Korsets seier* 13 January 1995, p. 21.

Johnsen, Berger N., 'Argentina', *Korsets seir* 15 July 1912, pp. 110-11.

—'Argentina', *Korsets seier* 22 August 1936, p. 5.

—'Argentina', *Korsets seier* Eastertime 1938, pp. 10-11.

—'Fra Argentina', *Det gode Budskab* 15 December 1910, pp. 95-96.

—'Fra Argentina', *Det gode Budskab* 1 August 1917, p. 58.

—'Fra Argentina', *Det gode Budskab* 15 September 1936, p. 2.

—'Fra Sydamerika', *Det gode Budskab* 1 June 1911, p. 42.

'Jones, Klara Ellen', *Norsk Misjonsleksikon*. Vol. 2 (Stavanger: Nomi forlag – Runa forlag, 1966).

'Jones, Spencer Norman', *Norsk Misjonsleksikon*. Vol. 2 (Stavanger: Nomi forlag – Runa forlag, 1966).

'Juan Carlos Ortiz fra pinsebevegelsen til presbyterianerne', *Korsets seier* 6 August 1993, p. 6.

Kastberg, Nils, 'Juan Carlos Ortiz forandrer menighetslivet', *Korsets seier* 25 May 1977, p. 2.

'Katolikkene i Latin-Amerika er ikke som de europeiske', *Korsets seier* 27 September 1996, p. 15.

Kihle, Ragnhild, *Mitt livs historie: Kallets tjeneste* (Horten: R. Kihle, 2015).

Kjeilen, Rolf, 'På reise i Brasil 1985-4', *Det gode Budskap* 1 Novem-ber 1985, pp. 10, 15-16.

Kjellås, *Ruth,* 'En hilsen fra Paso Cadena, Paraguay', *Korsets seier* 6 December 1958, p. 779.

'Kommentarer', *Korsets seier* 3 May 1978, pp. 7, 15.

Kornmo, Morgan, 'Til Bolivia', *Korsets seier* 20 March 1965, p. 6.

'KS i samtale med Anna Strømsrud om fortjenestemedalje og det daglige slit for en misjonær', *Korsets seier* 23 April 1975, pp. 5, 15.

Küng, Andres, 'Norsk pinsemisjon i Bolivia', *Korsets seier* 16 March 1977, pp. 6-7.

Lange, Solveig Barratt, *T.B. Barratt. Et Herrens sendebud* (Oslo: Filadelfiaforlaget, 1962).

Larring, Kjell, 'Jorunn og Lars Førland ble feiret. Misjonærer i 40 år', *Korsets seier* Christmastime 2001, p. 31.

Larsen, Rudolf Leif, 'Innvielse av skole i Curuguaty, Paraguay', *Korsets seier* 17 January 1986, p. 7.

Lie, Geir, 'Apostler og aposteltjeneste i internasjonal pinsekristen-dom', *Refleks – med karismatisk kristendom i fokus* 1.1 (2002), pp. 3-11.

—*Fra hellighetsbevegelse til norsk karismatikk.* Vol. 1 (Wyoming, MI: Akademia forlag, 2024).

—Interview with Anita and Jan Bjarne Skrøvje, 18 Novem-ber 2024.

—Interview with Benjamin Jensen, 8 June 2024.

—Interview with Gro and John Agersten, 29 October 2024.

—Interview with John Yngvar Jones, 11 November 2024.

—Interview with Kjellaug Palma Sjølund, 21 November 2024.

—Interview with Roar Eriksen, 4 April 2024.

—Interview with Sara Jensen, 7 November 2024.

—'New Life Mission', in Geir Lie (ed.), *Norsk pinsekristendom og karismatisk fornyelse. Ettbinds oppslagsverk* (Oslo: Refleks-Publishing, 2nd. ed., 2008), p. 121.

—(ed.), *Norsk pinsekristendom og karismatisk fornyelse. Ettbinds oppslagsverk* (Oslo: Refleks-Publishing, 2nd. ed., 2008).

—'Spansk- og portugisisktalende menigheter i Norge: En rapport', in Lemma Desta and Stian Sørlie Eriksen (eds.), *Migrasjon og misjon: Refleksjon og praksis* (Oslo: Norges Kristne Råds Skriftserie – No. 24), pp. 59-69.

—Phone conversation with Ole Bjørn Saltnes, 28. October 2024.

—*Tro og tanke før og nå: En selektiv gjennomgang av den kristne menighets historie* (Wyoming, MI: Akademia forlag, 2024).

Lie, Gunn Elisabeth, 'Misjonærsamling i Cochabamba', *Korsets seier* 6 March 1987, p. 16.

Lie, Trygve, 'Cubaneren Mario Fumero til Norge', *Korsets seier* 26 June 1971, p. 12.

Lindgren, Lennart, 'En missionärsson berättar om sin kallelse', *Evangelii Härold* 27 July 1961, pp. 6-7.

L., O., 'Berit og Torstein Tørre til ny periode i Bolivia', *Korsets seier* 30 July 1977, p. 2.

Losnegård, Magne, 'Fest og glede i Salta', *Korsets seier* 23 May 1997, p. 9.

Lunde, Deborah Selbekk, 'PYM endrer navn', *Korsets seier* 29 Sep-tember 2007, pp. 10-11.

Mangersnes, Frantz, 'En hilsen fra Nord-Paraguay', *Korsets seier* 13 June 1959, pp. 377-79.

—'Hilsen fra Formosa, Nord-Argentina', *Korsets seier* 23 March 1963, p. 187.

—'Vel framme i Brasil', *Korsets seier* 20 January 1949, p. 28.

Mangersnes, Frantz, and Per A. Pedersen, 'Fra Brasils innland', *Korsets seier* 11 February 1950, p. 90.

Manus, Max, *Sally Olsen: Fangenes engel i Puerto Rico* (Oslo: Luther forlag, 5th. imp., 1986).

Marciano, Kappaun (ed.), *Da Suécia ao Brasil. Uma história missionária* (Campinas, Brasil: Convenção das Igrejas Batistas Independentes – CIBI, 2012).

Martinsson, Erik, 'Intens IBRA-aktivitet på misjonsfeltene', *Korsets seier* 3 March 1962, p. 131.

McGee, Gary B., *Miracles, Missions, & American Pentecostalism* (Mary-knoll, NY: Orbis Books, 2010).

'Med merkelapp på ryggen til postboks i Brasil', *Korsets seier* 5 November 1999, p. 32.

Meistad, Tore, *Methodism as a carrier of the Holiness tradition in Norway* (Alta: ALH-forskning, 1994:2).

Melbostad, Kirsti, 'Fra Chile', *Det gode Budskab* 1 August 1913, p. 60.

Menighetens utvikling i Nord- og Sør-Amerika (Tananger: Stiftelsen Skjulte Skatters Forlag, 2022).

Mentzen, Egil, *Jubileumsboken om Sarons Rose og Sally Olsen – Fangenes engel' på Puerto Rico … men Gud ga vekst* (Oslo: Nye Luther Forlag, 1987).

'Mexico', *https://oks.no/mexico/* [Accessed 24 October 2024].

'Miguel E. Ardiles: Misjonslege i Argentina', *Det gode Budskap* 1 February 1990, pp. 10-11.

'Misjonen', *Korsets seier* 14 December 1974, p. 10.

'Misjonærene May-Lise og Gunnar Standal flyttet til Brasils hovedstad, Brasilia', *Det gode Budskap* 10-20 July 1976, p. 6.

'Misjonærer hilser', *Korsets seier* 10 January 1981, p. 14.

'Misjonærer i bilulykke', *Korsets seier* 20 September 1972, p. 1.

'Misjonær fra Brasil', *Jesus mitt liv. DFEFs sommerstevne 10.-15. juli 2007 Åkrahallen, Karmøy*, p. 3. Supplementary to *Det gode Budskap* no. 5 2007.

'Misjonærer til Honduras', *Korsets seier* 2 February 1966, p. 4.

'Misjonærkontakt med Chile', *Det gode Budskap* 1 August 1969, pp. 10-11.

'Misjonær Marit Moen', *Det gode Budskap* 10 November 1977, p. 8.

Mitchell, Robert Bryant, *Heritage & Harvest. The History of Inter-national Ministries of Open Bible Standard Churches* (Des Moines, IA: Open Bible Publishers, 1995).

Mitchell, Robert Bryant, and Marietta Mitchell Smith, *Jennie and the Song of the Meadowlark* (Weaverville, CA: Isaiah Sixty One, 1988).

Mjåvatn, Helga, 'Argentina', *Korsets seier* 13 July 1946, p. 446.

—'Argentina', *Korsets seier* 30 April 1949, p. 187.

—'Hilsen fra Argentina', *Korsets seier* 12 May 1956, p. 298.

Moen, Marit, 'Marit Moen vel fremme i Argentina', *Det gode Budskap* 10-20 April 1973, p. 9.

—'Misjonskandidat for Argentina', *Det gode Budskap* 10 November 1971, pp. 4-5.

Møller, Arvid, *Liv Haug. Norsk misjonær, ordfører og anleggsbas i Amazonas-jungelen* (Oslo: J.W. Cappelens Forlag A/S, 1987).

Mossberg, Hardy, 'På langreise i Syd-Amerika', *Korsets seier* 5-12 July 1952, pp. 335-36.

Mossberg, Hardy and Karin Mossberg, 'Hilsen fra Chile', *Korsets seier* 20 June 1948, p. 356.

Mossberg, Karin, *Ved foten av Andes-fjellene* (Oslo: Filadelfiaforlaget, 1962).

Mossberg, Karin and Hardy Mossberg, 'Guds ord har framgang i Chile', *Korsets seier* 20 January 1962, pp. 44-45.

—'Hilsen fra Chile', *Korsets seier* 19 August 1950, p. 520.

—'Hilsen fra Chile', *Korsets seier* 1 September 1950, p. 419.

—'Til Chile på ny', *Korsets seier* 2 July 1955, pp. 426-27.

Mydland, Harald (ed.), *Liv Margrethe Haug - misjonær og samfunnsbygger blant urbefolkningen i Peru* (Kjeller: Hermon forlag, 2021).

'Nicaragua: Menigheten mer enn fordoblet', *Misjonsbilag* p. 10 as supplementary to *Korsets seier* 14 May 1993.

Nilsen, Oddvar, 'Larsen, Severin', in Geir Lie (ed.), *Norsk pinse-kristendom og karismatisk fornyelse. Ettbinds oppslagsverk* (Oslo: Refleks-Publishing, 2nd. ed., 2008), pp. 97-98.

—'Paraguay et av våre nyere misjonsfelt', *Korsets seier* 21 January 1970, p. 4.

—'Til Brasil for tredje gang', *Korsets seier* 5 May 1962, pp. 284-85.

—*Ut i all verden. Pinsevennenes ytre misjon i 75 år* (Oslo: Filadelfia-forlaget, 1985).

Nordmo, Siman, 'Det vokser i Brasil', *Det gode Budskap* 15 August 1981, p. 11.

Nordmoen, Bergljot, 'Fra Guarani-indianernes land, Paraguay', *Korsets seier* 8 April 1961, pp. 220-21.

—'Hilsen fra Paraguay, Sør-Amerikas hjerte', *Korsets seier* 17 October 1953, pp. 650-51.

—'Opplevelser i Sør-Amerika', *Korsets seier* 9 June 1956, pp. 363-64.

'Norge er ikke lenger verdensmester i misjon', *Korsets seier* 25 July 1997, p. 24.

'Norges Frie Evangeliske Missionsforbund', *Korsets seir* 1 February 1916, p. 21.

Norheim, Bergljot, 'Arbeidet vokser blant indianerne i Paraguay', *Korsets seier* 21 January 1967, p. 12.

Norheim, Olav, 'Til Paraguay', *Korsets seier* 7 December 1963, p. 774.

Norrmann, Evy, interview with missionary Lennart Lindgren, 30 October 1996. Available as a pdf from the Institute for Pentecostal Studies in Sweden.

Nupen, Helge, 'Avvikler barnehjemmet', *Det gode Budskap* no. 2 2012, p. 30.

Nyborg, Geir Magnus, 'Tragedier møtes med kjærlighet', *Ekko. Korsets seiers utenriks- og misjonsmagasin* February 1988, p. 12.

'Nye misjonskandidater for Argentina', *Korsets seier* 16 March 1968, p. 9.

'Nye misjonærer', *Korsets seier* 26 June 1965, p. 11.

'Nye misjonærer', *Korsets seier* 1 January 1966, p. 4.

'Nye misjonærer', *Korsets seier* 19 January 1977, p. 8.

'Nye misjonærer for Brasil', *Korsets seier* Eastertime 1963, p. 222.

'Nye misjonærer til Bolivia', *Korsets seier* 26 October 1968, p. 7.

'Nye misjonærer til Paraguay', *Korsets seier* 10 December 1966, p. 7.

'Nye regionssekretærer i PYM', *Korsets seier* 11 July 2008, p. 24.

'Ny menighet dannet i Argentina', *Korsets seier* 21 May 1977, p. 2.

'Ny menighetsarbeider i Chile', *Korsets seier* 31 January 1976, p. 11.

'Ny misjonær', *Korsets seier* 11 February 1961, p. 91.

'Ny misjonær', *Korsets seier* 25 February 1961, pp. 110-11.

'Ny misjonær', *Korsets seier* 23 November 1963, pp. 738-39.

'Ny misjonær', *Korsets seier* 18 October 1967, p. 3.

'Ny misjonær til Argentina', *Korsets seier* 8 April 1967, p. 12.

'Ny misjonær til Argentina', *Korsets seier* 23 September 1972, p. 4.

'Ny misjonær til Bolivia', *Korsets seier* 23 March 1966, p. 2.

'Ny misjonær til Bolivia', *Korsets seier* 10 September 1966, p. 4.

'Ny misjonær til Chile', *Korsets seier* 22 November 1972, p. 5.

'Ny norsk skole i Argentina', *Korsets seier* 17 November 1989, p. 9.

Nyseter, Gustav, *Jordens ytterste ender. En virkelighetsskildring fra et mangeårig ophold i Beringstredet* (Kvinesdal: Kvina Trykk, 1976).

Olsen, Bjørn S., '100-års misjonsjubileum i Brasil', *Det gode Budskap* no. 3 2012, p. 31.

—'DFEF har satt fotspor i Brasil', *Det gode Budskap* no. 3 2012, pp. 32-33.

—'Eventyret i Amazonas', *Det gode Budskap* no. 4 2017, pp. 2-3.

Opheim, Gunnvald, '40 år i misjonens tjeneste', *Korsets seier* 7 December 1966, p. 4.

Opheim, Julie-Marie, and Gunnvald Opheim, 'Hilsen fra Salta, Argentina', *Korsets seier* 23 May 1959, pp. 328-29.

—'Misjonen tar radioen i bruk i Nord-Argentina', *Korsets seier* 3 January 1968, pp. 3, 6.

Opsahl, Kari, 'Jesu befaling er å lære dem', *Korsets seier* 6 May 1972, p. 7.

Østbye, Knut, 'Takk, Turid!', *Det gode Budskap* no. 1 1998, p. 22.

'Our history'. *https://www.team.org/ourstory#:~:text=TEAM%20 began%20under%20the%20name,East%20Africa%2C%20Swaziland% 20and%20Mongolia* [Accessed 15 March 2024].

Øvrum, Ingjerd, 'Blant skogens indianere lyder evangeliet', *Korsets seier* 6 March 1968, p. 8.

Øya, Martha, and Helge Magne Øya, 'Framsteg i Argentina', *Korsets seier* 1 September 1976 p. 7.

'På besøk i Argentina', *Korsets seier* 13 January 1973, p. 2.

'Paraguay', *Korsets seier* 12 March 1999, p. 11.

Pedersen, Palma, and Per A. Pedersen, 'Hilsen fra Sør-Amerika', *Korsets seier* 15 March 1952, pp. 130-31.

Pedersen, Per A., *Blant indianere i Chaco* (Oslo: Filadelfiaforlaget, 1972).

'Peru: Flodevangelisering og bibelmaraton', *Misjonsbilag* p. 10 as supplementary to *Korsets seier* 14 May 1993.

Pettersen, Gottfred Leonard, *Blant folkeslag i Sør-Amerika: Misjons- og reiseskildringer* (Oslo: Filadelfiaforlaget, 1947).

—'Bolivia', *Korsets seier* 11 April 1953, pp. 234-35.

—'Brasil – Sør-Amerika', *Korsets seier* 2 January 1954, p. 11.

—'En del glimt fra misjonsarbeidet i Brasil', *Korsets seier* 17 February 1951, p. 82.

—'En del glimt fra misjonsarbeidet i Brasil', *Korsets seier* 3 March 1951, p. 105.

—'Glimt fra et nytt misjonsfelt i Sør-Amerika', *Korsets seier* 20 November 1965, p. 7.

—'Norsk pinsemisjon representert i 7 land: Sterk utvikling i Latin-Amerika', *Korsets seier* 25 July 1970, p. 8.

—'Nye misjonærer til Brasil', *Korsets seier* 18 November 1961, p. 728.

—*Pinse over grensene* (Oslo: Filadelfiaforlaget, 1989).

—'Utsendermenighet for misjonærene Spjøtvold', *Korsets seier* 14 December 1966, p. 15.

Pettersen, Ragna, and Gottfred Leonard Pettersen, 'Hjemme igjen fra Brasil', *Korsets seier* 13 October 1945, pp. 395-96.

Pinsemisjon i 100 år (Oslo: De norske pinsemenigheters ytremisjon, 2010).

'Pinsevennenes Ytre Misjons prosjekter ved Aksjon Håp', *Korsets seier* 25 June 1980, p. 8.

'Pionerarbeid i Argentina', *Korsets seier* 31 May 1959, p. 9.

Reite, Jarle, 'Guds kraft forandrar indianarane', *Korsets seier* 22 September 1971, pp. 4-5.

Rike, Tarald, *Blyfoten. Historien om misjonær Leif Andersen* (Hovet: Hermon Forlag, 1993).

Ringås, Tore Bjørn, 'Jeg kunne ha nøyd meg med å strikke sokker for misjonen', *Korsets seier* 13 February 2004, pp. 12-13.

Ritse, Erling, 'Fra Sør-Amerika', *Korsets seier* 8 November 1952, p. 541.

Robeck, Cecil M., *The Azusa Street Mission & Revival: The Birth of the Global Pentecostal Movement* (Nashville, TN: Nelson Reference & Electronic, 2006).

Rodgers, Darrin J., *Northern Harvest: Pentecostalism in North Dakota* (Bismarck, ND: North Dakota District Council of the Assemblies of God, 2003).

Rodli, Agnes, *Strait gate. A norse saga: Mission to the Diomede islands in the 1920's* (Enumclaw, WA: WinePress Publishing, 1999).

Rosten, Lasse, 'Vekst og behov i Nicaragua', *Korsets seier* 28 October 2005, pp. 12-13.

Ruud, Kjell, '30 år i Herrens tjeneste', *Korsets seier* 1 September 1956, p. 533

Saltnes, Ole Bjørn, *Som et stormvær. En bok om Maran Ata vekkelsen* (Tofte: Misjon Europa Forlag, 2017).

Samuelsen, Solveig, 'Årskonferanse for nordiske pinsemisjonærer i Bolivia', *Korsets seier* 20 February 1982, p. 9.

—'Feltkonferanse for PYMs misjonærer i Bolivia', *Korsets seier* 24 November 1976, pp. 9, 15.

—Input and corrections to an earlier version of this book manus-cript.

—'Internasjonal familie fra Halden til Honduras', *Korsets seier* 12 November 1975, p. 11.

—'Levende menighet i vekst i La Paz', *Korsets seier* 30 September 1994, p. 12.

—'Lisbeth og Mario Fumero', unpublished manuscript, September 2024.

—'Med misjon som livsstil', *Korsets seier* 22 September 2006, p. 30.

—'"Pinsevennenes evangeliske grunnskole" i Gonzalo Moreno, Bolivia fyller 15 år', *Korsets seier* 13 April 1977, p. 11.

Samuelsen, Solveig, and Roger Samuelsen, 'Tilbake til Bolivia igjen', *Korsets seier* 9 January 1998, p. 11.

Sandli, Birger, 'Avskjed for Martha og Helge Magne Øya i Argentina', *Korsets seier* 15 October 1980, p. 14.

Sandli, Britt, and Birger Sandli, 'En trofast Herrens tjener legger årene inn', *Korsets seier* 15 October 1983, pp. 14-15.

—'Vekkelsesrapporten fra Ing. Juarez', *Ekko. Korsets seiers utenriks- og misjonsmagasin* May 1987, p. 4.

Sandli, Elisabeth, and Roberto Sandli, 'Nye misjonærer til Guatemala', *Korsets seier* 14 April 2000, p. 28.

Saracco, J. Norberto, 'Argentine Pentecostalism: Historical Roots, Current Developments, and Challenges for the Future', in Vinson Synan, Amos Yong, and Miguel Álvarez (eds.), *Global Renewal Christianity*. Vol. 2: *Latin America* (Lake Mary, FL: Charisma House, 2016).

Schjander, Fredrik, *I samtale med Håkon Haug: Mitt liv i tjeneste* (Oslo: Filadelfiaforlaget, 1988).

Schølberg, Oddvar, *Med Bibel og moped i Paraguyays jungel. Et møte med pionermisjonæren Anna fra Løten* (Oslo: Ibra Media Norge, 2008).

Sjølund, Kjellaug Palma, 'Ambulerende bibelskole', *Korsets seier* 17 March 1989, p. 13.

Ski, Martin, *Fram til urkristendommen. Pinsebevegelsen gjennom 50 år*. Vol. 1 in a 3 vols. series (Oslo: Filadelfiaforlaget, 1956).

Søderberg, Gustav, 'Underhold av misjonær Erling Andresen, Argentina', *Korsets seier* 22 October 1932, p. 5.

—'Vedrørende misjonær Erling Andresens underhold', *Korsets seier* 28 January 1933, p. 6.

Solås, Berner, 'Jesus lever!', *Det gode Budskap* 20 July 1979, pp. 1, 5.

Solvoll, Oddwin, 'Eva og Geirr Standal klare for utreise til Brasil', *Det gode Budskap* no. 2 2012, p. 31.

—'Menigheten begynte i stuen', *Det gode Budskap* no. 1 2015, p. 22.

—'Misjonsmøte ble frelsesmøte med barnevelsignelse', *Det gode Budskap* no. 1 2015, p. 23.

—'Misjonsmøte torsdag', *Det gode Budskap* no. 7 2017, pp. 20-21.

—'Misjonær Ragnhild Kihle har skrevet sin selvbiografi', *Det gode Budskap* April 2016, pp. 30-31.

—'Misjonær Ragnhild Kihle: Pensjonist og kirke-bygger', *Det gode Budskap* no. 1 2014, pp. 24-25.

—'Tredjegenerasjons indianerpastor', *Korsets seier* 5 March 2010, p. 22.

'Sør-Amerika – feltet med 30% av våre misjonærer', *Korsets seier* 12 April 1980, p. 1.

'Sør Amerika-konferansen', *Korsets seier* 9 March 1946, pp. 157-58.

'Sør-Amerika-konferansen i Halden', *Korsets seier* 9 June 1951, pp. 275-76.

'Sør-Amerika-konferansen i Lillestrøm', *Korsets seier* 16 November 1946, pp. 739-40.

'Sør-Amerikakonferansen i Sarpsborg viser framgang', *Korsets seier* 2 June 1976, pp. 20, 19.

Sørensen, Sten, 'Pensjonister hjelper gatebarn i Argentina', *Det gode Budskap* 15 April 1991, p. 9.

—'Æresborger av Mogi das Cruzes', *Det gode Budskap* no. 6 2017, pp. 26-27.

'Sørheim, Anna', *Norsk misjonsleksikon*. Vol. 3 (Stavanger: Nomi forlag – Runa forlag, 1967), p. 883.

'Sørheim, Jahn', *Norsk misjonsleksikon*. Vol. 3 (Stavanger: Nomi forlag – Runa forlag, 1967), p. 883.

Sørheim, John, 'Fra Brasilien', *Korsets seir* 20 October 1925, p. 7.

—'Kjære Korsets Seir's læsere', *Korsets seir* 17 March 1928, p. 6.

Søvde, Anne Lise, 'Toleranse og misjon', *Korsets seier* 11 January 2013, p. 7.

S., M., 'Hjem fra Peru', *Korsets seier* 12 November 1975, p. 11.

Spjøtvold, Henry William, 'Besøk på en utpost i Argentina', *Korsets seier* 11 December 1965, p. 10.

—'Karismatisk vekkelse i Argentina: Stort behov for undervisning', *Korsets seier* 13 January 1971, pp. 6-7.

—'Vekkelsens vinder blåser i Argentina', *Korsets seier* 13 May 1967, p. 12.

Staalstrøm, Bjarne, 'Nye misjonskandidater for Argentina', *Det gode Budskap* 10 September 1965, pp. 3-4.

Standal, Geirr, 'Rektor for voksende bibelskole!', *Det gode Budskap* no. 3 2006, pp. 34-25.

Standal, Gunnar, 'Avskjedsmøter og fest på floden i Brasil', *Det gode Budskap* 10-20 February 1973, p. 6.

Standal, May-Lise, and Gunnar Standal, 'Framgang og vekst for arbeidet i Recife', *Det gode Budskap* no. 14 1998, pp. 18-19.

—'Glimt fra misjonsarbeidet i Brasilia', *Det gode Budskap* 10 June 1979, p. 1.

—'I Brasils hjerte - 'Brasilia'', *Det gode Budskap* 10 May 1976, pp. 6-7.

—'Nytt misjonsfelt i Brasil', *Det gode Budskap* 15 January 1992, p. 13.

—'Takk til vennene fra misj. Standal og frue', *Det gode Budskap* 10-20 December 1969, p. 10.

Stø, Helge, 'Avskjed og velkomst i Gonzalo Moreno, Bolivia', *Kor-sets seier* 11-15 January 1967, p. 7.

Stokes, Louie W., *Historia del Movimiento Pentecostal en la Argentina* (Buenos Aires, Argentina: The author, [n.d.]).

'Store beløp til Latin-Amerika', *Korsets seier* 27 September 1996, p. 16.

'Store forandringer i Pinsevennenes Ytre Misjon', *Korsets seier* 4 October 1996, p. 4.

'Stort behov for nytt lokale i Aguaray, Argentina', *Korsets seier* 15 February 1978, p. 6.

Strømsrud, Anna, 'Bibelskolestart i Paraguay', *Korsets seier* 28 April 1989 p. 1.

—'Indianere får høre evangeliet for første gang', *Korsets seier* 21 October 1967, p. 12.

—'Radioarbeid på tale i Paraguay', *Korsets seier* 16 February 1972, pp. 1, 8.

Stuksrud, Hilde, 'Misjonærbarn i Atyra: Vi trives bedre i Sør-Amerika enn i Norge', *Korsets seier* 12 April 1980, p. 9.

Stuksrud, Ingrid, 'Norsk skole på misjonsmarken', *Korsets seier* 23 February 1974, p. 8.

Sundal, Norvald, 'Nye misjonærer til Bolivia', *Korsets seier* 6 May 1964, pp. 201-202.

Surland-Hansen, Georg, 'Anbefaling', *Korsets seier* 2 December 1961, p. 763.

Svartdahl, Hans, 'Agronom på Eben-Ezer, Paraguay', *Korsets seier* 8 September 1976, p. 2.

—'Betel bibelinstitutt i Argentina', *Korsets seier* 12 June 1987, pp. 5, 21.

—'Nasjonale overtar oppgaver i Paraguay', *Korsets seier* 21 August 1987, p. 8.

Svendsen, Leif Frode, 'Geirr Standal står i en rik tjeneste!', *Det gode Budskap* 1 June 2001, pp. 18-20.

—'Ingen kan hjelpe alle, men alle kan hjelpe noen', *Det gode Budskap* no. 6 2007, pp. 32-33.

—'Møtesal med plass til 600 stoler', *Det gode Budskap* no. 11 2004, p. 33.

—'Vunnet for Jesus av de "norske" – i dag vinner de tusener for Jesus', *Det gode Budskap* no. 6 2010, pp. 8-9.

'Syd-Amerika', *Korsets seir* 15 November 1913, pp. 174-75.

'Syd-Amerika', *Korsets seir* 15 March 1915, p. 47.

Synan, Vinson, Amos Yong, and Miguel Álvarez (eds.), *Global Renewal Christianity: Spirit Empowered Movements. Past, Present, and Future.* Vol 2: *Latin America* (Lake Mary, FL: Creation House, 2016).

Talaasen, Per G., 'Mangeårig misjonskasserer trekker seg tilbake', *Korsets seier* 8 January 1972, p. 7.

Tangen, Kjell, 'Åpning av Misjonsskole i Cordoba', *Det gode Budskap* 15 May 2003, pp. 36-37.

Thoresen, Thor J., 'Barnearbeidet - åpen dør til hjemmene', *Korsets seier* 13 August 1975, p. 2.

—'Blant incaindianernes ætlinger', *Korsets seier* 16 October 1968, p. 4.

—'De frie pinsemenigheter i Chile', *Korsets seier* 18 December 1968, p. 5.

—'Sentralisering av vårt radioarbeid i Sør-Amerika', *Korsets seier* 30 June 1973, p. 9.

—*Talende tårn* (Oslo: Filadelfiaforlaget, 1980).

'Thorleif Overhalden med familie til Paraguay', *Korsets seier* 21 July 1973, p. 2.

'Til Argentina', *Korsets seier* 19 October 1946, pp. 674, 678.

'Til Argentina', *Korsets seier* 19 January 1964, p. 37.

'Til Argentina', *Korsets seier* 28 July – 4 August 1956, pp. 474-75.

'Til Argentina', *Korsets seier* 2 July 1977, p. 2.

'Til Bolivia', *Korsets seier* 7 September 1963, pp. 567-68.

'Til Bolivia', *Korsets seier* 7 March 1964, pp. 156-57.

'Til Bolivia', *Korsets seier* 18 April 1964, p. 213.

'Til Bolivia', *Korsets seier* 26 September 1964, p. 627.

'Til Bolivia', *Korsets seier* 11 December 1965, p. 9.

'Til Brasil', *Korsets seier* 27 July 1946, p. 481.

'Til Brasil', *Korsets seier* 1 February 1947, pp. 73-74.

'Til Brasil', *Korsets seier* 20 June 1948, pp. 355-56.

'Til Brasil', *Korsets seier* 16 February 1963, p. 104.

'Til Norge etter 4 år i Brasil', *Det gode Budskap* 20 August and 1 September 1979, p. 12.

'Til Sør-Amerika', *Korsets seier* 10 November 1956, pp. 697-98.

Tollefsen, Gunnerius, 'Misjonsnytt', *Korsets seier* 30 November 1948, p. 611.

—'Misjonsnytt', *Korsets seier* 2 May 1953, p. 283.

Tolås, Kjell Arve, 'Glimt fra turen til Argentina', *Det gode Budskap* 1 May 1997, pp. 10-12.

Torp, Jan-Aage, '"Gode nyheter"' i fattigkvarteret', *Korsets seier* 26 January 1983, p. 12.

Tørre, Berit, and Torstein Tørre, 'Misjonsarbeidet i Bolivia: Folke-skolen åpnet vei', *Korsets seier* 24 March 1971, pp. 3, 6.

Trannum, Ivar, 'Ung styrmann fra Hvaler med sin svenskfødte hustru pionermisjonær i Bolivia', *Korsets seier* 27 May 1961, pp. 336-37.

'Tribute to our founders'. Brochure, published by Open Bible Church in San Fernando, Trinidad [n.d.].

'Turid + Karl = Sant!', *Det gode Budskap* no. 2 2006, p. 48.

'Turid og Jakob utvider i Sao Paolo', *Det gode Budskap* no. 11 2004, pp. 32-33.

'Turid Sneve – ny misjonskandidat', *Det gode Budskap* 20 June 1976, p. 4.

'Tusener lytter til evangeliske radioprogram i Chile', *Korsets seier* 17 October 1964, p. 23.

Tveito, Ingebjørg, 'Misjonærene i Paraguay trenger hjelp', *Korsets seier* 31 January 1968, p. 8.

Twetan, Arnt, 'Vekkelsen i Argentina', *Det gode Budskap* 20 April 1955, p. 90.

—'Vekkelsen i Argentina', *Det gode Budskap* 1 May 1955, pp. 101, 104.

'Unge søker Gud i det urolige Nicaragua', *Korsets Seier* 6 Novem-ber 1987, p. 5.

'Ut med evangeliet', *Korsets seier* 14 December 1966, p. 16.

Van Cleave, Nathaniel M., *The Vine and the Branches. A History of the International Church of the Foursquare Gospel* (Los Angeles, CA: International Church of the Foursquare Gospel, 1992).

'Våre misjonærer', *Korsets seier* 7 September 1963, p. 570.

'Våre misjonærer', *Korsets seier* 12 October 1963, p. 652.

'Våre misjonærer', *Korsets seier* 13 March 1965, p. 6.

Vedøy, Sverre, 'Historisk dag i Argentina', *Det gode Budskap* 15 April 1993, p. 8.

'Vel framkomne i Paraguay', *Korsets seier* 9 January 1971, p. 9.

Vestvik, Einar, *Gud skal ha æren. Olaug og Berner Solås* (Veavågen: Den frie evangeliske forsamling Klippen, 2016).

—'Møtet med folk og kultur i Bolivia sjokkartet', *Korsets seier* 17 February 1982, p. 9.

Viumdal, Andreas, 'Førstegrøden som ble pastor', *Korsets seier* 18 June 2004, pp. 16-17.

—'Hele Bolivia skal dekkes med kristne radio-program!', *Korsets seier* 17 May 1980, p. 6.

Waern, Claes, 'Bibelskolen i Bolivia har en positiv utvikling', *Korsets seier* 3 June 1981, p. 12.

Waern, Claes, and Solveig Samuelsen, 'SIDA satser 5 millioner på skoleprosjekt i Bolivia', *Korsets seier* 11 July 1981, p. 8.

Walker, Luisa Jeter de, *Siembra y cosecha. Las Asambleas de Dios de México y Centroamérica.* Vol. 1 (Deerfield, FL: Editorial Vida, 1990).

Western, Halvor, 'Fra Jevnaker til Chile – historien om misjonæren Nils Gunstad', *Årbok for Hadeland.* Vol. 40 (2007), pp. 66-72.

Westgård, Peder, 'Effektivt radioarbeid i Honduras', *Korsets seier* 7 January 1978, pp. 1, 15.

Wilhelm, Eva, and Rudolf Wilhelm, 'Det bygges i Honduras', *Korsets seier* 16 August 1969, p. 6.

—'Høytidsdager i Honduras', *Korsets seier* 28 January 1970, p. 5.

Wilhelmsen, Jean, *Trails through Trinidad* (Los Angeles, CA: The Go Ye Fellowship Inc., 2nd. pr., 1973).

'Wilhelmsen, Kåre', *Norsk Misjonsleksikon.* Vol. 3 (Stavanger: Nomi forlag – Runa forlag, 1967).

Wingeler-Rayo, Philip, 'A Third Phase of Christianity: reflections on One Hundred Years of Pentecostalism in Mexico', in Vinson Synan, Amos Yong, and Miguel Álvarez (eds.), *Global Renewal Christianity: Spirit Empowered Movements. Past, Present, and Future.* Vol 2: *Latin America* (Lake Mary, FL: Creation House, 2016), pp. 7-11.

Ystebø, Asle, '200 misjonærer klare til utreise nå', *Korsets seier* 17 August 2007, pp. 16-17.

MISSIONARIES

Aardalen, Gerda-Lillian (1930-2016). To Brazil in 1959 and to Bolivia in 1965. Later also Paraguay. Sending church: Betania, Notodden.

Aas, Ivar (1936-2021) and Liv (1936-1985), maiden name Bekke-lund. First time to Bolivia in 1964. Ivar's sending churches were Filadelfia, Gjøvik and Betania, Tønsberg while Liv was sent out by Filadelfia, Gjøvik. Liv died in a car accident in Bolivia in 1985. Later, Ivar married Astrid Tveter, who was a widow and had worked in Kenya with her husband Arne. Ivar and Astrid worked together for a few months in Bolivia and many years in Spain.

Aateigen, Edith (1942-2010). To Peru in 1969. Sending church: Filadelfia, Kristiansand.

Abrahamsen, Alf Viggo (b. 1955). To Brazil under the auspices of New Life Mission in 1987. There in Mogi das Cruzes he founded the organization Vida Nova with emphasis on work among children living on the streets.

Abrahamsen, Janni (1929-2016). First visit to Brazil in 1991 but returned for a lengthier stay in 1993. She had no sending church, but was part of the organization Vida Nova, founded by her son Alf Viggo.

Adolfsen, Eva Marie (b. in Stavanger 1945), maiden name Steiner and Helge (b. in Hvaler 1946). Helge went to Bolivia for the first time in 1968, while Eva followed the following year. They married in Bolivia in 1971. Eva Marie's sending church: Salen, Ullerøy. Helge's sending church: Salen, Halden.

Agersten, Gro (b. in Oslo 1944), maiden name Spangebu and John Herbert (b. in Bollnäs, Sweden 1940). Went to Peru for the first time in 1966. Sending church: Salem, Oslo. Lived in Cuba during 2003-2006.

Alegre, Ariel (b. 1984) and Rakel Ystebø Alegre (b. 1984). To Argentina i 2023. Sending church: Tabernaklet, Bergen.

Andersen, Hanne Miriam (b. 1961), maiden name Innvær and Tor Inge (b. 1955). Tor Inge had a six-months missionary stay in Peru before he married Hanne Miriam in 1984. They traveled together to Peru in 1985 and worked there until 1988. In the period 1990-1998 they worked in Nicaragua and were in Spain from 2002 to 2006. Hanne Miriam's sending church was Tabernaklet, Hauge-sund while Tor Inge was sent out by Filadelfia, Kristiansand.

Andersen, Leif Gunnar (1916-2006) and Olaug Marie (1918-2017), maiden name Ludvigsen. First time to Brazil in 1949. Have also been missionaries to Portugal, including Madeira. Sending church: Salem, Oslo.

Andreassen, Erling (1931-2007) and Inger Marita (1933-2024). Inger Marita was born in Borås, Sweden with the maiden name Düring. First time to Bolivia in 1957. Sending church: Salen, Uller-øy.

Andresen, Alvina (1898-1980), b. in Austrheim and Erling Samuel (1902-81), b. in Oslo. First time to Argentina in 1926. Sending church: Filadelfia, Sarpsborg.

Andresen, Alice (b. 1933) and Per (1932-2017), sent out under the auspices of the Free Evangelical Assemblies to Brazil in 1962. Sending church: Logen, Moss.

Arca, Hanne Carina (b. 1972) and Victor (b. 1970 in Paraguay). Hanne Carina is the daughter of Finn and Hanne-Berit Jensen. To Paraguay in 1993. Sending church: Betania, Notodden.

Ardiles, Miguel (b. 1955) and Turid (b. 1949), born Sneve. Formally sent out together under the auspices of the Free Evangelical Assemblies to Argentina in 1990. Sending church: Salem, Mandal. Turid, however, had previously been sent out as early as 1976.

Asplund, Kitty (1938-2023), maiden name Skaug and Knut Egil (1935-2018). First time to Paraguay in 1973. Sending church: Betania, Rakkestad. During 1995-1998 Salen, Halden was their sending church.

Axell, David Anders (b. 1968) and Elisabeth (b. 1970). Elisabeth is the daughter of Brith-Lajla and Rudolf Leif Larsen. To Brazil in 1995. Have also been to Paraguay and Mosambique. Sending church: Betania, Larvik.

Bakke, Arne Eilif Sverre (b. in Lenvik 1941) and Aud (b. in Older-dalen 1940), maiden name Ballovarre. Aud was sent out to Argen-tina in 1974 by Filadelfia Hammerfest. Arne was sent out in 1977 by Filadelfia, Tromsø.

Bauge, Laila (b. in Auklandshamn1955), maiden name Jacobsen and Oddvar (b. in Bremnes 1952). To Bolivia in 1979. Sending church: Filadelfia, Auklandshamn.

Bauge, Robert (b. 1976) and Åshild (b. 1978). To Bolivia in 2003. Sending church: Filadelfia Auklandshamn.

Bergli, Ågot (b. in Mo i Rana 1946). To Peru in 1981. Sending church: Filadelfia, Mo. In 2003, she defended her doctoral disser-tation at NTNU in Trondheim, wherein she analyzed texts from two Peruvian Quechua languages.

Bjervøy, Lisbeth Østmo (b. in Rjukan 1958). To Paraguay in 1983. Sending church: Filadelfia, Rjukan.

Bjørfjell, Ada Johanne (b. 1939), maiden name Bjørstad and Jan Fred Olsen (1939-2013). They eventually took Bjørfjell as their last name. Ada went to Bolivia the first time in 1961 sent out by Filadelfia, Tromsø. Jan was sent out in 1965 by Tabernaklet, Skien.

Bjørnevoll, Inge (b. in Lindås 1944) and Inger Johanne (1944-2021), b. in Fana with the maiden name Strøm. First time to Paraguay in 1970. Sending church: Tabernaklet, Bergen.

Blindheim, Jorid (b. 1960). To Paraguay in 1989 as a teacher at the Norwegian school. Sending church: Saron, Sandefjord.

Bølum Kjørstad, Camilla (b. 1980) and Thomas (b. 1980). To Paraguay in 2016. Sending church: Betel, Trondheim.

Børjesson, Eldbjørg (b. in Rjukan 1956) and Vidar (b. in Rjukan1954). To Paraguay as boarding parents at the Norwegian school in 1982. Sent out by PYM.

Brænne, Henny Marie Rasmussen (b. 1951). First time to Paraguay in 1979. Sending church: Betania Notodden.

Bu, May Britt (b. 1976) and Tom Georg (b. 1973). Tom Georg went to Paraguay in 1997 and May Britt in 2001. Sending church: Taber-naklet, Bergen.

Bullen, Vidar (b. 1962). To Argentina in 1988. Sending church: Betania, Berger.

Byberg, Arnt Rune (b. 1961) and Liv (b. 1962). To Paraguay in 1999. Sending church: Evangeliehuset, Egersund.

Byberg, Liv (b. 1960). First time to Paraguay in 1985. Sending church: Klippen, Jørpeland.

Byberg, Oddmar (b. in Sola 1935) and Sigrunn (b. 1935). First time to Brazil in 1964, thereafter Paraguay. Sending church: Klippen, Sandnes.

Bye, Gerd (1937-2011), maiden name Myhre and Tom Levi (1929-2006). To Chile in 1963. Sending church: Filadelfia, Kristiansand.

Cueto, Øyvor (b. in Nannestad 939), maiden name Skjennum. To Peru in 1976. Sending church: Betania, Bjerke.

Dahl, Daniel (1931-2019) and Tordis (1933-2016). Sent out under the auspices of the Free Evangelical to Argentina in 1966. Sending church: Klippen, Veavågen.

de Jong, Martha (1946-2023), b. in Rotterdam, Netherlands. To Peru in 1978. Sending church: Filadelfia, Alta.

Delgado, Oscar (b. 1960). Paraguayan, married to Aina Førland in 1984. Sent out as a missionary to Paraguay by Salem, Lørenskog in 1986.

Draganchuk, Evelyn (b. in Brazil in 1950), maiden name Pedersen and Pedro (1944-97), b. in Argentina. Missionaries to Argentina from 1972. Sending church: Filadelfia, Kristiansand.

Drageland, Signora (1895-1947), maiden name Tjelsund. First time to Argentina in 1929 with financial support from friends in Norway and Sweden.

Dysjaland, Tone (b. 1965). To Argentina in 1991 under the auspices of the Free Evangelical Asseblies. Sending church: Ebeneser Verdalen, Jæren.

Edvardsen, Ranveig Annie (1933-2016). First time to Argentina in 1964. Sending church: Tabernaklet, Skien.

Elvik, Frank (b. 1965) and Solfrid (b. 1965). To Argentina under the auspices of the Free Evangelical Assemblies in 2001. Solfrid's last name is now Anglevik Træet. Sending church: Sion, Moster-hamn.

Emberland, Ella (1929-2016), maiden name Ritse. As a missionary her last name was Ritse, but when she later married she took the name Ritse Emberland. To Argentina in 1959, and to Bolivia in 1961. Sending church: Bærum pinsemenighet.

Enoksen, Margit (1916-98). First time to Brazil in 1976. Sending church: Filadelfia, Oslo.

Eriksen, Berit (1914-2013). First time to Brazil in 1953. Sending church: Tabernaklet, Bergen.

Eriksen, Erling (b. 1944) and Solfrid (b. 1945). To Peru in 1970 under the auspices of Maran Ata. Sending church: Maran Ata, Oslo.

Eriksen, Roar (b. in Ski 1946) and Solfrid (b. in Oslo 1947). First time to Argentina in 1970. Sending church: Betel, Ytre Enebakk.

Fereira, Hugo (b. 1976) and Marianne (b. 1973). To Paraguay in 2001. Sending church: Filadelfia, Sarpsborg.

Figueredo, Candido (b. in 1955 in Paraguay) and Eva (b. in Bodø 1945), maiden name Sagen. Eva left for Paraguay the first time in 1971 where they married in 1973. They then moved to Norway, until they returned to Paraguay as missionaries in 1979. Sending church: Smyrna, Kirkenes. Later Betel, Nøtterøy became their sending church.

Flatland, Vigdis (b. in Rjukan 1954). To Peru in 1975. Sending church: Filadelfia, Rjukan.

Flatøy, Helge (b. 1973). To Paraguay in 1999. Sending church: Filadelfia, Kristiansand.

Forberg, Astrid (b. in Bø, Telemark 1941). First time to Paraguay in 1978. Sending church: Filadelfia, Sarpsborg.

Førland, Aina (b. in Oslo 1959), married to Oscar Delgado in 1984. She is the daughter of Jorunn and Lars M. Førland. To Paraguay in 1982. Sending church: Salem, Lørenskog. They were sent out together in 1986.

Førland, Jorunn (1935-2004), maiden name Westli and Lars Meling (1934-2018). To Brazil in 1961 and to Paraguay in 1967. Jorunn's sending church was Salem, Lørenskog while it was Salemkirken, Oslo which sent out Lars.

Førland, Lars Morgan (b. 1965) and Lourdes Nathalie (b. 1966). Lars Morgan is the son of Jorunn and Lars M. Førland and grew up in Paraguay, while Lourdes is Paraguayan. Sent out by Salem, Oslo in 1990. Most of the time was spent in Paraguay, but they also had 16 months of missionary praxis in Saramiriza, Peru (1993-94) in addition to working as missionaries in Piura/Ignacio Merino, Peru during 2000-2003.

Fosse, Godtfred (b. 1947) and Ragna Julianne (b. 1949). Have been missionaries to Congo (1988-90) and Paraguay from year 2000 as teachers as well as boarding parents at the Norwegian school. Sending church: Filadelfia, Arendal.

Fosli, Signe Marie (b. 1966). To Paraguay in 1986. Sending church: Filadelfia Dalen. Later she was married and took Stenseth as well as Fosli as her last name.

Fumero, Lisbeth (b. in Halden 1945), maiden name Jensen and Mario (b. 1940 in Cuba). Lisbeth was sent to Chile in 1966 by Salen, Halden. Mario had been ministering in different Latin American countries since 1964. In 1971 they were married and moved to Honduras as missionaries. In 1983 they relocated to Spain. Mario now lives in Honduras.

Gill, Gwen (b. 1952) and Svein (b. 1952). Sent out under the auspices of the Free Evangelical Assemblies to Argentina in 1978. Sending church: Betania, Lyngdal.

Granseth, Kolbjørn (1929-2019) and Margit (1926-2022). Sent out under the auspices of Maran Ata to Peru in 1967 with financial support from the Maran Ata churches in Arendal and partly from Telemark. They have also been missionaries in Bolivia and El Salvador.

Grønvold, Esther Sofie (1903-73), maiden name Kihl and Sigurd (1904-32), b. in Røyken. Sigurd went to Argentina as a missionary in 1927 but returned shortly afterwards to Norway. I 1930 left once again for Argentina. It is uncertain whether Esther accompanied him.

Gundersen, Hilde Stuksrud (b. 1964) and Ole Kristian (b. 1964). To Paraguay in 1997. Sending church: Misjonskirken in Kristian-sund. Hilde is the daughter of Ingrid and Knut Stuksrud. Her last name is now Stuksrud.

Haddal Dyb, Liv Helene (b. in Sykkylven 1946). First time to Chile in 1973. Sending church: Filadelfia, Ålesund.

Hansen, Kaleb Hindar (1911-1996). To Argentina in 1934. Relocated to Paraguay during 1937-38. Self supporting.

Håskjold, Reidun (b. 1943) and Åge (b. 1935). To Argentina under the auspices of the Free Evangelical Assemblies in 1968. Sending church: Klippen, Sætre in Hurum.

Haug, Håkon Arthur (1916-90) and Ruth Elisabeth (1917-2009), maiden name Landmo; parents to Liv Haug. First time to Peru in 1975 to assist Liv. Several brief periods in Peru.

Haug, Liv Landmo (b. in Drammen 1943). First time to Peru in 1971. Sending church: Filadelfia, Kristiansand.

Haug, Ruth (b. in Eidsberg 1937). To Paraguay in 1975. Sending church: Eben Ezer, Volda.

Hauge Karlsen, Signe Johanna (b. 1940), maiden name Hauge. To Chile in 1966. Sending church: Tabernaklet, Bergen.

Haugsvær, Kari (b. in Høyland 1940), maiden name Opsahl and Ragnvald (b. 1946). Kari was first time in Bolivia in 1967. Sending church: Zion, Stavanger.

Henriksen, Else-Marie (b. 1950). To Paraguay in 1985. Sent out by PYM.

Hjelpdahl, Alf (b. in Trondheim 1937) and Gerd (b. in Orkdal1940). To Paraguay in 1978. Sending church: Sørum pinse-menighet.

Hjelpdahl, Åslaug (b. 1934). To Paraguay in 1978. Sending church: Betel, Trondheim.

Hofstad, Jarle (b. 1969) and Yngvild (b. 1972). To Honduras under the auspices of Youth With A Mission in 1998. They remained in Honduras until 2012.

Høiland, Arnt Rino (b. 1972) and Rose (b. 1974). To Mexico under the auspices of Youth With A Mission in 2000. After a period in Norway they went out under the auspices of the Free Evangelical Assemblies in 2002 but still in cooperation with Youth With A Mission. Sending church: Smyrna, Tønsberg.

Iversen, Gunvor Lilly (1930-2000), maiden name Johansen and Josef Timoteus (1925-2006). Gunvor went first to Brazil in 1955, one year later to Paraguay. After their marriage in 1961, they were sent out together to Paraguay in 1962. Sending church: Filadelfia, Sarpsborg.

Iversen, Heidi Eunice (b. 1965). To Paraguay in 1987 and in 1992 to Argentina. She was sent out by PYM. When she together with her husband was sent out to Kenya in 1999, however, Betania, Notodden was her sending church. Heidi is the daughter of Gun-vor and Josef Iversen. Her last name now is Viken.

Iversen, Levi Peter (b. 1962) and Norma (b. 1962). Levi Peter is the son of Gunvor and Josef Iversen while Norma is Paraguayan. To Paraguay in 1995. Sending church: Filadelfia, Sarpsborg from 1995 to 1998. Then Salen, Halden became their sending church.

Janøy, Esther (b. 1954), maiden name Engh and Jostein (b. 1946). To Paraguay in 1986. Sending church: Tabernaklet, Skien.

Jelmert, Arve (b. 1954) To Bolivia in 1981. Sending church: Evangeliehuset Porsgrunn.

Jensen, Astrid Hennie (b. 1936), maiden name Woie and Roald Arthur (1932-2023). First time to Argentina in 1972. Sending church: Betel, Nordliland.

Jensen, Benjamin Oscar (b. 1965) and Ragnhild Linda (b. 1968), maiden name Haugen. Benjamin grew up in Argentina and was first sent out as a missionary to Paraguay and Bolivia during 1986-88. Together with Linda he went to Argentina in 1991. His sending church was Filadelfia, Mysen while Linda's sending church was Salen, Halden.

Jensen, Finn (b. in Eydehavn 1938) and Hanne-Berit (b. i Mysen 1940), maiden name Johansen. Finn went to Argentina the first time in 1962. His sending church was Filadelfia, Eydehavn. Hanne-Berit went to Argentina the first time in 1964. She had the same sending church.

Jensen, Kari (b. 1967) and Kai Roger (b. 1967). To Paraguay in 1998. Sending church: Filadelfia, Askim.

Jensen, Sara (b. 1994). To Mexico under the auspices of Back2Back Ministries in 2019. She returned to Norway in 2024. Sending church: Sentrumskirken, Strømmen.

Johannesen, Elsa Palma, married name Øgaard (b. in Kristiansand 1950). To Argentina in 1981. Sending church: Filadelfia, Kristian-sand.

Johansen, Astrid (b. in Fredrikstad 1948), maiden name Thor-valdsen and Kjell Arne (b. in Sarpsborg 1949). First time to Paraguay in 1972. Sending church: Filadelfia, Sarpsborg.

Johansen, Laila (b. in Sarpsborg 1956). To Bolivia in 1984. Sending church: Salen, Ullerøy.

Johansson, Ruth (1926-2023), maiden name Ingelsrud. First time to Brazil in 1951. Sending church: Filadelfia, Vestmarka.

Johnsen, Berger N. (1888-1945). Missionary to Argentina since 1910, founded the mission station in Embarcación.

Jones, Klara Ellen (1922-99), maiden name Hansen and Spencer Norman (1916-85). They had previously been missionaries to India. They arrived in Trinidad in 1955 and remained until 1957.

Jorud, Anne Lise (b. in Eidanger 1944), maiden name Langangen and Ole Johannes (b. in Trøgstad 1940). First time to Paraguay in 1974. Sending church: Trøgstad pinsemenighet.

Juliussen, Gunn Lisbeth (b. 1953), maiden name Hjertebråten and Johan Isak (b. 1955). To Paraguay in 1986. Sending church: Råde pinsemenighet.

Kihle, Ragnhild (b. 1934). Previous salvationist officer and missionary to Brazil since 1969. Sent out under the auspices of the Free Evangelical Assemblies to Brazil in 1981. Sending church: Betel Horten.

Kjellås, Ruth (1900-68),b. in Trøgstad. To Brazil in 1956. Left for Paraguay the same year. Sending church: Filadelfia, Sarpsborg.

Krogtoft, Birgitte (b. in Vestvågøy 1959). To Peru in 1983. Sending church: Betel, Nordliland. Later married to David Lindgren from Sweden.

Kvalsund, Flora Heredia (b. in Riberalta, Bolivia 1951) and Oddvar (b. in Herrøy, Sunnmøre 1942). Flora is Bolivian and came to Norway together with Ada and Jan Bjørfjell. First time to Paraguay in 1976. Sending church: Betania, Breivik.

Kvarstein, Kjell Torgeir (b. 1949) and Luisa Ester de Navarro (b.1955 in Paraguay, where she died in 2024. To Paraguay in 1991. Sending church: Klippen pinsemenighet, Bykle. Kjell had been to Paraguay prior to that.

Langåker, Irene (b. 1977) and Jan André (b. 1971). To Argentina under the auspices of the Free Evangelical Assemblies in 2006. Sending church: Saron, Åkrehamn.

Larsen, Brit-Lajla (b. in Tranøy 1946) and Rudolf Leif (b. in Bodø 1948). First time to Paraguay in 1976. Sending church: Filadelfia, Bodø.

Larsson, Solveig (1907-37), b. in Oslo with maiden name Hansen.To Argentina in 1936. Sending church: Filadelfia, Charlottenberg, Sweden. Married to Evert Larsson from Sweden.

Lie, Gunn Elisabeth (b. in Svarstad 1949). First time to Bolivia in 1974. Sending church: Betania, Notodden.

Lie, Synnøve (b. 1956). To Bolivia in 1982. Sending church: Saron, Hokksund.

Lund, Judith (b. 1953). To Paraguay in 1982. Sent out by PYM.

Madsen, Mildrid (1924-2016), b. in Gamvik. To Paraguay in 1983. Self supporting.

Mangersnes, Frantz Johan Wolf (1912-2001). First time to Brazil in 1948. He has also been a missonary to Argentina and Paraguay. Sending church: Bærum Pinsemenighet.

Maruyama, Shigeji (b. in Osaka, Japan 1931) and Ågoth (1915-2001), maiden name Berge. Ågoth had previously been a missionary to China and Japan. First time to Brazil in 1962, later once again in Japan. Sending church: Klippen, Sandnes.

Midtun, Kristine (b. 1974) and Rune (b. 1973). To Brazil under the auspices of the Free Evangelical Assemblies in 1994. Sending church: Eben Eser, Skudeneshavn.

Mjåland, Anna (b. in Åseral 1937). First time to Paraguay in 1975. Sending church: Eben Eser, Volda.

Mjåvatn, Helga (1904-73), b. in Østre Moland. First time to Argentina in 1937. Sending church: Filadelfia, Hamar.

Moen, Marit (b. 1947). To Argentina under the auspices of the Free Evangelical Assemblies in 1973. Sending church: Salem, Mjøndalen. To Spain under the auspices of the *Pinsebevegelsen* with Betania, Mjøndalen as the sending church.

Mølland, Borgny (1937-2023). Married to Antonio Barbosa Da Silva after having completed her missionary term. She uses Mølland Barbosa Da Silva as her last name. To Bolivia in 1966. Sending church: Filadelfia, Kristiansand.

Mondaca Cabrera, Eduardo (b. 1961) and Doris Nuñez (b. 1963). To Chile in 1998. Sending church: Filadelfia, Kristiansand.

Moseid, Dag Helge (b. 1950). First time to Bolivia in 1984. Sending church: Betania, Tønsberg.

Mossberg, Hardy Wilhelm (1902-82), b. in Halden and Karin Maria Eleonora (1901-83), b. in Stockholm with maiden name Lundberg. First time to Chile in 1947. Sending church: Salen, Halden.

Navarro Rivera, Claudio José (b. in Valparaíso, Chile 1953) and Else Margrethe Navarro (1947-2024), b. in Oslo with the maiden name Ekornaas. Else went to Chile the first time in 1974, sent out by Salem, Oslo. Since their marriage they have both had Salem, Oslo as their sending church.

Næsland, Geir (b. 1952). To Brazil under the auspices of the Free Evangelical Assemblies in 1984. Sending church: Betel, Horten.

Nilsen, Ann Merete (b. 1974). To Paraguay in 2001. Sending church: Lista Pinsemenighet.

Nilsen, Astrid (1935-2020), b. in Skjeberg with maiden name Myhrvold. To Paraguay in 1966. Sending church: Philadelphia, Seattle, USA.

Nordfjell, Anne Groven (b. 1965). To Paraguay in 1994. Sending church: Filadelfia, Namsos.

Norheim, Bergljot (1914-96), b. Nordmoen and Olav (1915-1997), b. in Nes, Romerike. Bergljot went the first time to Paraguay in 1952. She has also served in Argentina. Sending church: Vestby evangeliske menighet, Trysil. Olav went to Paraguay the first time in 1964. Sending church: Betel, Haga.

Nysand, Marit (b. 1960) and Stefan (b. in Finland 1961). To Brazil under the auspices of the Free Evangelical Assemblies in 1990. Sending church: Arken, Sira.

Nyseter, Gustav (1886-1961) and Laura (1881-1930), b. in Steigen, maiden name Volden. In 1921 they went to Alaska where Laura died. Gustav returned to Norway in 1930. No known sending church.

Olsen, Sally (1912-2006), b. in Bergen. Missionary to Puerto Rico from 1952. Founded Rose of Sharon Foundation, with financial support from Norway and the U.S.

Omdal, Anette (b. 1983) and Øyvind (b. 1978). To Bolivia in 2005. Sending church: Betania, Sokndal.

Opheim, Gunnvald (b. in Follafoss 1930) and Julie-Maria (1934-87). First time to Argentina in 1956, later to Spain. Sending church: Vestby pinsemenighet.

Opsahl, Kari (b. in Høyland 1940), maiden name Opsahl and Ragnvald Haugsvær (b. 1946). Kari kept Opsahl Haugsvær as her last name after marrying in 1995. She was sent out to Bolivia in 1967, while they went out together in 1995. Sending church: Zion, Stavanger.

Overhalden, Rigmor Margrethe (b. in Lillehammer 1942), maiden name Smelien and Thorleif (b. in Lillehammer 1943). First time to Paraguay in 1973. Sending church: Betania, Fjellstrand.

Øvrum, Ingjerd (b. in Porsgrunn 1943). To Argentina in 1967. Sending church: Tabernaklet, Skien.

Øya, Helge Magne (b. in Notodden 1940) and Martha (b. in Hammerfest 1938), maiden name Kvalsvik. Martha went to Argentina the first time in 1968. They went out together in 1973. Helge Magne's sending church was Evangeliehuset, Porsgrunn while Martha was sent out by Filadelfia, Alta.

Øyrås, Solveig (1938-2013), b. in Froland. To Paraguay in 1968. Sending church: Filadelfia, Arendal.

Pedersen, Adela Sofía Draganchuk (b. in Buenos Aires, Argentina 1958) and Carlos (b. in Embarcación, Argentina 1954). Carlos is the son of Per and Palma Pedersen. Missionaries to Argentina from 1977. Adele's sending church was Vestby pinsemenighet while Carlos was sent out by Sion, Lindesnes.

Pedersen, Cyril (b. in Narvik 1944) and Mirtha Josefa Ebeling (1946-2024), b. in Argentina. Cyril is the son of Per and Palma Pedersen. Missionaries to Argentina from 1964. Sending church: Tabernaklet, Skien.

Pedersen, Karin (b. 1954) and Samuel (b. in Argentina 1963). Samuel was sent out to Argentina in 1982 and Karin as a Swedish Pentecostal missionary in 1981. They married in Argentina in 1983. Samuel's sending church was Sion, Lindesnes whileKarin was sent out by the Pentecostal church in Järbo, Sweden.

Pedersen, Palma Louise (1924-2012), maiden name Halvorsen and Per Adrian (b. in Skien 1918-2012). To Brazil in 1949. That same year they went to Argentina ministering in Embarcación until retirement. Palma's sending church was Vestby evangeliske menighet, Trysil while Per was sent out by Tabernaklet, Skien.

Pedersen, Torkel (b. 1962). To Trinidad in 1996 with his wife Kathleen, who was born there. Together they built a rehabilitation center for drug users. They were supported both by the Evangelisenteret and the Tabernaklet, Bergen.

Pettersen, Arild (b. 1949) and Nilda (b. 1965, b. in Paraguay). Arild went to Paraguay in 1996. Sending church: Sion, Vanse.

Pettersen, Elsa Karin (1950-2019) and Gunnar (1953-2016). Gunnar went to Paraguay in 1985 and Elsa the year after. Sending church: Sion, Voss.

Pettersen, Gottfred Leonard (1907-95) and Ragna (1903-83), b. in Brandval, Solør with maiden name Sjølie. First time to Brazil in 1936; to Bolivia in 1953. Sending church: Salen, Ski.

Raaholdt, Nils Emanuel (1932-2000). To Bolivia in 1973. Sending church: Filadelfia, Oslo.

Ranta, Kari Juhani (b. 1967) and Marka Eeva Anneke R. (b. 1965). To Mexico in 1997. Sending church: Filadelfia, Oslo.

Ringås, Astrid Elisabeth Iversen (b. 1964) and Tore-Bjørn (b. 1965). To Argentina in 1991 and Paraguay in 1995. Astrid is the daughter of Gunvor and Josef Iversen. Sending church: Filadelfia, Elverum.

Røine, Finn (b. in Hønefoss 1946) and Reidun (b. in Borge, Lofoten 1942), maiden name Berntzen. First time to Bolivia in 1977. Finn's sending church was Filadelfia, Hønefoss while Reidun was sent out by Betel, Vestfossen.

Røine, Jael Dayer de (b. 1977) and Per Morten (b. 1973). Per Morten is the son of Finn and Reidun Røine. Per Morten went to Bolivia in 1995. His sending church was Betel, Vestfossen. In 1998 he married Jael in Argentina, and they returned to Norway in 2002.

Samuelsen, Roger (b. in Halden 1946) and Solveig Maria (b. in Lårdal 1949), maiden name Helgestad. Solveig went to Bolivia the first time in 1969 and Roger in 1971. Sending church: Salen, Halden.

Sandli, Birger (1942-2018) and Britt (b. 1949). First time to Argentina in 1978. They have also been missionaries to Nicaragua and Guatemala. Sending churches: Salem, Grorud and Bærum pinsemenighet.

Sandli, Elisabeth (b. 1978) and Roberto (b. 1978). To Guatemala in 2000. Sending church: Filadelfia, Ålesund.

Sjølund, Kjellaug Palma (b. 1942). First time to Paraguay in 1969. She has also been a missionary to Brazil. Sending church: Salem: Skudeneshavn.

Skau, Karin (b. 1946). To Puerto Rico in 1967. In 1975 she was married to Egil Mentzen (1944-2003), who had arrived in Puerto Rico that same year. She has since remarried. Her last name is now Skau Colón.

Skoland Stø, Berit (b. in Flekkefjord 1946), maiden name Stø. To Bolivia in 1969. Sending church: Salen, Flekkefjord.

Skretting, Gunvor (b. in Sandnes 1948), maiden name Hegrestad and Ingvald (b. in Sandnes 1948). First time to Paraguay in 1972. Sending church: Klippen, Sandnes.

Skretting, Olav (b. 1970) and Sheila Ann (b. 1964). Olav is the son of Gunvor and Ingvald Skretting. To Paraguay in 1994. Sending church: Betesda pinsemenighet, Heddal.

Skrøvje, Anita (b. 1968), maiden name Solås and Jan Bjarne (b. 1965). To Argentina under the auspices of the Free Evangelical Assemblies in 1993. Sending church: Betania, Vigeland.

Smidsrød, Jan (b. in Tønsberg 1960) and Åse-Miriam (b. in Bolivia 1959). Åse-Miriam is the daughter of Erling and Marita Andreassen. First time to Bolivia in 1987. Sending church: Betania, Tønsberg.

Solås, Berner (b. 1944) and Olaug (b. 1945). To Argentina under the auspices of the Free Evangelical Assemblies in 1972. Sending church: Klippen, Veavågen.

Sørheim, Anna (1894-1986), b. in Lanvetter, Sweden with maiden name Johannesson and Jahn (1899-1964). After having completed the Salvation Army's College for Officer Training in 1922 Jahn was sent out as a salvationist missionary in 1924. He went to Sweden in 1929 and returned to Brazil one year later, where he became a Pentecostal missionary. In 1932 he married Anna in Rio de Janeiro.

Spjøtvold, Henry (1938-91) and Ruth Mildred (b. in Bergen 1942) Former salvationist missionaries to Argentina; Pentecostal missionaries to Argentina from 1964. Henry's sending church was Klippen, Sandnes while Mildfred was sent out by Zion, Stavanger.

Standal, Geirr (b. 1972). To Brazil under the auspices of the Free Evangelical Assemblies in 2000. After marriage to Eva (b. 1977) in 2002, maiden name Gamst, they went out together in 2003. Sending church: Betania, Spangereid.

Standal, Gunnar (b. 1945) and May-Lise (b. 1944). To Brazil under the auspices of the Free Evangelical Assemblies in 1969. Sending church: DFEF, Drammen.

Steger, Hanne Synnøve Førland (b. 1962). To Paraguay in 1987, sent out by PYM. Hanne is daughter of Jorunn and Lars Førland. In Paraguay she was married to Reinaldo E. Dure Steger (b. 1962), who, similar to her, was working at Hogar Norma.

Stensland, Frank (b. 1967) and Marion (b. 1972). To Bolivia in 1999. Sending church: Sion, Sellebakk.

Stigen, Asta (b. in Egersund 1930), maiden name Hadland. To Bolivia in 1964. Sending church: Evangeliehuset, Egersund.

Stø, Greta (1937-2022), maiden name Pettersen and Helge (b. 1938-2017). First time to Bolivia in 1964. Greta's sending church wasSion, Vikna while Helge was sent out by Salen, Flekkefjord.

Stokland, Karl (b. 1959) and Turid Dahl Stokland (b. 1955). Turid went to Brazil under the auspices of the Free Evangelical Assemblies in 2002. Sending church: Klippen, Vedavågen. In 2006 she was married to Karl, who from that point worked alongside her in Brazil.

Strømsrud, Anna Pauline (1930-2006). First time to Paraguay in 1961. Sending church: Eben-Eser, Lårdal.

Stuksrud, Arne (b. 1963) and Marie Ask (b. 1963). To Argentina in 1989. Sending church: Saron, Sotra.

Stuksrud, Ingrid (b. in Lillehammer 1935), maiden name Overhalden and Knut (b. in Gausdal 1934). First time to Paraguay in 1967. Sending church: Evangeliesalen, Lillehammer.

Talaasen, Per G. (1888-1972), b. in Trysil. He went to Argentina in 1917 but returned to Norway after one year due to contracting malaria.

Tande, Sara (b. 1985) and Torbjørn (b. 1979). To Mexico in 2009 to work with orphaned children under the auspices of Back2Back Ministries and Youth With A Mission. Sending church: Betania, Stathelle.

Thoresen, Eldbjørg, (b. in Bergen 1945), maiden name Aase and Thor Johnny (b. in Halden 1946). Thor Johnny left for Chile in 1968 and Eldbjørg one year later. Eldbjørg's sending church was Tabernaklet, Bergen while Thor Johnny was sent out by Salen, Halden.

Thorjussen, Helge (b. 1946) and Turid Haave (b. 1947). To Bolivia in 1990, although they had been visiting the country in 1980, 1981 and 1985. Sending church: Tabernaklet, Skien.

Thorkildsen, Lorentze Wilhelmine (1905-81), b. in Svolvær. First time to Brazil in 1946. Sending church: Filadelfia, Oslo.

Tolleshaug, Bjørg (b. in Tvedestrand 1936). First time to Bolivia in 1966. Sending church: Filadelfia, Alta.

Tønnesen, Per (b. 1952) and Torill (b. 1954). To Argentina under the auspices of the Free Evangelical Assemblies in 1990. Sending church: Betania, Arendal.

Torgrimsby, Tone (b. in Oslo 1954). To Bolivia in 1979. Sending church: Filadelfia, Oslo.

Torkelsen, Jorunn (b. 1977). To Argentina under the auspices of the Free Evangelical Assemblies in 2003. Her last name is now Sortland. Sending church: Sion, Mosterhamn.

Tørre, Berit Ellinor (b. in Skien 1942), maiden name Langerud and Torstein (1941-1989). First time to Bolivia in 1968. Sending church: Tabernaklet, Skien. They were boarding parents at the Norwegian school in Paraguay in the early 1980s. After Torstein's death Berit remarried and has Stokset as her last name.

Tørre, Berit (b. 1967) and Håvard (b. 1964). Håvard is the son of Berit and Torstein Tørre. To Argentina in 1991. Sending church: Betania, Fjellstrand.

Tørre, Vegard (b. 1968) and Aija (b 1978), b. in Latvia. To Bolivia in 1992. Vegard is the son of Berit and Torstein Tørre. Sending church: Tabernaklet, Skien from 1992 to 1994 and the Pentecostal church in Kviteseid from 1998 to 2006.

Urevatn, Odd-Jan. (b. 1953) and Turid (b. 1955). To Argentina under the auspices of the Free Evangelical Assemblies in 1987. Sending church: Betesda, Eiken and Eben Ezer, Byremo.

Vatne, Ingrid (b. in Forsand 1945), maiden name Helmikstøl and Reidar (1943-2021), b. in Strand. First time to Bolivia in 1974. They went to Peru in 1993 and returned to Bolivia in 1996. Sending church: Klippen, Jørpeland.

Vedøy, Edel (1946-2019) and Sverre (b. 1945). To Argentina under the auspices of the Free Evangelical Assemblies in 1992. Sending church: Saron, Åkrehamn.

Vervik, Leif Gunnar (b. in Jørpeland 1953) and Oddbjørg (b. in Bergen 1953), maiden name Wergeland. First time to Peru in 1973. Sending church: Klippen, Jørpeland.

Vevang, Jakob (1919-2022). To Paraguay in 1973. Sending church: Betania, Kristiansund.

Wåle, Karl Agnar (b. 1967) and Åshild Viken (b. 1965). To Paraguay in 1999. Åshild, however, had been one year in Paraguay in 1984.Sending church: Notodden pinsemenighet.

Westgård, Gunvor (b. in Tolga 1936). First time to Paraguay in 1969. Sending church: Røros og omegn pinsemenighet.

Wilhelm, Eva Alise (b. in Buksnes, Lofoten 1938) and Rudolf (b. in St. Antonien, Switzerland 1939). To Honduras in 1966. Moved to Peru in 1972. Sending church: Filadelfia, Alta.

Wilhelmsen, Kåre (1922-83) and Jean (1913-84), maiden name Mitchell. They were former missionaries to India but left for Trinidad 1954. They remained in Trinidad until 1960. From that point on they were missionaries in various Asian countries.

Winsvold, Anne (1908-93). Has passed brief periods in Paraguay. Self supported.